ALSO BY BENSON BOBRICK

Wide as the Waters:
The Story of the English Bible and the Revolution It Inspired

Angel in the Whirlwind:
The Triumph of the American Revolution

Knotted Tongues: Stuttering in History and the Quest for a Cure

East of the Sun:
The Epic Conquest and Tragic History of Siberia

Fearful Majesty: The Life and Reign of Ivan the Terrible

Labyrinths of Iron:
Subways in History, Myth, Art, Technology, and War

Parsons Brinckerhoff: The First Hundred Years

TESTAMENT

A
SOLDIER'S
STORY OF
THE CIVIL WAR

Benson Bobrick

SIMON & SCHUSTER PAPERBACKS

NEW YORK LONDON TORONTO SYDNEY

SIMON & SCHUSTER PAPERBACKS
Rockefeller Center
1230 Avenue of the Americas
New York, NY 10020

First Simon & Schuster paperback edition 2004

SIMON & SCHUSTER PAPERBACKS and colophon are registered trademarks
of Simon & Schuster, Inc.

For information regarding special discounts for bulk purchases,
please contact Simon & Schuster Special Sales:
1-800-456-6798 or business@simonandschuster.com

Maps by Paul J. Pugliese

Manufactured in the United States of America

1   3   5   7   9   10   8   6   4   2

The Library of Congress has cataloged the hardcover edition as follows:

Bobrick, Benson, 1947–
Testament : a soldier's story of the Civil War / Benson Bobrick.
p. cm.
Includes the Civil War letters of Benjamin Webb Baker.
Includes bibliographical references (p.) and index.
1. Baker, Benjamin Webb, 1841–1909. 2. Baker, Benjamin Webb, 1841–1909—Correspon-
dence. 3. United States. Army. Illinois Infantry Regiment, 25th (1861–1864). 4. Soldiers—
Illinois—Biography. 5. Illinois—History—Civil War, 1861–1865—Regimental histories.
6. United States—History—Civil War, 1861–1865—Regimental histories. 7. Illinois—
History—Civil War, 1861–1865—Personal narratives. 8. United States—History—Civil
War, 1861–1865—Personal narratives. I. Baker, Benjamin Webb, 1841–1909. II. Title.
E505.525th B63 2003
973.7'473'092—dc21
[B]
2003045565
ISBN 0-7432-5091-5
ISBN 0-7432-5113-X (Pbk)

To Hilary,
with devotion;
and to Alice Lackey, David Heck, and Mary Lou Bentley,
for their warmth and generosity
and help in preserving material of undying worth.

CONTENTS

PART ONE
THE WAR
1

PART TWO
THE CIVIL WAR LETTERS
OF BENJAMIN W. ("WEBB") BAKER
191

Acknowledgments, 251
Notes, 253
Bibliography, 261
Index, 267

B. W. Baker

Benjamin W. ("Webb") Baker, circa 1866.

PART ONE

The War

I have seen some pretty hard times, went hungry a good many days, slept many a night on the ground with a stone for a pillow & went some nights without sleep. But that is nothing for a soldier . . . We don't look for easy times here.
— Benjamin W. ("Webb") Baker, Rolla, Missouri, December 16, 1861

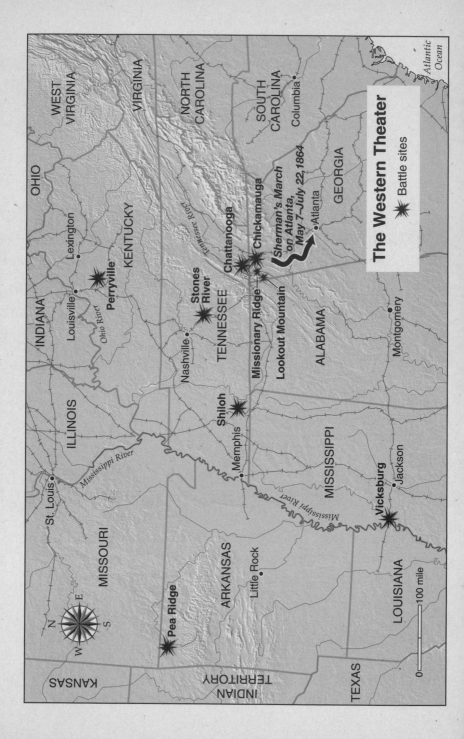

The Western Theater

✳ Battle sites

Sherman's March on Atlanta, May 7–July 22, 1864

OHIO

WEST VIRGINIA

VIRGINIA

NORTH CAROLINA

SOUTH CAROLINA

• Columbia

GEORGIA

• Atlanta

Chickamauga

Chattanooga

Tennessee River

Stones River

Missionary Ridge

Lookout Mountain

KENTUCKY

Lexington •

Perryville

Louisville •

Ohio River

TENNESSEE

Nashville •

INDIANA

ILLINOIS

Mississippi River

Memphis •

Shiloh

St. Louis •

MISSOURI

ALABAMA

Montgomery •

MISSISSIPPI

Jackson •

Vicksburg

Mississippi River

LOUISIANA

ARKANSAS

Little Rock •

Pea Ridge

TEXAS

INDIAN TERRITORY

KANSAS

N E W S

Atlantic Ocean

0   100 mile

CHAPTER ONE

I see a cloud, a little bigger now than a man's hand, gathering in the north, and in the west, and all around, and soon the whole northern heavens will be lighted up with a fire that you cannot quench." So Senator Benjamin Wade of Ohio warned his congressional colleagues on February 6, 1854, as a fateful bill, known as the Kansas–Nebraska Act, began to make its way through the chamber into law.

To one farm boy in Illinois, the idea of such a conflagration conjured up nothing so much as a prairie fire. Almost every year great sweeps of the prairies would catch, and the flames engulfing them would rush, roaring through the tall, coarse grass like thunder, sending up dense clouds of smoke and reddening the horizon with a flickering vastness that at night made the sky itself appear on fire. Nature's fearsome energy and power never ceased to astound him, for all the times he had beheld the scene. But always it stood in wild contrast to the arsenal of controlled pyrotechnics—the Roman candles, torpedoes, magic wheels, and wriggling serpents—that burst over the town common every Fourth of July.

The last such celebration he would ever view so simply would come and go in 1861.

This is a book about the Civil War. It is a book about the whole war, in a synoptic sense, and about its impact on the life and understanding of one man. That man was a Union soldier who fought almost the whole war through. His name was Benjamin W.

("Webb") Baker, and he belonged to Company E of the 25th Illinois Regiment of Voluntary Infantry, formed in August 1861 in response to one of Abraham Lincoln's first calls for volunteers. Webb answered that call.

From the day of his enlistment as a private at age nineteen, he served honorably until his discharge as a corporal on September 5, 1864. His company saw action early, almost from the moment it entered the field, and in the course of the war fought in a number of major engagements, including Pea Ridge, Arkansas; Perryville, Kentucky; Stones River, Tennessee; Chickamauga, Georgia; and on Sherman's decisive march to Atlanta, when the will of the South at last began to fail. In the end, battle-scarred and weary, partly disabled by his wounds, Webb also suffered one of the sharpest sorrows war can ever inflict. This book is his story, set within the epic of the war itself, and is based on various unpublished papers, including ninety remarkable letters he wrote from the field.

It is rare for a historian to come into possession of a hitherto unknown cache of material as rich and original as this archive is, especially in such well-tilled ground. And I am conscious of my debt. That ground is hallowed, and the letters alone, as a full and unique chronicle of the War in the West, possess, indeed, an objective importance far beyond my own poor power to add or detract.

In context they are also the testament of a life. And that life belongs to the Memory of the Land.

Webb was a farm boy. His forebears on both sides were of mostly English stock, and in the early to mid-1700s branches of the family had settled in Connecticut, New York, and Vermont. By the fourth generation, some had moved to the Midwest, and eventually (Webb's grandparents) to Coles County, Illinois. There Webb's father, John B. Baker, a schoolteacher, married Sarah Eliza

Adams on June 20, 1838. Three years later, on Thanksgiving Day, 1841, Webb was born. He had a sister, Mary, who died quite young, and a brother, John, born on December 20, 1843. The two boys grew up together with a kind of closeness that even among brothers might be counted rare.

Though Webb never put much stock in pedigree, there was also a touch of ancestral glory in his blood. His mother was the granddaughter of Elijah Adams, a soldier of the Revolution and, according to family tradition, a cousin of John Adams, second president of the United States. But in Webb's eyes, Elijah gave glory enough. As a soldier of the Continental line, he had reenlisted twice, fought in a row-galley under Benedict Arnold (when Arnold was still loyal) on Lake Champlain, and at the end of the Revolution, when Washington had Cornwallis trapped at Yorktown, helped secure the Mohawk Valley in hand-to-hand combat with Indians and Tories in the battles of Johnstown and Canada Creek. After the war, he moved from Connecticut to Ohio, and on April 11, 1833, was granted an annual pension of $79.95 a year. He lived to be eighty-nine and died on December 12, 1844, when Webb was three.

By then, the family had bought a forty-acre spread in Hutton Township, Coles County, and tried to make a living off the land. In those days, forty acres was about the smallest spread of farmland one could buy, and their own formed part of the vast level, unwooded tract or prairie that used to extend, almost without interruption, from Lake Michigan to the Mississippi shore. The land was high, dry, and rich; timber scarce, found mostly along the margins of rivers and streams; and the topsoil a black, friable, sandy loam. Beneath this, a thick red clay was finely mixed with sand. Webb loved to roam among the bushes of hazel and furze, small sassafras shrubs interspersed with grapevines, and everywhere in spring the immense profusion of flowers. In time he came to know by name the brilliant red tufts of the Judas Tree

(*Cercis camadensis*) and the *Lonicera flava*, or yellow-flowered honeysuckle, which, with yellow jasmine, sweetened the air. In the spring, too, thousands of acres were reddened with strawberries, and just as lower Illinois came to be called "Little Egypt" (from its delta-like features, reminiscent of the Nile), so Central Illinois had, in a manner of speaking, its own biblical Red Sea. Oddly (or aptly) enough, the land office where one recorded claims in that day was in a nearby town called Palestine.

The Baker plot was still unbroken sward, and in the first year was plowed with three or four yoke of oxen, the coulter turning up a furrow of turf about four inches deep and two feet wide. The sod was turned over completely so as to lay the grass down and one furrow fitted to another for sowing wheat. When summer came, corn was sown in every fourth row. The first crop was "sod corn"; at harvest it was cut up, stalk and all, and stacked for cattle feed. But by the next winter's frost, the turned earth had begun to crumble nicely as the grass beneath it decayed, and in subsequent years good corn was abundant, with fifty bushels to the acre an average yield. Thereafter, spring wheat was planted as soon as the ground could be cut, corn about mid-May, winter wheat in the fall. Along with corn, the family coaxed from each acre some forty bushels of oats and twenty-five more of wheat and rye. Irish potatoes and other vegetables also began to come up in the garden plots.

The work was hard, and in the mechanics of it hadn't changed much since "Ruth had gleaned in the fields of Boaz." The slow-going oxen, wooden-tooth harrow, and barshare plow were still in common use, but the cost of breaking up the land at least was cheap: about two dollars an acre in those days, when the whole spread had cost them fifty, plus forty dollars to build a cabin and eighty more for the thousand rails to fence their ground. A choice spot for the cabin had been found on a knoll near a spring, but the cabin itself was spare, with four rooms built around a central stone chimney and clapboards laid on joists to form a loft. The logs for the framing had been hewn, with the corners notched; the roof pitched. The walls themselves stood eight feet high to the square. Four windows (at first of oiled paper, later glass) were cut into the sides. Within, wide puncheons split from a hackberry tree had been laid out for the floor. Years later, a porch was added, then a two-room addition with a framed roof.

Coles County was destined to become "the Buckle on the Corn Belt," and, like most other homesteads round about, the Baker farm relied on the harvesting of grain. But it was also typically diverse. Webb's father built a large barn with fenced-in stalls for his livestock—horses, cattle, goats, pigs, and sheep—and a coop for the chickens and geese. There was also a root cellar for summer storage and a smokehouse for the winter preservation of meats.

In 1841, the little town of Charleston, the county seat, was not much bigger than a village, while all of Coles County had a population of about seven thousand scattered across twelve hundred miles of largely virgin land. Until recently, Hutton Township had been known merely as "Stringtown," from a row of buildings that included a grain mill, a brickyard, a sawmill, a couple of tradesmen's shops, and a general store. A one-room "hickory schoolhouse" (made of hickory logs) had doubled for a time as a place of worship, then two churches, one Baptist, one Methodist, had gone up. But the main route through the town was still the Old York Road or Indian trail that led southeast through Kentucky all the way to Cumberland Gap.

Even so, the rustic simplicity and homespun spareness of that world was soon to change. A first great wave of immigrants had come into the state after 1825 with the Erie Canal, followed by a greater wave in 1848, when a canal was cut from Michigan to Illinois. That, coupled with the railroad boom of the 1850s, spurred tremendous growth in the state. Illinois served as a magnet for enterprising folk of all kinds. "Come leave the fields of childhood,/ Worn out by long employ/ And travel west and settle/ In the state of Illinois." So began a bit of promotional verse, "Westward the Star of Empire Moves," that appeared about that time in the *Boston Post.* Come they did. The population of the state nearly doubled in a decade, Chicago was transformed from a mere boomtown into a city, and tiers of new farms sprang up in the heartland as the prairies began to disappear.

Webb lived the life of the ordinary farm boy of the period, attending school briefly during the winter months, where he learned to "read, rite and cipher to the rule of three." He learned to spell out of Noah Webster's *American Spelling Book*, to read from McGuffey's reader, and was taught facts about the world around him from a book called *The Science of Common Things*. As time allowed, he would go off to hunt and fish, swim in rock-bound pools, and on occasion, scour for arrowheads and bones on a path that meandered along Kickapoo Creek. At home, he often liked to romp with Moses, his favorite sow-belly pig. He was a formidable wrestler, not easily outboxed, a decent shot with a squirrel gun, and clever at catching wild quail with box traps set with four-figure springs. He also seems to have been adept at a game called bull pen, one of the many from which baseball evolved.

But it was the farm that demanded almost all of Webb's time and strength. Spring, summer, and fall, he cleared the ground for plowing, planted and plowed, bundled the sheaves of wheat for shocking, gathered and cribbed the corn. Always, he had to be on the lookout for wolves, raccoons, polecats, opossums, and other predators that menaced what the farm produced. The large black wolf, in particular, was a danger to livestock, prairie wolves and raccoons to poultry, raccoons and opossums to the growing corn. The otherwise harmless rabbit could quickly lay a garden waste.

Webb was tolerably good at his tasks, good at grating corn into meal for making corn pone and mush, at cutting cottonwoods for rails, and hollowing out the trunk of a sycamore for casks. Before winter came, he usually managed to pack the woodshed full with ricks of split hickory and oak. He had had to learn all these things quite early, in fact, for in 1845 his father suddenly died. Webb's mother tried to make a go of the farm with the help of her father, John Adams (Elijah's son), but she needed a husband to sustain it, and in 1850, when Webb was nine, she married a local farmer, Hezekiah Jones. Hezekiah died six years later, leaving her with three more children and a heavy debt, so in 1860 she married again, this time a well-propertied Irishman by the name of Robert Moore. It was an affectionate union between devoted friends. The Bakers and Moores had known each other for a long time, and Robert had some children from a previous marriage who were about Webb's age. One of them, Isaiah D. Moore (known as I. D.) would serve with him in the 25th Illinois. Another, John W. Moore (Little Johnny, as Webb called him), was close to Webb's own brother and would subsequently join the 123rd. The ties among them all ran deep, and even before marriage bound them formally together, they were nearly kin. Meanwhile, Webb had grown into a strong, able, self-reliant if somewhat headstrong young man, stout but fit, tall, fair-complexioned, with dark hair and hazel eyes. For more than half his life he had been "the man of the house," and from nine to nineteen, the mainstay of the farm. In 1860, he had even begun to think of starting a farm of his own.

Then the war came.

CHAPTER TWO

In 1861, the population of the United States was about 31.5 million, with an optimistic birthrate, a steady tide of immigration, and a robust, stable economy, nicely balanced, some would say, between the agrarian harvests of the South and Midwest and the industrial production of the North. Year after year, North, South, East, and West were being linked ever more closely by an expanding system of rail and river routes, and otherwise seemed to be knitting themselves together according to a national and integrated plan. The Union was apparently mighty: it had prevailed over the British Empire (yet again) in the War of 1812; had hugely enlarged its territorial demesne through the Louisiana Purchase; and from 1845 to 1848, through war and annexation, had wrenched vast tracts of land from Mexico to extend its continental boundaries from the Pacific to the Rio Grande. This was a democratic empire in the making, and one for which the Union itself was already a sacred, if not quite sacrosanct, idea. Politicians of every stripe embraced it as "an object of general worship"—especially on national occasions, such as the inauguration of a president or the Fourth of July—even as the people themselves looked to it as the pledge of their hopes. But for all that, a fault line ran through the body politic, cleaving it in two. The essential issue, shed of all others, was slavery, and the immediate theater of conflict was just that bounty of new land that had opened up in the West. Was it to be slave? Or free? The blessing and the curse of it went hand in hand.

At the nation's founding, several compromises had been carefully forged between the states to give the new Union traction, among them, the adoption of a federal Senate with a national House of Representatives to mediate between the claims of federal and state authority; related to this was a clause in the Constitution that allowed the South, in the apportionment of its representation, to count each slave as three-fifths of a man. These, together with the Fugitive Slave Law of 1793, which provided for the return between states of escaped slaves, had helped keep North and South together, while (it was hoped) slavery found its own best way to die. Even slaveholders like Jefferson, as well as pre-Abolitionists like John Adams, had imagined this might happen over time. But in the intervening years, two things occurred to dash that hope to the ground. First, the economic (or plantation) conditions that had long fostered slavery in the South were fatally reinforced by a new dependence on cotton; second, instead of consenting to the national and international trend toward abolition, the South not only clung to slavery for its own survival but sought to enlarge its domain.

According to guidelines laid down by Congress, new territories were supposed to "be disposed of for the common benefit" and "settled and formed into distinct republican states." The process for this was clear: a rudimentary legislature was to be elected by the settlers, a governor appointed by the president, and the new state with an approved Constitution admitted by congressional Act. Since 1789, free and slave states had been admitted together in pairs to ensure parity between the two interests, but in 1817 the demand of Missouri to be admitted as a slave state had threatened to tilt the scales. A compromise was reached in 1820 that allowed Missouri to come in as a slave state in conjunction with the free state of Maine, but it also prohibited slavery from all territory (Missouri excepted) north of the parallel 36/30, that is, from the great northwest. That immense region, no Southerner could fail to note, "was equal in size to all the slave states combined."

The Missouri Compromise appeared to save the day, but a geographical line had now been ominously drawn between the two sections, and the shrillness of the debate to which it had given rise had rung out across the nations, in Jefferson's memorable words, "like a firebell in the night." From that day forward, apprehension was in the air. "While the union lasts, we have high, exciting, gratifying prospects spread out before us," declared Daniel Webster. "Beyond that I seek not to penetrate the veil. God grant that, in my day at least, that curtain may not rise . . . on the broken and dishonoured fragments of a once glorious union; on States dissevered, discordant, belligerent; on a land rent with civil feuds, or drenched it may be, in fraternal blood!"

As the years passed, the population of the free states increased faster than that of the slave, giving them a numerical advantage in the House; in response, the slave states began to demand a federal guarantee of their minority rights. South Carolina's John C. Calhoun—once a nationalist, almost a Federalist—became, toward the end of his life, the insistent voice of that demand. He saw accurately enough that on either side of the divide there were now two communities essentially opposed to one another in just about every respect—yoked together, perhaps, by a constitutional alliance, but not united in fact. Beginning in 1831, he began to argue that the Federal Union was actually more of a compact among sovereign states, and that any one state could therefore "nullify" or declare an act of Congress unconstitutional unless a constitutional amendment (with two-thirds of all states concurring) could make it law.

The question was, What form of government had the Founders in fact created? A league? Or a national entity, commanding a fealty all its own? The Constitution itself was not clear on the matter, so it was left to the politicians to fight it out. In the end, they fought it to a draw. As Daniel Webster put it in a notable Senate speech: "Turn this question over and present it as we will—argue it as we may—exhaust upon it all the fountains of metaphysics—stretch over it all the meshes of logical and political subtlety—it still comes to this, Shall we have a general government? Shall we continue the union of the states under a *government* instead of a league? This is the upshot of the whole matter; because, if we are to have a government, that government must act like other governments, by majorities; it must have this power, like other governments, of enforcing its own laws and its own decisions; clothed with authority by the people and always responsible to the people, it must be able to hold its course unchecked." Otherwise, the Union would fail.

Slavery and states' rights, in its extremest form, now bound themselves together and would go down together as a losing cause. In the cities and towns, small and commercial farms of New England and the upper Midwest, "a kind of intense decency mingled with a robust materialism" demanded adherence to the principle of opportunity for all. Even if many Northerners could accept slavery in the South, as many did, its expansion into the unoccupied West remained unpalatable, because, if only in an opportunistic way, it seemed to limit what that land could become.

One crisis followed another: most notably in 1846 over the Wilmot Proviso, a second attempt in Congress to ban slavery from new lands; then in 1850 over the admission of California as a free state. The latter was ultimately resolved in a compromise that left open the destiny of New Mexico and Utah, banned the slave trade from the District of Columbia, but made the Fugitive Slave Law more stringent than before. It really settled nothing, and the whole issue reemerged with a vengeance when Congress had to decide what to do about the territories of Kansas and Nebraska in 1854. The upshot was the Kansas–Nebraska Act, sponsored by Stephen A. Douglas, a Senate Democrat from Illinois, which provided for their organization under the principle of popular sovereignty. That meant, simply, that the settlers in a territory could decide for themselves whether it would enter the Union as a free or a slave state. As innocuous as that may sound, its effect was to lift the ban against slavery above the line the Missouri Compromise had drawn. Douglas made his own position clear: "If Kansas wants a slave constitution, she has a right to it; if she wants a free state constitution, she has a right to it. It is none of my business which way the slavery clause is decided. I care not whether it is voted up or down." In fact, he seems to have expected (being too clever for his own—or the country's—good) that antislave settlers would ultimately overwhelm those hoping to plant slavery in the West. But he utterly failed to anticipate the clamor his proposal would arouse or the fervor with which it would be embraced by the South. Members of the Senate came to the chamber armed with bowie knives and pistols in an atmosphere of such violence as to almost stop debate. In the end, President Franklin Pierce placed the prestige of his administration on the line and the Act was pushed through, with catastrophic results.

Northerners poured into Kansas from the North, Southerners from the South. Civil war broke out between the two factions as both claimed the land as their own. Rival governments were established, and both appealed for recognition. Congress and the president, now James Buchanan, took opposite sides. From this blood-stained chaos, the Free-Soilers rose triumphant, along with the prospect of never-ending strife. Three years later their apparent victory was embittered and potentially reversed by the Supreme Court's decision in the Dred Scott case. That decision, which denied freedom to a fugitive black, also ruled that bans against the extension of slavery were unconstitutional, contrary to Fifth Amendment rights. In other words, the Court decided that slaves were property—movable property—that could be taken anywhere their owners wished. By extension, it was feared, even free states might be denied the right to prohibit slavery in their midst.

The major political parties began to crack. The Whigs split into two factions, one pro-, the other anti-slavery; the Democrats, into a Southern and a Northern wing. The Northern, led by Stephen A. Douglas, made popular sovereignty its creed. Meanwhile, in 1854, various antislavery advocates from sundry factions united to form the new Republican Party, which supplanted the Whigs as the second party in the land. Just two years later, in its first presidential bid, the Republican candidate, John C. Frémont, the "Pathfinder of the Rockies," carried all the free states save five. "A minor shift," it was noted, "would give these five states to the Republicans and make a President—without a single vote from the South!"

Ambivalence beset the population at large. Powerful banking and commercial interests in the North depended on cotton and were anxious to protect their investments in Southern states; working-class whites were concerned about competition from black labor; others were convinced, on constitutional grounds, that, for better or for worse, slavery in the South had been sanctioned by law. "Notwithstanding that slavery is a great wrong," one contemporary put it, "it had been permitted at the origin of our government and in justice to the Slave States, could not be abrogated without their consent. Yet it should not be extended into the Free States or into territory out of which Free States could be made." The hard truth of the Civil War was that it emerged from a collision of two fundamental and fundamentally valid principles of democratic government: the right of men to govern themselves, as embraced by the South in the form of states' rights, and the right of a national majority, as embraced by the North, to decide what kind of nation it would be.

Illinois was the fractured Union in a mirror: divided in its allegiance, north and south, by its own sectional slant. Most of the upper half of the state had been settled by New Englanders; the lower, by pioneers from Georgia, Kentucky, and Tennessee. In the senatorial election of 1858, the state, as one reporter put it at the time, was "in every respect . . . the Union for the time being"—the very place where "the battle of the Union will be fought." He was right. The two contestants were Stephen A. Douglas, the incumbent, who had a national reputation and a Southern following and, as chairman of the Senate Committee on Territories, stood as the acknowledged authority on all the issues under debate; and Abraham Lincoln, a relative unknown, with destiny, wisdom, and literary genius on his side.

Born in a log cabin in backwoods Kentucky to frontier drifters, Lincoln had grown up dirt-poor with almost no formal schooling and had learned to write with a piece of charcoal on a wooden shovel "scraped clean with a drawing knife." His access to books had been limited, but he devoured all he could get and went over and over *Aesop's Fables, Robinson Crusoe, Pilgrim's Progress*, Parson Weems's *Life of Washington*, and a short history of the United States. As he developed, he also read general history, philosophy, and poetry; trained his mind to logical demonstration by the study of Euclid; and immersed himself in the Bible—"retaining them all," recalled a friend, as if each one had been the study of his life. Physically imposing, rawboned and tall, "with large features, dark, shriveled skin, and rebellious hair," he had been famously strong as a youth, could "wrastle something fierce" and hoist a cask full of beer and drink out of the bunghole. But it was his inner strength and life that memorably marked his features as he aged. He loved a good story, possessed a ready wit, detested any kind of cruelty, and was deeply touched by the pathos of life and the mortality of all earthly things. From his constant preoccupation with such matters, his face acquired a grave and melancholy cast.

During his youth and early manhood, Lincoln had been somewhat shiftless and had lived in various towns in Kentucky, Indiana, and Illinois; eventually, he settled in Springfield. Meanwhile, his father, Thomas, and his stepmother, Sarah (Abe's own mother having died when he was nine), moved to Coles County just out-side of Charleston, and there, about ten miles from where Webb grew up, bought a farm. By then, Lincoln had been making his own way in the world. A livelihood had not come easily. At one time or another, he had managed a mill, split rails, tried his hand at invention, been a flatboatman, a farmhand, and a postman, and had worked in a general store. Along the way, however, he had also locked on to his star and had more or less constantly applied himself to politics and law. These ultimately worked in tandem, and by the time he obtained his license as an attorney in 1836, he was a member of the state assembly, where he served four terms. From 1847 to 1849 he also served in Congress, before settling down to the practice of law. As an advocate, he was diligent and successful, attracted clients high and low, covered the many coun-ties (including Coles) of Illinois's 8th Judicial Circuit, and pros-pered in the public eye. In 1854, he also briefly considered a run for the Senate after the Kansas–Nebraska Act aroused his ire.

In short, Lincoln was no novice, and if, as yet, his reputation was mainly local, Douglas, on learning of his nomination, said, "I shall have my hands full. He is the strong man of his party—full of it, facts, dates—and the best stump-speaker, with his droll ways and dry jokes, in the West. He is as honest as he is shrewd; and if I beat him, my victory will be hard won."

Even before Douglas said this, Lincoln had shown how strong he could be. In accepting the Republican nomination, he warned, "A house divided against itself cannot stand. I believe this govern-ment cannot endure permanently half slave and half free. I do not expect the Union to be dissolved. I do not expect the house to fall—but I do expect it will cease to be divided. It will become all one thing or all the other. Either the opponents of slavery will ar-rest the further spread of it, and place it where the public mind shall rest in the belief that it is in the course of ultimate extinction; or its advocates will push it forward till it shall become alike lawful in all the states, old as well as new—North as well as South." To such a distinct and commanding voice, the people lent their ears.

Douglas launched his campaign with a speech from the balcony of the Tremont House in Chicago on July 9. He paid tribute to Lincoln as a "kind, amiable, and intelligent gentleman, a good citizen and an honorable opponent," but challenged his categorical vision of the nation as either slave or free. That implied, he said, "a uniformity in institutions and local regulations that had never been contemplated by the framers" and invited "a war of sections," thus raising the specter of civil war. Douglas believed he had hit on an invincible theme, and his journey from Chicago to Springfield came to resemble a triumphal procession, with all the trappings of a postvictory parade. He traveled in his own special train, colorfully decorated with flags that proclaimed him "the Champion of Popular Sovereignty"; in tow was a six-pound cannon mounted on a flatcar that announced his arrival at each stop with a thunderous boom. At Bloomington, several thousand people waited at the station in the rain to greet him, and that evening, after an imposing display of fireworks, he addressed an immense crowd from a platform erected in the courthouse square.

Lincoln, somewhat underfunded, followed Douglas about the state as best he could and tried to rebut his remarks as soon as they were made. But he always seemed to be "trailing into town" on the heels of his opponent, only to be engulfed in the crowd that had assembled to hear him speak. Finally, he challenged Douglas to a series of joint debates; to his surprise, Douglas accepted, the encounters to take place at some prominent locale in each of the seven congressional districts of the state.

The first debate was held at Ottawa, Kendall County, on August 21; but it was the second, at Freeport in Stephenson County, on August 27, that really set the stage. In the course of it, Lincoln, who had denounced the Dred Scott decision, challenged Douglas to reconcile his support for the High Court ruling with the popu-

lar sovereignty he espoused. In what became known as the
Freeport Doctrine, Douglas replied that although a territorial
legislature could not prohibit slavery, for so the Court had declared, neither could it be forced to protect it. It could uphold it or
not by the laws it chose to enact. To many, that seemed as slippery
as an eel.

Lincoln was favored in the upper, Douglas in the lower part of
the state. It was therefore in the hotly contested central counties
like Coles that the campaign would have to be won. The Coles
debate was their fourth and marked the midpoint of their duel.
Neither, in fact, had the advantage when, on September 18, they
met at the County Fair Grounds just outside of Charleston before
a large and expectant crowd.

As it happened, Webb was there.

Both candidates had spent the previous night in nearby Mattoon, before proceeding to Charleston by different routes. Douglas was greeted by a two-and-a-half-mile-long cavalcade of
supporters, including thirty-two young couples on horseback,
each representing a state. The Lincoln parade, a slightly lesser
crowd, was led by the Bowling Green Band from Terre Haute, Indiana, and included a gigantic float bedecked with wildflowers and
covered with muslin and silk. Emblazoned along one side was the
motto "Westward the Star of Empire Takes its Way, Our Girls
link-on to Lincoln, Their Mothers were for Clay." This was
meant to remind the voters that the great statesman Henry Clay
of Kentucky, a man of hallowed name, had (by the Missouri Compromise and some other measures he had crafted) opposed the
spread of slavery to the West. On the float itself rode thirty-two
girls (again, one for each state) wearing blue velvet caps adorned
with a silver star; one, representing Kansas, was dressed in mourn-
ing garb. The streets of Charleston were festooned with flags and
pennants, many of them large and impressively unfurled, but all
were dwarfed by one remarkable banner over eighty feet long that

had been strung from the courthouse across the main square. This boldly proclaimed in big, blue letters "Coles County for Abe Lincoln" and featured a life-size painting of Lincoln as a young man driving an ox-drawn Kentucky wagon above the caption "Old Abe 30 Years Ago."

All through the morning and early afternoon a restive crowd had gathered, and by 2 in the afternoon it was said to be fifteen thousand strong. The people came from Hutton, Dog Town, Greasy Creek, Muddy Point, Paradise, Buck Grove, Farmington, Goosenest Prairie, Pinhook, and other towns and settlements. Webb and his brother, John, were among them, having come up with their mother, grandparents, and an uncle that morning in a farm wagon from Hutton, ten miles away. As the day promised to be a long, hot, sticky one, they had brought with them a large hamper full of garden vegetables to refresh them and (like many another) plenty of "cider to cut the dust." When they got to the Fair Grounds the crowd was already teeming as they made their way slowly toward the front, where the wide platform stood. Rough board seats had been provided for part of the audience, but most were obliged to stand. Some sixty people had also taken their places on the dais—Party leaders and other dignitaries as well as members of the press. In the assembled throng, partisans carried campaign placards and banners. Those for Douglas proclaimed him "the little Giant" (he was five feet two) or read, "The government was made for white men—Douglas for life!" Lincoln was hailed as "Honest Abe" and "Abe, the Giant Killer." Some showed him felling Douglas with a club.

The two men were oddly matched. Douglas was short, barrel-chested, and robust, had a rich, impressive, baritone voice, and strutted about the stage "with the air of a fighting cock." He was an enormously self-confident debater with a polished manner, and on that day was dressed "like a plantation owner or a cavalier." Lincoln, less elegant by far, was tall, stoop-shouldered, with a ramshackle build; he wore a faded coat a bit short at the sleeves and baggy trousers that lapped over the tops of his boots. Whereas Douglas had a smooth and pleasant face, Lincoln's was weathered and craggy, and in contrast to the sonorities Douglas could command, Lincoln had a backwoods twang to his voice that seemed almost crude. That voice, in fact, had an almost falsetto ring, "as high-pitched as a boatswain's whistle," which seemed strange in a man so large. Even so, it seemed to carry farther than Douglas's baritone.

The affair got off to a raucous start. After the speakers took their places, some Republicans rushed forward with a large banner showing Lincoln pinning Douglas to the ground and worrying him as a dog would a bone. Lest its meaning be missed, it bore the inscription "Lincoln Worrying Douglas at Freeport." Democrats objected and Lincoln supported them in this, saying, "Let us have nothing offensive to any man today." But then some Democrats rushed to the front with their own large banner showing Lincoln cavorting with a black girl. This was captioned "Negro Equality" and implied that miscegenation was Lincoln's real aim. Two of his supporters leaped from the platform to tear it down, and a scuffle ensued. When the commotion at length died down, the three-hour debate began—forty-five minutes late—at quarter to 3.

At Charleston, Lincoln was on both friendly and unfriendly ground. On the one hand, his father had lived out his days in the town and his stepmother and a number of relatives lived there still. Over the years, Lincoln's law practice had also brought him into contact with the community, and he was regarded locally as a good man. But the issues of slavery and racial equality were hotly debated in its precincts and did not favor him, because a majority of the townsfolk had Southern roots, having migrated north from Kentucky and Tennessee. At the same time, Coles County had certain traditions that inclined Lincoln's way. Organized in 1831, it had been named for Edward Coles, a former state governor best remembered for his antislavery views. As the son of a wealthy Virginia planter, he had grown up in the midst of slavery, conceived a hatred of it, and in April 1819 had set out for Illinois to free the slaves he owned. They descended the Ohio River together, and when he reached his destination, he not only released them all but gave to the head of each family over a hundred acres of land. In subsequent years he fought hard to keep Illinois from becoming a slave state, though he failed to prevent the legislature from enacting so-called Black Laws aimed at preventing free blacks from coming in.

Throughout the debates, Lincoln argued that the Declaration of Independence had envisioned the gradual improvement in the conditions of all men, blacks as well as whites. "I should like to know," he remarked on an earlier occasion, "if, taking this Declaration of Independence, which declares that all men are created equal upon principle, and making exception to it, where will it stop? If one man says it does not mean a Negro, why may not another man say it does not mean some other man? If that declaration is not the truth, let us get the statute book in which we find it and tear it out." But in Charleston he seemed to adopt a different stance.

It was not his finest hour. In the first five minutes of his opening remarks, he disclaimed any desire to bring about "in any way the social and political equality of the white and black races" and declared against allowing blacks to participate as voters or jurors in the nation's civic life. As for intermarriage, he coyly remarked, "I do not understand that because I do not want a Negro woman for a slave I must necessarily want her for a wife," which drew laughter and cheers. After that, Lincoln devoted almost an hour to elaborating a charge that Douglas had conspired to deprive the people of Kansas of the very popular sovereignty he espoused. When it came time for Douglas to speak, he accused Lincoln of being a chameleon on the whole issue of race relations and of adapting his pronouncements to wherever he happened to be in the state: "jet black" in the north, "a decent mulatto" in the center, and "almost white" in the south. Yet he also insisted that Lincoln was a "rank Abolitionist" at heart, and that part of the proof of it was the support he received from the celebrated black leader Frederick Douglass and others (black and white) who belonged to the Abolitionist camp.

The truth is, Lincoln's views on slavery were a little hard to pin down. His campaign was really based on the moral iniquity of slavery, not racial equality, and on the need to keep slavery out of the West. His argument, at least at the time, was that opposition to slavery did not imply social equality any more than opposition to the extension of slavery to the territories implied interfering with it where it existed in the states. Certainly, he had no notion then of its extirpation in the South. In his career as a lawyer, he had argued two slavery cases, one in 1841 on behalf of a Negro girl who had been held as a slave without proof of indenture, another in 1847 in Coles County on behalf of a slaveholder; but he had never been for slavery itself. In his adamant opposition to the Dred Scott decision as well as the Kansas–Nebraska Act, he had been second to none. But the strength of his repugnance and what he thought could be done about slavery in the legal sense evolved over time. One turning point seems to have come in 1841, when on board a steamer from Kentucky he saw a coffle of slaves shackled together "like so many fish on a trot line," a sight that haunted him for years. On the other hand, in the Illinois State Legislature and later, in his first year as president, he also expressed the view that neither the president nor Congress had the power under the Constitution to tamper with slavery where it had already taken root.

Yet, however qualified his stance, almost everyone seemed to agree that the difference between Lincoln and Douglas was not one of degree but kind. Douglas himself went out of his way to make this clear. He liked to talk about the "white basis" of America and how everything had been arranged, properly, for "the benefit of white men." He was prepared to see slavery made national. Lincoln thought no man, or class of men, should exist for the benefit of any other and held that the Constitution had recognized slavery only as a local institution, and that there it must stop. In the eyes of Douglas, such views made Lincoln almost a traitor to his race. When it came to the doctrine of popular sovereignty, Lincoln also tried to show the true divide. If the bloodbath in Kansas was an example of the fruits of it, he asked, what good could it be? It left the whole question of slavery unresolved. "When are we to have peace upon it, if it is kept in the position it now occupies? . . . If Kansas should sink today, and leave a great vacant space in the earth's surface, this vexed question would still be among us. I say, then, there is no way of putting an end to [it] . . . but to put it back upon the basis where our fathers placed it; no way but to . . . restrict it forever to the old States where it now exists. Then the public mind *will* rest in the belief that it is in the course of ultimate extinction." With that he returned to the great theme and some of the same language of his "house divided" speech.

Webb heard, and sifted, all this as best he could. He was sixteen at the time and probably didn't know any blacks—indeed, could scarcely have known what racial equality meant. But he did believe, or had been raised to believe, in the Declaration of Independence and thought, with Lincoln, that its words must point the way. The alternative seemed to hold out only the prospect of turmoil without end. Nor could Webb accept the notion that the Union was a "league." At least, when the break finally came, he would have none of "states' rights" in the sense that a state could claim some allegiance above that owed the central power. And so at the end of that historic day, with all these issues revolving in some heightened way in his young mind, he and his brother and their elders slowly made their way back home to Hutton, just as dusk was falling, along the crowded dirt road that looped southeastward toward their farm.

The election was close. Lincoln ran ahead in the popular vote; Douglas, or rather, his Party, carried the legislature and was therefore reelected by the rules that then applied. But the contest had made Lincoln a figure of national renown. He had emerged from the debates, as one writer put it, "one of the chief intellectual leaders of America, with a place in English literature; Douglas came out—a Senator from Illinois." Indeed, the "little Giant" had lost much of his standing. No longer much loved in the North, his equivocal Freeport Doctrine had also poisoned his name in the South, where former supporters now saw him as "some blind Samson pulling down their temple about their ears." The following year, John Brown's raid on the little Virginia town of Harper's Ferry shook that temple to the ground. As a self-styled armed prophet of Abolition, Brown had hoped to raise a general slave revolt. In that sense, his raid was a fiasco: no revolt was sparked, and he was trapped by federal troops brought up from Washington under a cavalry colonel by the name of Robert E. Lee. After his capture, he was tried and hanged. In the South, he was regarded as a criminal fanatic; in the North, some saw him as a "saint," born, wrote Emerson, "to make the gallows glorious like the cross."

America was on the cusp. Partisan feeling ran about as high as it could without exploding, yet still, even some extremists remained divided in their minds. One such was Alexander Stephens, who as a Whig had supported the annexation of Texas, the Compromise of 1850, the Kansas–Nebraska Act of 1854, and the institution of slavery; but he did not want to see the Union dissolved. On the morning of March 5, 1859, as he left Washington after having served in Congress as a representative from Georgia for sixteen years, he was asked by a companion whether he might one day return to Washington as a member of the Senate. "No," he replied, "I never expect to see Washington again—unless I am brought here as a prisoner of war.'"

The following April, as the presidential campaign of 1860 got underway, the Democratic convention that met at Charleston, South Carolina, produced two national tickets: one led by John C.

Breckinridge of Kentucky, the other by Douglas of Illinois. A sizable block of other Democrats with a pro-Unionist bent defected to form the Constitutional Union Party under John Bell of Tennessee. The Republicans turned to Lincoln, who had been critical of John Brown, had a Southern wife and Southern roots, and was considered a moderate in the antislavery camp. It was hoped that his conciliatory disposition might help keep the Union intact.

The campaign was almost a reprise of the Illinois race; all the familiar issues were rehashed. In the end, Bell emerged as the leading candidate of the upper South, in Virginia, Kentucky, and Tennessee; Breckinridge, in all the slaveholding states except Missouri; Lincoln, in all the free states but one. When all the votes were tallied, Lincoln fell well short of a popular majority, but his electoral margin was clear. That, however, made him a minority president. He had been raised to power by his Party, not the nation, which, even in less rending times, would have shadowed his right to rule. Indeed, although the South was not directly imperiled by his election (because he accepted slavery where it was), it was unwilling to accept a government essentially hostile to its way of life. From South Carolina on December 20 the signal rocket of secession went up; shortly thereafter, Mississippi, Florida, Alabama, Louisiana, and Texas followed suit. On February 8, 1861, delegates from all these states met to form a provisional government, framed a Constitution that recognized state sovereignty and upheld slavery, and chose as their president Jefferson Davis, a Mississippi Senator and former secretary of war. Alexander Stephens was made vice president and tried to give the practice of slavery a biblical spin. "The negro, by nature and by the curse against Canaan," he explained, "is fitted for the condition he occupies in our system . . . It is, indeed, in conformity with the Creator. It is not for us to inquire into the wisdom of His ordinances, or to question them. For His own purposes He has made one race to differ from another as He has made one 'star to differ from another star in glory.' The great objects of humanity are best attained when conformed to His laws, in the constitution of governments as well as in all things else. Our confederacy is founded upon a strict conformity with these laws. 'The stone which was rejected by the first builders is become the chief stone of the corner in our new edifice,'" quoting Matthew 21:42, but inverting the meaning of the text.

At least at first, Davis assumed a more plaintive tone. "We seek no conquest, no aggrandizement, no concession of any kind from the States with which we were lately confederated," he declared; "all we ask is to be left alone." Many in the North were prepared to oblige. But that would have meant allowing a gigantic "foreign power," as it were, to seize, control, and occupy the lower Mississippi Valley, which the rest of the Union could scarcely abide. With the act of secession, moreover, the principal issue changed. Slavery receded to be replaced by the legitimate claims of majority rule. In the face of Southern defiance, the whole future of democratic government seemed at stake.

James Buchanan, the outgoing president, seemed at a loss. On December 4, 1860, he sent a message to Congress in which he pronounced secession unconstitutional, but "denied his own right to oppose such a course." As one observer acidly remarked, he thereby "showed conclusively" that it was "the duty of the President to execute the laws—unless somebody opposes him; and that no State has a right to go out of the Union—unless it wants to." Perhaps Buchanan hoped passions would cool as a result of his inaction. Instead, in the South at least, they ran to a boil, as the new Confederate government took advantage of the interlude between administrations to consolidate itself politically and prepare for war. It promptly seized, or tried to seize, all federal property within its boundaries, including military installations such as arsenals, harbors, and forts, and it sent emissaries to Washington to request accreditation as the envoys of a foreign power.

Meanwhile, Congress panicked, and in a series of desperately proposed measures sought to appease the seceded states by extending the Missouri Compromise to the Pacific, admitting at least two new Western states as slave, and strengthening the Fugitive Slave Law still further until it was set with iron teeth. Congress was even willing to place slavery itself beyond the reach of constitutional amendment, enshrining it forever in the law. A resolution in support of all these measures actually passed the House and Senate by wide margins. But Lincoln refused to go along.

In an atmosphere of crisis, he made his way to the capital, entered it by night under threat to his life, and on March 4 was inaugurated under military guard. In his inaugural address, he promised to do everything in his power to preserve the Union and pledged to maintain the authority of the Federal government with respect to its own property in every state. At the same time, he promised to do this without "bloodshed or violence," unless these were forced upon him by the South. "In your hands, my dissatisfied fellow countrymen, and not in mine," he said, "is the momentous issue of civil war."

By the end of March 1861, all the issues pertaining to the government's authority were "linked to the fate of a tiny man-made island" built on a shoal in South Carolina's Charleston harbor, where Fort Sumter, garrisoned by a small number of Federal soldiers, stood. The Confederate authorities demanded their surrender; they refused. The fort was thereupon ringed with heavy guns, and to prevent any attempt by the Federal government to relieve it under cover of darkness, the Rebels installed powerful calcium lights on two adjacent shoals and moored scows piled with wood for burning at the harbor's mouth. In early April, with the garrison running out of food, Lincoln announced that he planned to send in provisions. On the morning of April 12, in a preemptive strike, the Confederate bombardment began. The shelling continued without cease for thirty-four hours until the fort was ablaze, and at noon on the 14th, the Stars and Stripes came down. The next day, Lincoln declared the seceded states in rebellion and issued a proclamation calling for seventy-five thousand three-month volunteers. Public sentiment in the North firmly coalesced around his action, but the immediate price of it was high, as Virginia, North Carolina, Arkansas, and Tennessee joined in the revolt.

The lines had now been drawn for war. Politically it was a civil war, but from a purely military point of view it was a war between two states. It would last almost four years, involve 3 million men, and kill six hundred thousand of them in two thousand engagements as the nation paid its awful toll to Mars.

The military or strategic objectives of the North were to master the Mississippi and cut off Louisiana, Arkansas, Texas, and, if need be, Missouri from the other states; to take Chattanooga and other positions in Tennessee, which commanded railway lines that bound the Confederate territory together; and to blockade the coast to prevent the South from receiving supplies or marketing its products abroad. The Mississippi River bore the same relation to the seceding states as the Hudson had to the colonies in the Revolutionary War; that is, it cut them in two. If the Union could control it, men from either side of the line would be hard put to support each other or come to each other's aid with arms and supplies. In or from the East, the general plan called for the reduction of the Confederate capital of Richmond, Virginia, after which Rebels could be pushed back to the southern end of the Appalachian Mountains, where armies east and west would join to end the task.

The South, on the other hand, did not have to conquer territory to secure its independence, but only persuade the North that it could not win. Should a military deadlock develop, the South might also look for the intervention of foreign powers—in particular, England and France—"who for various reasons would not be sorry to see the United States partitioned and control of the cotton trade wrested from Northern hands." Although the North controlled the seas and had an immense advantage in numbers, wealth, and industrial might, "it also had to do the invading," and the territory it had to invade—and subdue—had a thirty-five-hundred-mile coastline and 190 harbors and was as large as Portugal, France, and the British Isles combined. Long, tenuous lines of communication would be required to hold on to what was gained, backed by every bit of manpower advantage the North enjoyed. Finally, the North would also have to break the will of a proud people who, rightly or wrongly, had convinced themselves that they were fighting for their own heritage of freedom as well as hearth and home.

The outcome, in fact, was by no means clear.

The traditional military organization of the United States was based on the state militia, raised and trained by the states and led by state-appointed officers, with junior officers elected by the men. Almost all the senior officers on both sides had graduated from West Point and served in the Mexican War, on the Western frontier, and in the Indian Wars. Many had also been instructors at West Point. But they knew little about large-scale fighting and almost nothing about tactics. Even most generals with experience had commanded no more than two or three companies in the field. So they were ill-equipped to handle the vast citizen armies now abruptly entrusted to their care. At West Point, the curriculum had stressed mathematics and engineering over combat training; in practice, the lives of most soldiers had been given over to a routine of road building, post maintenance, and other like chores.

Neither side was prepared. The Federal army as it existed in 1861 was not even large enough to subdue a single Confederate state. Altogether it consisted of about sixteen thousand men, most of them dispersed among frontier posts in the West; a third of its officer corps at once defected to the South. The Federal navy, such as it was, consisted of just six screw-frigates, twenty sailing vessels, a handful of gunboats, and five steam sloops. Eleven of these vessels, moored at the Navy Yard at Norfolk, immediately fell into Confederate hands.

Neither side had enough arms to go around. In the beginning, some soldiers entered battle armed with old sporting rifles, shotguns, or 1812-style muskets, even as their generals puzzled over the topography of the ground. Unlike Europe, where, as a result of centuries of strife, military maps noted almost every road, stream, bridge, swamp, hamlet, and patch of forest, that part of America where most of the Civil War would be fought had never been thoroughly studied with respect to the movement of troops or war matériel. Due to the tangled character of the country, many of the battles would also come to resemble vast bush fights, which made it difficult to deploy and maneuver large forces in the field.

Both sides issued successive calls for volunteers, the Union again in July for up to half a million more to serve for three years. By August, both armies were over two hundred thousand strong. In the North, some naïvely predicted a swift Union triumph, but wiser heads demurred. As General William Tecumseh Sherman watched the raw troops come in, he dolefully remarked, "You might as well use a squirt-gun on the flames of a burning house." His opinion was promptly put to the test. On May 24, Federal troops crossed the Potomac, seized Alexandria and Arlington Heights, established their camp on the south side of the river, and entrenched their line before Washington along a broad front. General Winfield Scott, then in command of the Army of the United States and "the hero of two wars," was "the only man in America," notes one historian, "who had ever actually commanded as many as 5,000 men. But he was now too old for active duty, so Brevet-Major Irvin McDowell, an officer of the Adjutant General's Department, was made a brigadier general and given command of the forces on the Potomac's south bank." McDowell had never directed so much as a squad in the field. Nevertheless, his army of thirty-five thousand was the largest ever assembled on the continent. Meanwhile, twenty-five miles to the south at Manassas Junction, near a stream called Bull Run, Confederate General P. G. T. Beauregard had established his own, slightly smaller but equally green army to hold the Rebel line. The Northern public clamored for an attack, and on July 21 the two armies clashed. At first, the Federals made headway and turned the Confederate left flank. But then Brigadier General Thomas T. Jackson stood like a "stone wall" until, toward the end of the day, he massed his troops for attack. They roared forward, and the war began with a Union rout.

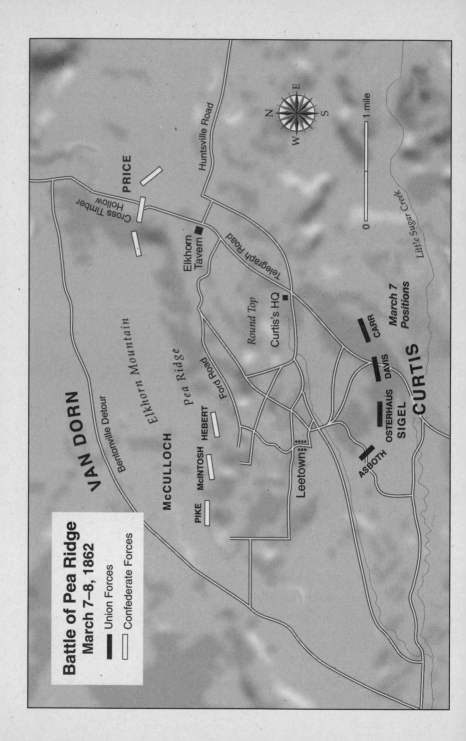

Battle of Pea Ridge
March 7–8, 1862

Union Forces
Confederate Forces

VAN DORN

PRICE

Cross Timber Hollow

Huntsville Road

Elkhorn Tavern

Telegraph Road

Bentonville Detour

Elkhorn Mountain

McCULLOCH

Pea Ridge

Round Top

Curtis's HQ

Ford Road

PIKE

McINTOSH

HEBERT

Leetown

ASBOTH

OSTERHAUS

SIGEL

DAVIS

CARR

March 7 Positions

CURTIS

Little Sugar Creek

N E S W

1 mile

0

CHAPTER THREE

That summer, when it looked as if the North would need every man it could get, Webb volunteered. Not everyone in the family wanted him to go, but he was his own man now, and so as not to draw out the parting he hurried on his way. In early August, he enlisted in a company led by Captain Westford Taggert (afterward promoted to major) and entrained for St. Louis, Missouri, where on August 9 he was mustered into service for three years at Arsenal Park. His company, Company E of the 25th Regiment of Illinois Volunteer Infantry, was composed almost entirely of Coles County men, most of them from Charleston, but included a number of friends from home, two cousins, and at least one stepbrother, Isaiah D. Moore, who joined at the same time. Isaiah was a drummer, one of the company's two musicians, and, like most musicians, would spend much of his time helping medics in the field.

St. Louis, MO. Aug. 7, 1861

Dear Mother:

I suppose you would like to know why I did not come by home as per agreement—Time would not permit—the company started on Monday (the 4) & I could not return home if I went with it. We arrived at St. Louis late in the evening—got supper at 10 P.M. Capt. Adam's company had only 40 men & was not received so I joined Capt. Taggert's company on the 6th. Am well satisfied with the change.

Some had enlisted for a lark. Webb was in earnest, and two days after being mustered in eloquently wrote his grandfather to explain:

St. Louis, MO. Aug. 11, 1861

Dear Grandfather:

. . . I ask forgiveness for going contrary to your wishes . . .
[but] I feel that I have only discharged a duty which as a good
citizen I owe to my country, to my friends & to liberty itself.
And now I ask your blessing as with my face to the enemy's
land I go forward—as long as this arm has strength to wield a
sword or handle a rifle; as long as these feet can carry me forward & these eyes can see to direct my steps I expect to march
forward unless they [the Rebels] submit to the Constitution &
laws . . .

If there was any doubt as to what Webb might have learned
from the great public debate, he put it to rest with this burst of
lofty passion that stamped him, like Lincoln, as a Union man all
the way.

At the same time, Webb's grandfather was apparently afraid he
might have been lured to the army by romantic ideas of war.
Webb promptly disabused him of any such concern: "I am already satisfied," he continued pointedly, "that a camp life is a
hard one & would not advise any of my friends to join the army
unless it becomes necessary." He would later come to feel, however, that some of those back home had not stepped forward as
they should.

St. Louis was the Union hub for the Western war, and Webb
had arrived just as the crucial struggle for Missouri was heating
up. The object of the Federal campaign in the West was to turn
the Confederate left flank. That flank was more or less traced by
the line of the Mississippi, and Missouri stood at its gate. If the
Rebels could take Missouri, Kentucky in turn would almost certainly fall, thereby adding 2.5 million people and a land mass the
size of Italy to the Rebel states. Enormous industrial resources
would also fall into Confederate hands and the war could be carried northward into Illinois. Indeed, Lincoln had moved at once

to secure Cairo, in the heart of "Little Egypt," to shut out secession from the southern part of the state.

In Missouri, Union troops in the field were commanded by Brigadier General Nathaniel Lyon, a red-bearded former infantry captain of boldness and panache, who had been decorated for bravery in the Mexican War. He regarded the Rebellion as a threat to "the great rights and hopes of the human race" and said he would rather die than see it prevail. At the outbreak of the war, he had been foremost in his fervor and had done much to establish Federal control in the state. He had secured St. Louis, driven the pro-Confederate Missouri State Guard out of Jefferson City, and helped chase them from Carthage and Booneville. On July 13, three weeks before Webb signed up, he then joined his forces to those of Colonel Franz Sigel, a Prussian-trained officer and artillery expert, who had been almost as energetic as Lyon in ousting the Rebels from their nests. But neither man at that moment enjoyed a large command. For though the Union had fifty-six thousand troops in the state, they had been rashly scattered among thirteen different posts. As a result, Lyon and Sigel had between them fewer than six thousand men. Meanwhile, the Confederate State Guard under Sterling Price had regrouped in the southwestern part of the state and had there combined with a larger force under Benjamin McCulloch that had been brought in from Arkansas to win Missouri for the South. The balance of power seemed at once to shift their way, for the recent Union defeat at Bull Run had emboldened the Rebels, even as their numbers grew.

Both Price and McCulloch were brigadiers. Price had a long career behind him in government service, first in Congress, then as governor of his state, and due to his venerable civic reputation was affectionately known as "Old Pap." McCulloch was cut from altogether different cloth. A former Texas Ranger and friend of Davy Crockett's, he had made a name for himself as the sheriff of

Sacramento during the Gold Rush and by his tough tactics against Comanches on the frontier. The two now set their sights on Lyon, who on August 1 had marched from Springfield in pursuit of Price. On the 3rd he encountered the Rebels in force in a valley called Dug Springs, and finding they had twice his strength, beat a quick retreat. Both armies followed the valley of Wilson's Creek northward, where, on August 8, twelve miles from Springfield, the Rebels went into camp.

The Federals were in a bad way. Lyon had almost no cavalry to screen his retreat, and the nearest reinforcements were at Rolla, 120 miles away. This was largely the fault of Major General John C. Frémont (the former Republican candidate for president), who had been running the Federal Department of the West ineptly since early July. Surmising that Price and McCulloch would probably overtake him in a day, Lyon turned to strike. On the evening of the 9th, he moved part of his force under his own command along one road to attack them in front; the other, under Sigel, moved around to hit them from the rear. As they were about to set out, Lyon told his troops, many of whom were green, "Men, we are going to have a fight . . . Don't shoot until you get orders. Fire low—don't aim higher than their knees. Wait until they get close. Don't get scared—it's no part of a soldier's duty to get scared."

At dawn, Sigel's column came within a mile of the Rebel tents, ascended the shrub-covered hills along the creek, and caught the Rebels at their breakfast, cooking corn. He brought his artillery into position and sent a shot into the middle of their camp. That was the signal for the battle to begin. As it unfolded, it seemed to go well for the Federals at first, not unlike Bull Run, but then the numbers told. Sigel found himself outflanked, lost five of his six cannon, and in the end his men ran. Lyon, meanwhile, gained a commanding eminence known as Oak Hill but could not hold the ground. His horse was shot from under him, his body carved with wounds, and as he swung his hat in a gallant gesture to lead a final charge, he fell, shot through the heart. In the manner and meaning of his death he would afterwards be compared to Joseph Warren, a hero of the Revolution cut down at Bunker Hill.

Wilson's Creek was the second major battle of the war and the first to see a Union general fall. Losses on both sides were proportionally stiff, but the victory gave the Rebels control for a time of southwestern Missouri and a lift to their adherents in the state. The Federals withdrew to Springfield and from there, unassailed, to the railhead at Rolla, their forward base. Five regiments were quickly dispatched to discourage the Confederates from advancing, and martial law was declared in St. Louis to keep pro-Rebel sentiment in check.

Throughout the state, but especially south of the Missouri River, "solitude and desolation reigned. Nearly all the houses and plantations had been deserted by their inhabitants," wrote one contemporary, and unharvested wheat, corn, and other grains rotted in the fields.

The day after the Union rout—as the news of it came in—Webb attended service in a field chapel where the chaplain took as his text for the day, "They that take the sword shall die by the sword" (Rev. 13:10), which did not comfort him much. But his patriotic ardor was not easily palled. He quickly adapted to the harsher realities of camp life, put up with the chronic diarrhea—"which is some what inconvenient, though not bad sickness"—that army rations gave the men, and matter-of-factly informed his brother, "We don't have more than half enough to eat." There also weren't enough rifles to go around, and his first night on guard duty (August 14) he was armed with a pick handle instead of a gun. On the 17th, blankets and muskets were handed out, with ten rounds of ammunition for each man. The order to march came down and "[we] took down our tents & got all ready at the expense of our dinners," but in the end were kept in place. Saboteurs were thought to be about and an attack threatened, so that

night "a double guard was put out." Webb was one of those selected to protect the Arsenal and took up his post at midnight, but
"we were disappointed, for there was no battle. [I] stood guard all
night with out sleep." These, he wrote his brother, with a touch of
stoic pride, are but "some of the particulars of soldier life so far as
I have tried it" (letter of August 18, 1861).

On August 23, just two weeks after being mustered in, Webb's
regiment left for Jefferson City, and from September 7 to 17, as part
of an operation against guerrillas, he scoured the countryside for
Rebel bands. During that time, he lived largely on peaches and
helped capture twelve horses but saw no direct action, though it
seemed to be getting near. Already, some of the raw recruits were
finding army life too much to bear. "I received yours of the 4th last
evening," he wrote his mother from Jefferson City on September
17. "It has been here, perhaps, several days. We are just in from a
ten day's scout. I am tired but send this that you may know I have
not forgotten you. How could I forget a Mother that has been as
good as you have been to me. I don't remember having said that Isaiah [his stepbrother, Isaiah D. Moore] was coming home. I heard
the Capt. say, however, that he, James Cartwright & several other
boys who are not strong would be sent home. But I don't think any
of them will come. Do not look for I. D. till you see him coming . . .
I should like to be at your apple cuttings very much . . . Mother can't
you write once a week. I love to hear from home so well."

After the Battle of Wilson's Creek, the Federals consolidated
their position at Rolla as Price struck north toward Lexington,
about eighty miles upriver from where Webb was encamped.
There, from September 17 to 20, Price besieged a Federal garrison, which Frémont had notably failed to reinforce. Conflicting
battlefield reports came in. First, he heard "that [Captain Thomas
A.] Marshall's cavalry & 500 Irish troops were taken prisoner,"
then that "our boys gained the day. They lost 800 men while the

secesh [secessionists] lost 4000. This is the news from Lexington last night at dark" (letters of September 17 and 21, 1861). The first (not second) report was true, and the fall of Lexington, the most important town between St. Louis and Kansas City, was judged a heavy blow. But Webb took heart. Like many volunteers, he viewed the war through the lens of his own ardor and was eager to show what he could do. "Now if Gen. Price wants fun," he wrote his mother with typical pluck, "let him come down here." With such bravado did he try to keep his courage up.

Frémont at last drew a substantial force together to advance on Price and on September 27 set out with a combined battery of eighty-six guns. Everyone expected to leave for Lexington to join the fray. "We are going up 20,000 strong, with Sigel at our head to see the fun," Webb wrote his grandfather. "Two companies went up the river, on the 'War Eagle,' scouting." Then he told a mischievous tale: "[These companies] were fired on & Lieut. Buckner had his shoulder straps cut off lest he should be selected as an officer & popped over. When they returned he went to the same lady that sewed them on in the first place & told her to sew them on a little stronger."

Instead of Lexington, his regiment was sent across the LaMine, Osage, and Pomme de Terre Rivers to Springfield via Sedalia, where there was also the prospect of a fight. Meanwhile, the men had received their uniforms—a simple blue overcoat, jacket, and pants "such as Doctor Lea wears"—but still no pay. "We have been expecting it," he wrote cuttingly, "tomorrow for several days." Mindful of the risk of scurvy, he was also consuming "plenty of apples, peaches & cider" in addition to his basic fare. Still, he told his mother, he was "not quite well." Though he looked for "a hard battle in the vicinity of Lexington" soon, he thought that even if it occurred it would be the last in the state that season before both sides hunkered down in winter camps. "If it [takes place] and I live," he added, she could expect to see him on furlough before too long. But that was not to be. Ahead of him lay a hard winter's war, which was only just beginning to take shape.

As combat threatened, he hankered for news from home. "Tell me whether any more of the boys have gone to war," he wrote his brother from Sedalia, "& whether you hug the girls any, & how the boys & girls get along on an average anyway." The bright, ordinary things of life helped to ease the strain. Meanwhile, in a tactical move, Price withdrew from Lexington toward the Arkansas frontier. The Federals gave chase, and Webb, who thrived on action, rebounded as it began.

Sedalia, Mo., Oct. 13, 1861

My Dear Brother:

. . . We left the Saline Bridge from where I wrote you last & moved up to Otterville 1½ miles. We were there just a week & then came here distance 14 miles. We came up on the [railroad] cars, but had to walk & push a good part of the way. It took all day. It seems that we start every time on Sunday. We expect to leave here tomorrow, or next day, following after Price. He is now a good ways ahead of us, & I think he will keep ahead, but reports are here that our fleet has taken New Orleans . . . I am as fat as ever I was, weigh 215 lbs. & think I am the best man in the Regt. Give my love to all.

Goodbye.
B. W. Baker

Webb's health (and heft) were amazing, given the daily ration he got. This consisted of twelve ounces of salt pork (or one pound, four ounces of salt beef), a pound and a half of flour or hardtack, and a little rice, navy beans, or peas. To this might be added three pounds of potatoes a week. It was pretty unpalatable fare. The pickled beef (or "salt horse," as it was called) had to be soaked before eating; the salt pork was flabby and the large, thick crackers called hardtack were often infested with weevils or blotched with mold. Ground rice sometimes served as a substitute for meal and pulverized peas for bread. Roots, tree buds, and even grass and weeds were occasionally simmered in a little water and consumed as soup and broth.

At this stage, everyone hoped and many believed that the madness of the war might soon be over. Rumors to that effect were rife. "Isaiah got a letter today from one of his friends in Washington," reported Webb, "who says that Gen. [Winfield] Scott has said that we shall all eat our Christmas dinners at home." In fact, Scott was one of the few men in the government who at the outset had predicted a four-years' war. In any case, Webb didn't put much stock in the report. (Eventually, he learned to question almost everything he heard.) Meanwhile, the realities of the war had begun to close in. In mid-October, he was called on, apparently with some success, to help impress "secesh teams" into service to haul the army's baggage and then proceeded to Warsaw, Missouri, in an effort to hem the Rebels in. He was in good spirits and full of grit: "We were three days marching to this place," he wrote his mother on October 19, "two of which it rained, making it a little disagreeable under foot as well as over head, but we had lots of fun anyway. It is said that we are [with] in 40 miles of Price, who is fortifying. If so perhaps we will have some real fun in a few days. If he keeps on retreating, & we follow, the next time you hear from me I shall be in Arkansas." Meanwhile, it had been blithely reported (falsely) that "Gen. [James Henry] Lane has captured McCulloch with all his army. Hope it is so."

Lane was a rough character, an Abolitionist in the John Brown mode, who a few weeks before had detected a Rebel cell in Osceolo and burned the town. A senator from Kansas, he had been commissioned a brigadier general but had declined the rank to keep his Senate seat. Nevertheless, he claimed the honorific and from the beginning of the war had been carrying on semi-independent, lawless depradations on the Kansas–Missouri frontier. His jayhawking escapades hadn't done the Federals much good and probably contributed to sentiment that, in late October, gave support to a rump convention at Neosho that voted to secede. Price was now said to be advancing on Springfield to make the vote stick. As the crisis deepened, Webb's unit was among those that hurried up from Otterville to Sedalia and from there 120 miles to Springfield to try to cut him off. Price got there first, briefly occupied the town, but then was driven out. "Our advance guard had a fight here with Gen. Price's rear guard," Webb wrote his mother from Springfield on November 1. "14 of our men were wounded & 15 killed out right. It is said that 100 rebs were killed." That seemed too good to be true, as battles went, "since our men charged." However, it was true. This was the famous Zagonyi Cavalry Charge, led by Major. Charles Zagonyi, a Hungarian expatriate, that secured the town ahead of Frémont's advance.

Soon thereafter, Webb was on the field. "The dead & wounded were taken care of," he reported, "yet the ground was sprinkled with blood. How queer one feels on a battle field. The feeling is very much the same as that felt on a fourth of July occasion when one hears the fife & drum. Price's camp is only 40 miles from here & we expect to have an engagement in the next five days. So the Col. told us today . . . perhaps in two. I almost feel anxious to be in a battle & yet I am almost afraid. I feel very brave sometimes & think if I should be in an engagement, I never would leave the field alive unless the stars & stripes floated triumphant. I do not know how it may be. If there is a battle & I should fall, tell with pride & not with grief that I fell in defense of liberty. Pray that I may be a true soldier."

Two days later, he learned that he would shortly be marching to Wilson's Creek, about ten miles from where he was encamped. "The Col. told us on dress parade this evening to pack our knapsacks & be ready for we would be ordered out before morning. I feel very brave now & when we get there, if I don't get weak in the knees shall do some good fighting." Having steeled himself for battle, he was plainly disappointed when he didn't get the chance. When they reached Wilson's Creek, Price wasn't there. (In fact, he was sixty miles away, near Neosho.) But the battlefield itself was still memorably littered with signs of Lyon's celebrated clash. "Hats, shirts, coats & clothing of all kinds are scattered all over the ground," he wrote his mother from Otterville on the 11th. "I saw the skull of one poor fellow who had been sent to his long home in a hurry by a ball entering just above the eye. Price has left the state and we expect to start for St. Louis in the morning. From St. Louis we go to Kentucky, or Tennessee."

Frustration clearly began to build in him, which came through in a letter he wrote to his Uncle Elijah on November 5, bringing him up to date: "Well, Uncle, we have traveled, almost all over the state of Missouri since I left home. We have been [with]in one day's march of a fight 5 or 6 times but have not got there yet, & guess we never will. Price escaped from Lexington & came to this place [Springfield] when we again came up with him after a toilsome march of 120 miles. Our advance guard consisting of 250 cavalry charged Price's rear guard and drove them out of town on the 28th of Oct. The report is that the rebels lost 100. The rangers lost 15 killed & 14 wounded. We got here the next day after marching 24 hours without sleep & but little to eat. We have been looking for a fight every day since." He wasn't the only one displeased. Lincoln was fed up with the way the battle for Missouri was going and, reported Webb, "news comes that Fremont is relieved by Gen. [David] Hunter & the policy is changed. Fremont is thought unsound."

Hunter lasted but a week, to be replaced by Major General Henry W. Halleck, "a military intellectual," who began to turn things around. Halleck correctly recognized that Price's whole strategy had been to tie up as many Federal troops as possible in defense of St. Louis and other centers to prevent a concerted campaign in the West. As General Sherman succinctly put it: "With a comparatively small force he holds in check five times his number . . . That is his game." After Frémont, Hunter, too, had played along, withdrawing his troops with improvident haste from Springfield, which ceded Price the southwest of the state. The latter moved at once to occupy the vacated ground. By mid-November, he had extended his lines as far north as the Little Osage River, built winter huts in Springfield and elsewhere for his men, and opened a recruiting camp.

The storms of winter now began to sweep the bleak Western prairies, as the Federals established their own fortified line. On November 17, Webb's regiment, under Franz Sigel, set out for Rolla, arriving on its outskirts on the 19th. Rolla was the very front of the Union position, and as Webb tried to adjust to its perils, he received a letter from his brother, John, with some gossip about the social life of Hutton and, to his dismay, hints of his own desire to enlist. Webb replied at once: "Glad that you are getting along so nicely with the girls. Squeeze them some for me." Then: "I am very well satisfied with my position, but let me tell you there is nothing desirable in a soldier's life & I would advise all that are at home to stay there for the present because there are more here than there is a place for this winter. I don't expect I will get to come home till my time is up but I can't help it." In short, *you* stay put.

Yet there was something about roughing it that Webb liked. On December 16, he wrote to his cousin Louisa, "I have been half over the state of Missouri since I left home, after 'Old Price' but the old fox is too cunning for our Dutch [German] Gen. Sigel so we have given him up & are going to Kentucky to try our skill in the cane brakes. I have seen some pretty hard times, went hungry a good many days, slept many a night on the ground with a stone for a pillow & went some nights without sleep. But that is nothing for a soldier. We are as jovial a set of fellows as ever you saw. We don't look for easy times here."

The times grew worse. The men began to get sick, first with measles—Webb got them "like sixty"—and other "children's diseases," to which farm boys like Webb were especially prone. Then smallpox ate through the ranks. At Rolla, about two-thirds of the men came down with it, with scant relief. "There is now but 300 able for duty out of 900 when we left Sedalia," he confided. "There are new cases of smallpox every day. As fast as one gets well another is taken . . . I reckon there is as merry a set of fellows here as ever you saw, what there is left of us." Webb had that droll way. Most of the recruits had been vaccinated, in fact, but the doctors, instead of using an animal virus, had drawn their serum from human scabs. As a result, ulcers or chancres appeared at the vaccination site, and in addition to the usual pustules and fever, there were lymphatic swellings in the armpits and groin. It did not help that Rolla itself was so bleak, for it seemed to Webb as if the barren, cinder-scarred landscape around their encampment almost invited disease. "No wonder there is sickness here," he wrote, "for this is the poorest country in the world. Willow Creek [a drybed in Coles] is a Paradise compared to it. Our camp is in a ravine between two high rocky, shrubby hills, desolate beyond compare, & this is a fair specimen of this part of the state. Nobody ever did live here & nobody ever can, but Uncle Sam's boys & they would starve if he did not send them something to eat."

The broader news was also grim: There were rumors that England might intervene in the fighting after two Confederate envoys to Europe had been seized off an English boat, which was bound to prolong the war; in that case, "we will get to stay three years without any trouble," Webb caustically remarked. Meanwhile, he had "read in the local paper," much to his surprise, that Lincoln might free the slaves: "Don't believe it. Don't care if he does." This, of course, was a year before emancipation. Webb's response was an enlightened one, even for a Union soldier, at this stage of the war.

He tended to accept what came. Homesick though he was at times, his stoic nature inclined him against complaint. But his mother, bewailing his absence, seldom failed to remind him how bereft she felt. On the whole, he met this with perfect understanding, but now and then, as he could do nothing to change his situation, her complaints got under his skin. About this time he received an especially mournful letter from her, and replied with a gentle rebuke: "You ought not to indulge in your lonesome spells, they render you unhappy & everybody with whom you associate, at least to some extent. My happiest moments are spent in thinking of home & how I may surprise you by coming in unexpected. I may get to come home this winter though there is no such prospect now . . . My health is not so good as it has been sometimes. [But] the weather is pleasant & warm, & we are very comfortable in our new quarters. There is a great deal of solid comfort in the wild rough life of a soldier. It is true there are a great many hardships to be endured, but those I expected to find, & in them I find pleasure in the tendency they have to develop the unselfish in one's character."

One cannot but admire him. His whole regiment was now a debilitated wreck. On top of measles and smallpox, it was now beset by mumps—this at a time when "children's diseases" could kill. The weather had also turned bitterly cold. Things got so bad he thought it would be best, in fact, if his unit were just "disbanded," and noted that one of his officers, Captain William J. Salee, was even then back at Coles recruiting replacements for the dwindling men. "If boys don't want to see the elephant [battle]," he added, "[they'd] better stay at home. [I] have all the war I want." But it took more than ill health to discharge a unit in this war, especially just then in Missouri, when the War Department was trying to hold on to all the men it could.

The struggle for the state had reached an impasse. The Federals held St. Louis, maintained a grip on the Missouri River valley, and more or less controlled the central and northern portions of the state. The Confederates held Springfield, were ensconced along the Osage River, and sent raiders as far north as Mount Zion and Silver Creek. For Lincoln, this was intolerable, especially as Missouri had not seceded after all and was supposed to serve as a bridgehead for the Western advance. Halleck therefore decided to mount a major offensive to drive the Rebels out. For the task, he chose Brigadier General Samuel R. Curtis, a West Pointer who had served under Zachary Taylor in the Mexican War. In subsequent years he had prospered as a lawyer and engineer in civilian life, been elected to Congress as a Republican in 1856, and when the Civil War began, led the 2nd Iowa Regiment into the field. He was promptly promoted from colonel to brigadier general and assigned to St. Louis, where he served on Frémont's staff. Lincoln thought well of him and had secretly consulted him in October on Frémont's fitness to command.

Curtis established his headquarters at Rolla, a railhead that was the obvious starting point for a movement south. Two divisions belonging to Sigel (now a brigadier general) and General Alexander S. Asboth, an officer of Hungarian birth, manned the town fortifications and hillside camps; a third division, commanded by Colonel Jefferson C. Davis (unrelated to the Confederate president), lay near Sedalia and Otterville to the west. Davis, who had come up through the ranks, had been a private in the Mexican War and an artillery lieutenant at the bombardment of Fort Sumter, before his promotion; two other able colonels were also on staff, Peter Osterhaus and Eugene A. Carr, who had both fought at Wilson's Creek. Under Curtis, all the forces now assembled were rechristened the Army of the Southwest; it would later be said that "for hard fighting, long and weary marches, as well as privations and sufferings endured, no army could show a better record, or one deserving greater credit in the war."

Sigel was second in command. A rather wily tactician, he had been schooled at the famed Military Academy of Karlsruhe in his native Germany, became a champion of German unity in the years of democratic turmoil, and had served as minister of war in the Revolutionary government of 1848. In 1852, he had come to the United States, where for several years he had taught at the German-American Institute in St. Louis and edited a military magazine. When the Civil War began, he organized a Missouri regiment and kept the St. Louis arsenal (packed at the time with twenty-one thousand weapons) from Rebel hands. Whatever his faults as a commander (today still under debate), "his prompt and ardent espousal of the Union cause," as one writer put it, was a critical factor in uniting the large German population of the North, including Missouri, on the Union side. Many non-Germans, like Webb, also revered him—"I fights mit Sigel" was a proud phrase—and in his knowledge and use of artillery he had few peers.

Between the two opposing armies lay extremely harsh terrain. A midwinter campaign across it would almost certainly be deemed unthinkable by Price and, it was presumed, catch him off guard; but there were also considerable risks on the Federal side. Every step south would take the men farther from their base, including the branch line that ran from St. Louis to Rolla. But that was only part of the supply line Curtis had to hold. Beyond it lay the Ozark Mountains, "a massive limestone uplift" that extended southward into northern Arkansas. From Rolla in the center of Missouri onward for 113 miles Curtis would have to rely on wagons struggling along primitive roads winding through a hostile and barren domain. He would also "have to travel light," carrying a minimum of food and equipment, each man, including junior officers, being allowed two shirts, one change of underwear, two blankets, and

four pairs of socks. In the end they would need more than that, of
course, as well as military items, which would have to get to them
through snow, mud, wind, and rain. The man charged with man-
aging the difficult logistics of all this was Philip H. Sheridan, then
a lowly captain in Curtis's command. He would prove his mettle
as a quartermaster and commissary of the Army long before fame
crowned his valor in the field.

The main route across the Ozarks was a narrow dirt road origi-
nally constructed for the supply of frontier forts. In the winter of
1838–39, it had formed part of the Trail of Tears that had taken
thousands of Indians westward into exile to the territory north of
Texas, where a quarter of them died. Later, it served as a postal
route for the wayside communities that began to spring up; then,
in 1860, a telegraph line had tried to thread them all together, after which it became known as the Wire (or Telegraph) Road. That
road led straight through Springfield and would mark the main
line of the Union advance.

Webb was eager to march. His malaise had passed and all the
"boys [are] in fine spirits," he wrote his mother, and "drill three
hours a day." I.D., he added, was "as fat as a buck but can't jump so
far." But the still uncertain health of his unit as a whole kept it
back. There is "talk of our going—don't believe it—wish it were
so—tired of camp" (letter of January 26, 1862). Two days later it
was ordered forward and he predicted "a battle inside of two
weeks." He was now feeling "very brave" and thought, "if we
thrash Price," he would be home by the Fourth of July "to have a
big time." Meanwhile, Sigel had given a big boost to the regiment's morale. He told the men that as long as he had the 3rd
Missouri, which he had organized, and the 25th Illinois, he could
"whip two to one." But Webb had already begun to look a little
beyond the war. Since entering the service, he had embarked on a
program of self-improvement (one, in fact, he would never for-
sake), had pushed ahead with mathematics, for which he had a

gift, and was being tutored in grammar by his staff sergeant, "a fine fellow," Joseph B. Spence. He wanted still more to read and asked his uncle to send him several books, including a copy of *Bullion's Grammar* as a guide.

There is a time for every purpose, however, and Webb soon turned to polishing his bayonet. Time, in fact, was of the essence, as Curtis moved with dispatch to get his army midway, to a town called Lebanon, where it could pause to regroup. But the going proved slow. A freezing rain poured down and drenched the men, then froze them over and turned their tents into islands of ice. The primitive roads were hard and sharp as stone, until a sudden thaw turned them ankle-deep with mud. As the men slogged along, the thick muck sucked at their feet and new shoes just issued "ripped apart from the uppers" and had to be held together with bits of string. The army's heavy eight-yoke wagons, or prairie schooners, floated along behind on a river of slime. A week after starting, one regiment and all its wagons were "mired down" in mud between Rolla and the Gasconade River and all "the life," Webb wrote his uncle Elijah, "pulled out of the mules."

On February 7, Webb wrote his mother from Sharon, Missouri: "Got orders to march Saturday night & Sunday morning took up our beds & walked." The regiment marched twelve miles through a steady snow, then tried to scrape the snow away from the ground for pitching camp. The men set up their sheet iron stoves in their tents, but in the morning found themselves sleeping in mud where the stoves had thawed the ground. At the same time, where the fire had gone out, their blankets were "frozen fast." On the second day, they marched another fifteen miles; on the third, thirteen more, and finally crossed the Gasconade. That night they tried to sleep through an icy rain, marched still another ten, cut brush to sleep on so they wouldn't sleep in the mud, and at dawn pressed on for one more stretch before making camp near

Lebanon, as the temperature continued to drop. Meanwhile, reports had come in that the Confederate force was larger than previously thought, but, said Webb, "we talk of giving them some blue pills" (i.e., laxatives, meaning "scare the shit out of them"), "& if they don't give me a dose I expect the scare will serve as well for physic," which was fair enough. "Love to all, especially the girls," he wrote his mother. "Believe me ever your son."

Curtis had started out with about twelve thousand men and fifty heavy guns. One regiment had been left at Rolla to guard it and another two to protect the rest of his line of supply. That left him with a force of 10,250 organized into four divisions. These were led by Osterhaus, Asboth, Davis, and Carr. Sigel was the brigade commander of the first two, which included Webb's regiment in the 1st Division, and had four batteries of artillery under his special care. The Union troops were spoiling for a fight, and as Springfield came into view on February 12, hurried forward for the prize. Price, caught off-guard, quickly withdrew from Springfield to the south, tempting an energized Curtis to give chase. That did not seem a risky thing to do, but then, nothing in what followed turned out as it seemed. Before Webb had much chance to write home again, the two armies would clash in one of the fiercest battles of the war.

Price had never been as strong as rumor had it, but he was about to be far stronger than the Federals could have dreamed. In Arkansas he was joined by eleven regiments under Ben McCulloch—largely made up of tough mountain folk inured to the hardships of the wilds—and by an Indian Cavalry Brigade under a Grand Mason by the name of Albert Pike made up of Choctaw, Cherokee, and Creek. Estimates of this combined force at the time ranged up to thirty-five thousand, though afterwards, the Rebels chose to revise down their numbers. However, it is probably safe to say that the Federals were outnumbered by almost two to one. The Rebels had also brought in a new and dashing Confederate general to lead them: Earl Van Dorn.

A grandnephew of Andrew Jackson, Van Dorn was a diminutive, vain, impetuous but able officer who had broken many a Southern damsel's heart. In his Indian fighting days and as a lieutenant in the Mexican War, he had garnered two brevets for valor, along with five wounds, and at the beginning of the Civil War in Texas had negotiated the surrender of Union troops in that state. As a division commander in the Army of Northern Virginia, he had earned his brigadier's stars, but the thirst for rank had grown with its own satisfaction, and he frankly yearned for more. With his recent promotion to major general, he had also been given a new department command.

No one had more exalted ideas than Van Dorn as to what that might mean. "Who knows but that yet out of the storms of revolution," he wrote his wife, "I may not be able to catch a spark of the lightning and shine through all time to come, a burning name! I feel a greatness in my soul!" His ultimate goal was the capture of St. Louis, which he thought, not implausibly, he could take if the army of Curtis were crushed. "I must have St. Louis," he exclaimed, "then Huzza!" As a general, his strength was speed and surprise; his weakness, a lack of care in preparation and, despite chastening lessons, a failure to understand that "the hell-for-leather methods he employed against bands of Plains Indians were not particularly well suited for conventional war."

Curtis had chased Price a little too far. On February 13, the Stars and Stripes had been raised again over Springfield, but instead of pausing to regroup, Curtis had pressed on. As his men slogged along the muddy roads at twenty miles a day, they almost caught up with Price on a number of occasions, the Federal advance guard just catching sight of the Rebel rear. But supplies over the roads could not be moved at the same rate, and after Curtis crossed into Arkansas on the 18th, the men began to depend on daily forage for their food. By the 23rd he had pushed as far as Fayetteville, where the Wire Road came to an end.

Osage Springs, Ark., Feb. 23, 1862

Dear Mother:

   Have not had an opportunity to write to you since we left Lebanon—We have been making forced marches in pursuit of Price, but did not catch him. He is largely reinforced since he got into this state. We are waiting for recruits & as soon as they come up we are going to follow him to the Gulf, or catch him. The boys are generally well & anxious to march . . .

Curtis's supply line, however, was now stretched to the snapping point. Ahead of him stood the pathless ridges and wild ravines of the Boston Mountain Range, where Price had taken refuge in a place called Cove Creek. There McCulloch's reinforcements had come in. To follow risked disaster, while the strength of Curtis's own army, despite Webb's chipper zeal, was in some ways almost spent. In a month it had marched 240 mountain miles through snow, sleet, gales, and freezing rain, and for the past ten days had kept up the chase almost at a run. It needed time to rest and recoup, but war, and Van Dorn, declined to grant it that reprieve.

   On March 2, Van Dorn rode into the Rebel camp to a forty-gun salute (consistent with his rank) and at once announced his intention to attack. He assembled the troops in hollow squares for a rabble-rousing speech and told them to pack up three days' rations with one blanket but no tent. He was a man in a hurry, and on the 4th he began to march them out of the hills. At the time Curtis was at Cross Hollow, near Bentonville, busy writing a letter in his tent, when (as story has it) a civilian scout named Wild Bill Hickok arrived to alert him to Van Dorn's advance. He called in his divisions, then foraging far and wide, and ordered them north (still inside Arkansas) to a point where the Wire Road crossed Little Sugar Creek. The valley of this creek had hills on either side, and on the north these included a plateau of high tableland with farms and open fields known as Pea Ridge. There, and between the creek and ridge, Curtis began to entrench. Trees were felled to close the road, and earthworks (a compound of dirt and logs) prepared on the bluffs of the creek's north side. If the Rebels advanced along the road, as Curtis thought they would, they would have to cross the creek near his entrenchment and come under his organized fire. For the moment at least, he held the high ground, and over the next day and a half, as his divisions came up, he placed them in fortified lines.

Sigel's division came up last. At the time the order had gone out to regroup, Webb's regiment, with several others, was encamped five miles south of Bentonville in a cluster of fields known as McKisick's Farm. A courier reached Sigel on the night of the 5th, and soon reveille was rasping through the dark-enshrouded tents of his command. Some of the regiments quickly got themselves together. Webb's was a little slower to respond. As Webb tells it, it had just gotten "looped." The night had been unusually cold and to warm things up "the 37th suttler" had brought over a barrel of whiskey and "a good many of the boys got drunk." About midnight they fell into a stupor; at 1 in the morning, they were suddenly roused and told to get up and march. "We were just off of a spree & in poor condition to," wrote Webb, and "Gen. Sigel got many curses for ordering us out so early. We thought there was no danger & we were very tired & sleepy. Every time we halted the boys tumbled down & went to sleep even though it was snowing hard." At dawn, the snow stopped "& the sun shone brightly all day." They got to Little Sugar Creek about noon, after marching sixteen miles in ten hours on almost no sleep; but just as they began to look forward to food and rest, they were told to take up their arms again, face round, and double back to Sigel's aid.

Sigel had been making haste more slowly than he should.

When he came up to Bentonville with the rear guard, he had six hundred men with him, but, thinking them not at risk, had "strolled over to the Eagle House, a hotel near the southwestern corner of the square," for a breakfast of ham and eggs. The sun was out, the sky was clear, but the temperature was below freezing, so his troops had stacked their arms, built a bonfire in the town square, and gone to sleep. And there a band of Texas cavalry almost scooped them up.

Just after 10, as he emerged from his repast, Sigel saw horsemen drifting up "like a black cloud across the smooth and treeless prairie" to the south. They came on with such speed that some gained the wooded hills behind or above him, cutting him off from Pea Ridge. His men managed to shoot their way through, but the Rebels were now in greater numbers on their heels. Before they could catch up, Sigel planted a battery in the woods at a bend in the road, and as the Rebels came round, let loose a burst of canister and grape. The whole front of the Rebel column crumbled, and those coming up behind found their way blockaded by the bodies of the slain. Meanwhile, "though we were very tired, we were rested [i.e., revived]," wrote Webb, "by the excitement of a prospect of a battle [and] soon got back 4 miles [where] we met Gen. Sigel & cheered him & then returned to camp."

Curtis spent the rest of the day strengthening his line; he barricaded the Wire Road near Leetown, a small hamlet under the shadow of Pea Ridge, and threw up still more earthworks where the road followed the hollow of the creek. He also took over Elkhorn Tavern, a two-story frame house to the northeast where the telegrapher lived; converted a place called Pratt's Store, south of the tavern, into a Federal command post; and turned a large barn near the tavern into a depot for supplies. There were a number of farms in the area where battle lines could form, most notably, Ford's farm to the west, near a part of the Ridge known as Big Mountain; Clemon's farm to the east; and, between them to the south, Cox's field and Ruddick's field. All these he carefully surveyed. As the Federals assumed their posts, Curtis and Carr occupied the left, Davis and Osterhaus the center, Sigel and Asboth, near Leetown, the right.

Webb's unit was encamped on Ruddick's field. The men had had nothing to eat for two days, and it wasn't until midnight, according to Webb, that they even got so much as a little flour. "Our teamster brought us a keg of lard so we had shortening for our biscuit. We slept well for the remainder of the night with our guns for pillows & the canopy [of heaven] for a tent." Meanwhile, the Confederates had come up, and across from the Federals, that is, on the south side of the creek, were making their own camp. A company of Cherokees dressed in buckskin, hunting shirts, and leggings and adorned with rattles and bells came through on their Indian ponies, their faces painted and their long straight hair tied back in queues. Some carried rifles, others tomahawks and knives. These were among the Indian auxiliaries that Pike had brought in.

Both armies were dead tired. Van Dorn had been driving his own men hard, and over the past three days they had covered more than fifty miles in snow and freezing rain. But they were not done yet. Van Dorn could see no point in assailing the defense works Curtis had thrown up, so after nightfall "he sent half his force in a wide arc around the north side of Pea Ridge, then down the road past Elkhorn Tavern for a dawn attack on the Union left rear." As the men moved out they left their long line of campfires blazing to conceal their march. Meanwhile, Van Dorn prepared to file the rest of his force around the ridge in the opposite direction to surprise the Federals at the Leetown end. Despite some delays, Van Dorn got his men into place and Curtis awoke to face a vanished host. Vanished, but not gone. From scouts he at once grasped what Van Dorn had done and swung his troops around. All the fortifications they had constructed were suddenly at their back, and the valley of the creek no longer between them and the foe. Retreat was impossible, as the route north to Springfield, which his lines had protected, was now almost straddled by Van Dorn. And so the battle began with the Federals having almost to form their new defense line under fire. The rear at once became the front, the right the left, the left the right.

"Carr was sent at once to meet the threat beyond Elkhorn Tavern," writes Shelby Foote,

> Osterhaus moved up past Leetown to protect the western flank, and presently . . . Curtis sent Davis to support him, while Asboth remained under Sigel, in reserve . . . Carr stood where the first blow was about to fall.
>
> At 10:30 it fell, and it fell hard. Tired and hungry after their stumbling all-night march, but keyed up by the order to charge at last, Price's men came crashing through the brush along both sides of the wire road, guns barking aggressively on the flanks and from the rear. Carr had prepared a defense in depth, batteries staggered along the road and a strong line of infantry posted to support the foremost while the other three fired over their heads. Presently, though, they had nothing to support. A well-directed salvo knocked out three of the four guns and blew up two caissons, killing all the cannoneers. Unnerved, the infantry fell back on the second battery, just north of the tavern, where they managed to repulse the first attack, then the second, both of which were piecemeal. Bearded like a Cossack, Carr rode among his soldiers, shouting encouragement. Out front, the brush was boiling with butternut [Confederate] veterans forming for a third assault.

All this was taking place at the Elkhorn end, in the critical contest for a foothold atop Pea Ridge and control of the road. Against a force far larger than his own, Carr contended for several hours with all the skill and enterprise he could muster, but he could not hold the ground. Repeatedly, he appealed for reinforcements, but Curtis, deceived by a feint to his right, felt he could spare only a part of his own bodyguard and the light mountain howitzers they carried in their train. Toward the end of the day, however, he at last moved a battalion of infantry and seven guns under Asboth to Carr's aid. By then, the third Rebel onslaught had come and Carr had been driven back, now well below the tavern, three miles from where the lines had first been drawn. Before long Confederates "were whooping around the tavern itself and drinking from the horse trough in the yard." Meanwhile, at the south or Leetown end of the ridge, McCulloch had made early headway against Osterhaus and Davis, and Pike's Indian brigade had overrun a battery of Union guns.

Sigel alone remained in reserve. "We were up early & got our breakfast," wrote Webb, "& then provided two days rations of biscuits in our haversacks." By then, the battle had begun and for some time "we had listened . . . to the continual rattle of musketry & roar of cannon & were anxious to join the fray." Sigel was ready, "with shotted guns," and drew up his men in battle formation; but the assault he expected never came. As the day wore on, Webb found himself in the odd circumstance of having to "[hunt] a place to fight. Over hills & hollows," he wrote, "through brush & over fields we went from point to point. Once or twice we halted while our battery threw a few shell[s]" toward the enemy lines. Not far from where they were, the battle was constantly shifting: just over the horizon, in fact, as Osterhaus and Davis suddenly gained the upper hand. After a Federal soldier, an Illinois private named Peter Pelican, picked off Ben McCulloch, who had ridden into battle wearing sky-blue britches and a velvet vest, his now leaderless troop broke. At about the same time, Pike's Indians also lost heart and scattered into the woods.

At length, as evening fell, darkness settled across Pea Ridge and brought an end to the first day's fight. By 7 P.M., all that remained of it were "occasional flashes of artillery fire [that] lit up the smoky battlefield like heat lightning on a summer night." The outcome had been inconclusive. Van Dorn had gained the Union rear, but in the process the two wings of his army had become separated and could not give each other support. His left was intact and he had gained strategic ground, but his right (under McCulloch) had been mauled. Even so, he thought he had won the day. The Federals, after all, had been pushed back several miles, could hardly retreat without risk of annihilation, and had lost much of their camp equipage and stores. Van Dorn's headquarters were now where Curtis's had been, and his campfires flared up to the elkhorns on the rooftree in the yard.

There was gloom in the Union camp. Outnumbered if not outgunned and apparently trapped, the soldiers well knew that the fate of the Union cause throughout Missouri lay in their faltering hands.

At 8 o'clock, Webb's unit "settled down for the night, on the picket line. Many of the boys," he wrote, "had thrown [away] their blankets [during the day] & consequently suffered for it was very cold." But weariness overwhelmed them. "Part watched at a time & the rest slept cold or no cold for we had slept but little for three days & two nights. We remained in our place till 3 o'clock in the morning when we were relieved & taken to a place where we could build fires & warm ourselves. We remained there till eight o'clock. Prisoners that we took that morning said that Price made them a speech before the battle began in which he told them that a half hour's fighting would give them the victory, that we were surrounded (& we were) & could not hold out long."

So it seemed. In a conference held that night, most of the Union officers advised a "slashing retreat." But Curtis demurred. His left had held and was no longer in danger; he still had most of his guns. That would enable him to concentrate most of his forces on the right. Intuition as much as anything else also told him that the Confederate strength was drained. As dawn broke on March 8, smoke from the previous day's battle still draped the fields and mountains, and the slowly rising sun shone through it with a copper glare. The Confederates held Pea Ridge, the field below it, and Elkhorn Tavern in an irregular crescent that stretched east of the Wire Road for about a mile; the Federals faced them in a concave arc. Carr and Davis held the right; Sigel, the left. Both armies drew their lines tight. If Sigel had done little on the previous day, he would make up for it now, and if Webb had searched in vain for action, he would soon be in the thick of it, in one of the signal actions of the war.

It was the intent of Curtis to envelop—and hammer—both of Van Dorn's flanks. In a critical action of this plan, Sigel skillfully extended his ranks beneath the ridge, then wheeled his two divisions around to face the enemy right. He placed his infantry in front, his artillery behind: thirty guns, by Webb's count, carriage to carriage, in a seamless line. The infantry flattened on the ground. Each of Sigel's gunners took a tree for his mark until he had gained the range, and as Sigel rode down the line, he occasionally dismounted to personally sight a gun. This was his hour. Artillery was the one thing he knew how to use, and for sighting cannon no one in the Union army had a better eye. "At eight," wrote Webb, the Rebels "opened the ball expecting to have the victory soon." Sigel's guns responded, and there followed "the most sustained artillery barrage ever to take place on the North American continent up to that time." Both sides had about fifty cannon all told, but the Federals had more and larger shot. And they did not spare its use. The duel was so intense that single explosions could not even be heard, as the firing blended into one great volcanic roar. "Billows of smoke swirled across the plateau and drifted over the crest of the mountain . . . The shriek of projectiles of every size and shape, and the clatter of shrapnel and the debris nearly overpowered the senses of the troops." All the while, Sigel's guns kept "firing as fast as they could," wrote Webb. "The rebels were firing at us with a large number also, the shot & shell rained thick around us, the air was full of blue streaks marking their tracks in both directions." But the Union gunners had the better aim. The Rebel guns were blasted from their emplacements; battery after battery was silenced and the ranks about them pulverized by shot. For two hours, Webb and the other infantry crawled forward on the ground. Behind them followed Sigel's line of guns. The range of those guns grew shorter and shorter and ever more potent their aim. The machine-like progress of the two together horrified the Rebels as they watched its inexorable advance across the yellow plain. At length, the order was given to rise, and the infantry rose together, all in one motion, like a field of unflattened grain. The spirits of the men were now up, and some of them, according to one, "as lively as if going to a corn husking." "We advanced in the face of the enemy at a double quick," wrote Webb, "first east a quarter [mile] across a field & then north a quarter [mile] through thick brush. The rebel shell shot the tops off of the brush but fortunately overshot us." As Sigel watched his men sweep forward over one critical patch of ground, he exclaimed, "Oh, dot was lofely." Webb and his brethren now broke into a trot. "We double quicked across the field a quarter [mile] farther," even as "the grape whistled" by; when in turn those guns were silenced, "we stripped to the canteen, fixed bayonets & again started on a bayonet charge into a hazel thicket. We advanced into the thicket about a hundred yards when the musketry opened on us at 70 yards. Such a rattling of musketry & such a whistling of bullets I do not want to hear again. Of course we did our best to return the compliment."

In the midst of this exchange, Webb was shot twice. As he knelt to reload—"I was on my knees with a cartridge in my teeth"—two bullets whisked past his scalp and plowed across his back: "one [cut] the skin right on the shoulder blade the other took quite a large piece of flesh out between the shoulder blade and the backbone. I would rather the wound had been somewhere else." Then it was all over. That volley had been almost the Rebels' last gasp. A few minutes later, "the rebs skedaddled & the victory was ours." But as Webb got slowly to his feet, some others did not rise. One was Mike Waltrip, a friend from his youth, slain. Another, Enoch Frost, lay with a shattered right arm. Twenty-one others from his unit alone were among the killed and wounded that day.

At 12 noon, the victorious wings of the Union Army met and embraced where the Rebels had stood just fifteen minutes before. Around them lay shattered wagons, dismounted cannon, caissons "blown to fragments" and shattered trees. Body parts covered the ground. "To add to the horrors of the scene," wrote one, "the woods, which had been set on fire by the shells, now began to blaze up in various directions." Many of the wounded were dragged safely away from the flames, but a few, "who had fallen in secluded places, or crawled off to thickets, were overtaken by the fire, and their charred and blackened corpses were afterward found lying amid the ashes and cinders of the woods."

The Confederate rout was absolute. As Van Dorn's army fell back toward the Boston Mountains, they flung aside everything that might impede their flight: blankets, knapsacks, even their guns. Indeed, they seemed to vanish so completely that Curtis remarked that it was as if they had "sunk into the earth." Meanwhile, the Federals had pushed through the heavily wooded tract east of Elkhorn Tavern, and emerging met a happy General Curtis, cavorting about on his horse and shouting "Victory! Victory!" to his equally elated men.

Thus ended the Battle of Pea Ridge. For many on either side, it had been a hard introduction to the realities of war. Though its human toll was less than that of some other battles, the wreckage it left in its wake was frightful enough. The Federals lost about fourteen hundred men, of whom 203 were killed outright, though 150 others later died. The Confederate toll was much higher but less certain, as no formal accounting was made; it is thought to have amounted to a quarter of those engaged. Some of the Union dead near Leetown were afterwards found to have been scalped and hacked up by Pike's Indian troops, which drew a strong remonstrance from Curtis; much was made of this at the time. But it is hard to imagine anything more gruesome than the carnage wrought by the more modern weapons of war. Some men were so shot to pieces they resembled debris and could only be lifted in a blanket and poured into a grave. The whole area abandoned by the Confederates was also covered with shallow pits of the dead, several dug in such haste that feet could be seen protruding from the ground.

For the wounded, there was often little the doctors could do. "It is redicklous how bad they is taken care of," complained one soldier; another, speaking of a dying friend, said, "I don't believe he could have suffered any more if he had been burnt up." Indeed, it was the singular misfortune of the soldier, as Bruce Catton noted, that this war erupted when medicine was still primitive but the killing power and efficiency of weapons "had been brought to a brand-new peak." As a result, the soldier

got the worst of it both ways. When he fought, he was likely to be hurt pretty badly; when he stayed in camp, he lived under conditions that were very likely to make him sick; and in either case he had almost no chance to get the kind of medical treatment which a generation or so later would be routine. When a man was wounded and the wound was dressed, doctors expected it to suppurate; they spoke of "laudable pus" and supposed that its appearance was a good sign. The idea that a surgical dressing ought to be sterilized never entered anyone's head . . . If a surgeon's instruments were so much as rinsed off between operations at a field hospital, the case was an exception. In camp, diseases like typhoid, dysentery, and pneumonia were dreaded killers. No one knew what caused them, and no one could do much for them when they appeared. Doctors had discovered that there was some connection between the cleanliness of a camp and the number of men on sick call, but sanitation was still a rudimentary science, and if a water supply was not visibly befouled and odorous, it was thought to be perfectly safe.

All that, of course, did not make the suffering of the soldiers any easier to bear. At Pratt's Store, for example, surgeons "were busy cutting and carving like butchers" for twenty-four hours straight. Other local buildings and dwellings, such as Elkhorn Tavern, as well as most huts, cabins, and private homes within miles around were converted into hospitals and marked with yellow flags. That flag was often merely symbolic, as both armies were woefully short of bandages, dressings, surgical implements, and other medical supplies.

A few days after the battle, Curtis wrote his brother: "The scene is silent and sad. The vulture and the wolf have now communion, and the dead, friends and foes, sleep in the same lonely graves." He said this with true, impartial feeling, as wrung from an ecumenical heart.

But his victory had been no such neutral thing. The Battle of Pea Ridge, the largest battle of the war west of the Mississippi, not only secured Missouri for the Union but prepared the way for subsequent campaigns into Kentucky and Tennessee. Webb had wanted a battle, and he got it. For the sake of the Union—for the sake of liberty itself and "the Constitution & laws"—he had fought the good fight. He had two furrowed wounds, one the size of his fist, along his back to prove it and the knowledge that he had not faltered under fire. He had been, as he had prayed he would be, brave and true, and for that he would be grateful all his days.

In conjunction with Pea Ridge, other points along the left flank of the Confederate line had also been seized. On January 27, 1862, troops and a flotilla of armed river craft, including ironclad gunboats under Commodore Andrew Foote, had assembled at Cairo, Illinois, and advanced with Ulysses S. Grant against Fort Donelson on the Cumberland River and Fort Henry on the Tennessee. Fort Henry was taken on February 6, Fort Donelson on the 16th. The day after Donelson fell, Bowling Green, Kentucky, was evacuated by the Rebels, and three days after that, Nashville passed into Federal hands.

With the fall of Donelson and the unconditional surrender of ten thousand men, Grant's profile was first raised in the public eye. The Confederate general Simon Bolivar Buckner had defended the fort stoutly enough, but in Webb's home district it was claimed, in malicious jest, that, as the battle approached, he had hedged his bets. It was said that he had provided himself with two flags—one black, one white—tied to opposite ends of a pole. The black one stood for defiance; the white one, consisting of a lady's shift, for surrender. Before the Federals arrived, he had boldly unfurled the black, "but as they approached, he—shifted—."

After Fort Donelson, Grant moved up the Tennessee to Pittsburg Landing, was there attacked, and on April 6 and 7 fought the Battle of Shiloh, named for a nearby church. Grant's army almost got the worst of it and might have been destroyed if reinforcements under General Don Carlos Buell had not arrived on the second day and swept the Rebels from the field. The victory at Shiloh coincided with the capture by General John Pope of another important river fort on the Mississippi, known as Island No. 10. Confederate power in the West seemed almost to be hanging by a thread.

Webb nursed his wounds, both of which had been made by a slug called the minié ball. This was a new and more deadly kind of bullet that had been developed just prior to the war. It had a cone-shaped top with a hollow base, as opposed to the round shot of the past, and had been designed by Captain Claude E. Minié of the French army for the new percussion-lock rifles that had become the infantry norm. Minié had called his projectile a "cylindro-conoidal ball"; others called it the minié, and the "Minié principle" was soon adopted in both Europe and the United States. U.S. ballistics experts then refined it and made it even more powerful, with a base that expanded with the powder blast. This new minié engaged the rifling of the barrel, was more accurate, and could kill at one thousand yards. It also tended to spread on impact, and, unlike the bullets of today, which tend to pass clean through, to lodge in the lacerated tissue after splintering bone.

Webb had been lucky. Had the second bullet lodged where it struck, his wound would have been considered inoperable and would probably have resulted in his death. As it was, his torn flesh was simply dressed, and he was given an opium pill for his pain. In the end, he didn't seem to need much more than that, and eventually he regained almost all his oxlike strength.

Just two days after the Pea Ridge fight, he did his best to recount his regiment's part in it all (much quoted above) in a letter to his mother dated "Benton Co., Ark. March 10, 1862. Camp on the Battlefield." "Dear Mother," it began, "Through a well directed train of providence, I am again permitted to write you . . . We enjoyed the privilege of going into a battle." His wry, good-natured wit seemed often to keep the terrible at bay. In closing, he said simply: "My back is so sore I can hardly write. Please send me some postage stamps. Write soon & often to your affectionate son, B. W. Baker."

CHAPTER FOUR

After Pea Ridge, Webb's unit was attached to the 1st Brigade, 1st Division of the Army of Southwest Missouri, which soon began a circuitous march that would culminate in the siege of Corinth, Mississippi, at the end of May.

"We are in Dixey, in a land of heathendom!" he wrote proudly, perhaps provocatively on March 17 from Camp Wilfley to his cousin Amos, who was then in Bible school.

We do not get any papers or anything else to read except now & then a letter from a friend up in God's land. This life is harder on me at present from the fact that I am not able to drill . . . Though my wound is doing well as could be expected & I am ready for another battle, whenever necessity calls for it, yet I am hardly well enough to do anything . . . Battles are becoming more frequent now. I was out at the dress parade & listened to a long letter of praise & thanks for our conduct as a regt. in the battle. You have little conception of soldiers' feelings when he receives the approbation of an able general, one that is greatly beloved. After three days of cold March weather's hard fighting during which time we had little rest & little to eat & no time to warm; after the hardships of a winter campaign, covering a thousand miles march, in the midst of winter's exposures, over the rocks & hills of Mo. & Ark. After having been shut out from society & deprived of its luxuries; after have been exposed to all the dangers & diseases incident to a winter's campaign & battle, then to receive the approbation of our commander for having discharged every known duty, I tell you, it makes a fellow feel well.

Webb was energized. He didn't know what the generals had planned for him next, but he was glad when General Sigel, whom he revered, told the men they would soon pitch their tents "on the banks of the Arkansas [River], ere two more weeks have passed. I expect to go with the regt. We are expecting a speedy peace. What is the prospect. We common soldiers know nothing. You at home know more of the situation than we do. Though we thrashed the rebs. at Pea Ridge."

Four days later, the men were back in Missouri in Barry County, at Camp Hoffman, and Webb's wounds were healing "as fast as could be expected; & I can use my gun well enough now," he told his mother, "to give the secesh another turn" (letter of March 21, 1862). But for all his readiness for action, he had already seen enough of war to wish it might end, "if it could be done honorably," even in compromise. The total number of Union killed and wounded at Pea Ridge was still being assessed, but the report in camp was that it now came to 1,331. Meanwhile, reinforcements were supposed to be on their way from Kansas, and Webb expected to hear any day that Grant had taken Memphis, which he hoped would hasten the war to a close. So far, in any case, he felt he had done his country proud. "Ours is the crack regt. down here," he wrote his mother. "What kind of reputation has it up there?" and asked her to send him press reports of the Pea Ridge fight. Not much mail, however, was getting through. "The last letter I got from you was dated Feb. 18 . . . The mail has been robbed from both ways by marauding bands."

A week later, he wrote her again: "It is rather discouraging. Every letter I get complains that you get no letters from me. I write every week. I get a letter once a month. The latest is from

John dated March 12th. I received the socks you sent me today. Am very thankful. Was just out [of those I had]. Threw away my last yesterday. Clothing is scarce." That was the kind of thing his mother cared about, not whether the 25th Illinois was accruing fame. Beyond that, she was scared for his safety, of course, and her letter had apparently dwelt on this at length, and as always he did his best to ease her mind: "The rumor is that we are going to Little Rock as soon as Grant takes Memphis. But I was talking with Major [Richard H.] Nodine yesterday & he says it is his opinion that we will never be in another engagement; & that he would sooner think that we would be ordered back to St. Louis. We are in fine spirits because we think that we will be at home by the middle of the summer. I think you will hear me bragging at a large rate by the time your apples are ripe." Then he scolded her somewhat for her morbid fears: "Don't be down hearted. Look on the bright side. Don't borrow trouble. The secesh bullet has not been molded that is to kill me . . . My back is nearly well. I never felt better in my life. I am getting fat . . . Now cheer up Mother, all will be well in a few weeks" (letter of March 28, 1862).

But two days later he wrote more frankly to his brother to ask if there was any end to the war in sight. "I am getting tired of this kind of life," he confessed, and yet he also had to admit there was something in being a soldier that cast its spell. The troops had been out on general inspection that morning, and "the sight of the army on a great field amid martial display" had seemed to him "truly sublime"—so exciting, Webb said, as to make a soldier "rash." Afterwards, abashed at himself, he had gone to a field church to hear a sermon on the birth of Christ. Meanwhile, he had been devouring a book on Napoleon Bonaparte and his marshals, which his sergeant had lent him. "If what I have been reading is true, the opinion I had formed of the *Noble Chieftain* is very incorrect. Instead of being an ambitious tyrant, he was the noble defender of France. And a greater warrior or genius history gives no account of." During his brief convalescence, he had also been thinking about life after the war. "The weather is warm & nice; it makes me feel like getting ready to go plowing," he wrote. "[But] I never intend to plow any more. I shall learn to be a machinist when I am through with the army. Our orderly Sergeant is one & has told me about it. I would like to have you learn it too . . . My wound is nearly well. It would do me the most good in the world to be at home about this time . . . I don't know how long we will remain here . . . I don't know which way we will go when we leave." He enclosed $10 ("All I have saved since I came into the service") with a fond farewell.

Dreams of home faded, along with those of a quick end to the war. The victory at Pea Ridge had mattered, but not as much as the men liked to think. They remained in pursuit of Price, whom rumor now put in Mississippi, though their principal duty just then was to patrol the Arkansas–Missouri frontier. To protect Springfield, Curtis had taken up a position at Forsyth and from time to time sent out parties to forage and scout. In early April, he marched back into Arkansas and advanced to the southeast, toward Little Rock. He moved quickly, first to Salem, then toward Batesville on the White River, skirmishing with guerrilla bands. On the 8th, his army crossed the James River at Galena, on a pontoon bridge. Webb described for his brother the grueling progress of their march:

Forsyth, Tany County, Mo., Ap. 11, 1862

Dear John:

We left camp Hoffman Ap. 5, came up to Cassville & thence eastward 9 miles where we camped. The next morning we marched up a hollow whose sides were precipitous rocks 3 or 400 feet high with but now & then a place it would be possible to climb out. The bottom was very narrow, wide enough for one wagon to pass, more or less. I began to think that we had

all got into the narrow path way if it was very crooked & it certainly was. Almost noon we began to ascend the mountain.
Took us till three o'clock to get to the top. There are beautiful
pine forests here. Spruce, the tallest timber I ever saw. How
they ever grew is more than I can tell. Some of them look like
they come up out of solid rock. It took till night to get down
the hill, we then camped on Flat Creek, about the size of [the]
Hurricane [River]. We marched 25 miles without anything to
eat. I slipped out to a house & got my supper. There are half
dozen houses where we camped. The only houses we saw all
day. When I got back the boys had got some meal & killed a
hog, & had their suppers ready. Provisions are very scarce. We
rested the next day & all went a fishing. The next day we
marched 13 miles to Galena the county seat of Stone County.
Here we crossed the James River. We made a bridge of wagons. Strung them across the river, took out the endgates, & laid
in rails to splice them, letting them stand eight feet apart. It
took 25 wagons to make the bridge. It took the troops all night
to cross. To start with, in the morning we waded Flat Creek a
little more than knee deep, & then as the day before we
marched up hill & down, along deep ravines & over small
creeks wading them. I think this has been the most interesting
march that we have had. We expect to cross the river in the
morning & go to Batesville; & then to Pocahontas to fight
Price. Nothing certain about it. We hear that Island No. 10 is
taken, & that Gen. [James] Shields has gained a decisive victory at Winchester. Our news is only rumor. Have not heard
from you for more than a month, or just a month. Did you get
the ten dollars.

Love to grandfather & grandmother
—your affectionate brother,
Webb.

At Forsyth the troops were almost flooded out by rain. It
rained for ten days straight and "it is raining today," he wrote
John on the 20th. "I don't know when it will quit. We seem to
be cut off from all communication & living on what we can for-

age. Keep writing, anyway. I will get a letter from you after a while."

Curtis's army was now broken up. Most of the troops in Webb's division had already left for the advance on Corinth, via Cape Girardeau; his own company remained in Forsyth, which had become a hardship post. "We have had little to eat, & poor at that," he told his mother, "corn meal and blue beef." Still, he was holding up all right. But an acquaintance from home, Brink Brandenberg, was mortally ill "with lung fever. Out of his head most of the time" (letter of April 21, 1862). Webb stayed with him through the night and tried to nurse him through, but later the next morning he died. Meanwhile, he learned of the Confederate evacuation of New Madrid and of the hard victory won at Shiloh near Pittsburg Landing and had confirmation of the capture of Island No. 10. In a sense, they were all of a piece. The victories at Pea Ridge and Shiloh and the fall of the river forts, "though not conclusive," wrote General Sherman, "gave the keynote to all subsequent events of the war. They encouraged us and discouraged our too sanguine opponents, thereby leading to all our Western successes which were conclusive of the final result."

That day was still far off. On April 21, Webb's unit received "marching orders to go eastward, as soon as the creeks are favorable" (i.e., fordable; they were currently swollen with rain) and a few days later entrained for Fulton County, Arkansas, though the reason for the move remained obscure. By Webb's account, the train was almost useless and it might have been quicker to march. "The country is so rough . . . it takes all day to go a little distance"—from Forsyth to Camp Salem took a full seven days. "[I] expect to go southward tomorrow." "I. D. is getting so fat," he added with impish affection (Webb and his stepbrother were both big men), "he can hardly see" (letter of April 30, 1862). Curtis kept them on the go. On May 2, at 2:30 in the morning, the men broke camp and marched for twenty-five miles until dark, rested for a few hours, broke camp again at 1 in the morning, and marched another thirty-eight to Batesville before pausing to catch their breath. As he marched, Webb looked around. "This is pretty good country," he wrote John on the 5th. "Corn up & plowed once. Wheat is in head & there is a pretty good prospect for something to live on. Arkansas is a better country than Mo." "As I write my mind goes back to our merry days at home . . . Do you remember those times, or are you so full of present pleasure that old times are forgotten." There was sudden, real hurt in this, for he hadn't heard from John since March 12. "[It] seems a long time," Webb remarked to his mother. "I suppose it can't be helped" (letter of April 30, 1862). But he almost seemed to be suggesting that John ("so full of present pleasure") wasn't doing his part. He hadn't meant it that way, and it was an inference he would regret.

Webb was out of sorts. After marching and countermarching for over a month—"900 miles over a very rough country. We have traveled all kinds of weather, at all times of night & under all kinds of circumstances"—he was feeling futile, not for the last time. Then his regiment received orders to report to Cape Girardeau. The men set out on May 9, arrived on the 20th, and two days later, at noon, embarked on the transport *Henry Clay* for Pittsburg Landing by way of Cairo and Fort Henry, now firmly in Federal hands. "Expect we will have it hot down there," he wrote John. "The butternuts will have a good time when they run against the Pea Ridge boys. It is raining & the paper blots so I can't write any more now" (letter of May 23, 1862). Meanwhile, he had received his pay "& for fear of not having a chance better than this, I send you $20."

Webb was back on a major front. From Pittsburg Landing on the 26th, his regiment was shifted to Corinth, where P. G. T. Beauregard had taken refuge after the Battle of Shiloh and where, since the end of April, Union forces had mounted a month-long siege. The next day, Webb joined the siege lines on the town's outskirts, where they "waited for three days momentously & anxiously expecting a battle. Now & then a shot kept us stirred up. The pickets were firing all the time. On the night of the 30th the firing ceased; & the next day we found the rebs. gone." Everyone was surprised. Beauregard had with him an army of seventy thousand men—far fewer than Halleck, it is true, but still a very large force, and after his reverse at Shiloh had been expected to fight. Jefferson Davis had expected it too and never forgave him for abandoning Corinth the way he did. "So we marched in & took possession," Webb wrote his mother on June 1. Not only had the Rebels fled, "they left camp equipage, guns, & everything. We were told that they were on the point of starvation, but they have plenty of provisions left anyway in the camp. [General John] Pope [who commanded the left wing of the Union Army] is after them & the report says that he has many prisoners. I wish he would get all of them . . . Give my love to all the pretty girls for I don't expect to see them soon."

Webb's unit joined in the pursuit of the Confederates as far as Boonesville, then on June 6, now reassigned to the 1st Brigade, 4th Division of the Army of the Mississippi, was ordered to Jacinto to help dislodge Beauregard from Tupelo, his new base. From Jacinto, Webb was sent out on reconnaissance expeditions to scour the country round. "Since I wrote you last we have been out toward Memphis," he wrote his mother on July 6. "We made a kind of circuit. We were out five days. We are constantly on the move. Though we do not go far, we keep going. The dust is shoe mouth deep . . . I should have written immediately [upon our return] but have been quite sick with fever & ague & diarrhea." However, he assured her, he was now "all right . . . [I] expect to march with the regt. at 3 P.M. The capt. says we are to go to Va.

We hear that the Pea Ridge gen., I mean Gen. Sigel, made the grand charge at Richmond. We made Beauregard get out of Miss. & if the Pea Ridge boys go to Va, Jeff [Jefferson Davis] will have to get from Richmond. Please Mother, send me a letter. It seems a long time since I had one from you . . . John's letters are so short."

"The Pea Ridge boys"—Webb liked the sound of that. In the army of the West, the phrase had become almost proverbial for troops that got things done. But in the East, the Rebels had managed to parry whatever was thrown their way. They had done this repeatedly, as Federal soldiers from Mobile to St. Louis looked on in dismay.

On July 22, 1861, the day after the battle of Bull Run, Lincoln had put General George McClellan in command of all forces in and about the capital, and by October had also made him general in chief. He had seemed perfect for the job. He was smart and had ranked second in a strong West Point class, in which Stonewall Jackson had ranked seventeenth; had witnessed and intelligently analyzed military action abroad, including British tactics in the Crimean War; and his "brief but brilliant" operations in West Virginia earlier that summer—at Philippi, Beverly, and along the Cheat River—had caught the imagination of the North. He had a fine soldierly bearing, an engaging manner, and at thirty-five the energy, it was thought, requisite to his command. His immediate task was to organize and drill the mass of new recruits, and at that he did a splendid job.

For several months he had a free hand. A complicated plan, known as the Peninsular Campaign, was developed under his direction. It included an overland advance between the York and James Rivers and a series of expeditions by sea against points along the Southern coast. By May 1862, most of the important seaports of the South, among them New Orleans (taken by amphibious assault), and with it the Mississippi River as far up as Port Hudson, had been occupied by Union troops. Even so, public impatience began to grow when McClellan failed to destroy or dislodge the main Confederate Army under Joseph E. Johnston, which defended Richmond, the Rebellion's official heart. By October, Johnston had also succeeded in establishing batteries on the lower Potomac that "effectively sealed up Washington as a port." McClellan's army was actually twice as strong as Johnston's, but he could not be persuaded that this was so. He refused to attack, as Lincoln demanded, and as a result a stalemate developed on that front. For the South, a stalemate was a kind of triumph and gave the Confederate strategists real breathing room.

At length, McClellan was replaced by General Pope. A collateral descendant of George Washington and linked by marriage to the family of Lincoln's wife, Pope had graduated from West Point in 1842, served with distinction in the Mexican War, and at the beginning of the Rebellion was made a brigadier of volunteers. In March 1862, he was promoted to major general during the campaign that opened the Mississippi almost to Memphis, and in May, as Halleck's army inched toward Corinth, he had commanded its left wing. There was therefore no blot on his record, and in June he was given charge of all the forces in the East except the core Army of the Potomac, which was under McClellan's immediate command. Meanwhile, Robert E. Lee had taken over for Johnston, who had been wounded in the Battle of Seven Pines. Nothing if not confident and brash, Pope expected to humble Lee even as he demoralized his own troops by upbraiding them for not having done better in the past. Lee paid his boasting no mind. He quickly maneuvered Pope into retreat north of the Rappahannock River, stunned his army with flanking blows, and managed to divide and reunite his own force in position for what would become the Second Battle of Bull Run. Pope attacked Lee's lines on August 29, mistook a tactical withdrawal by Stonewall Jackson for a retreat, and was badly beaten on the following day. Three days later he was relieved of command.

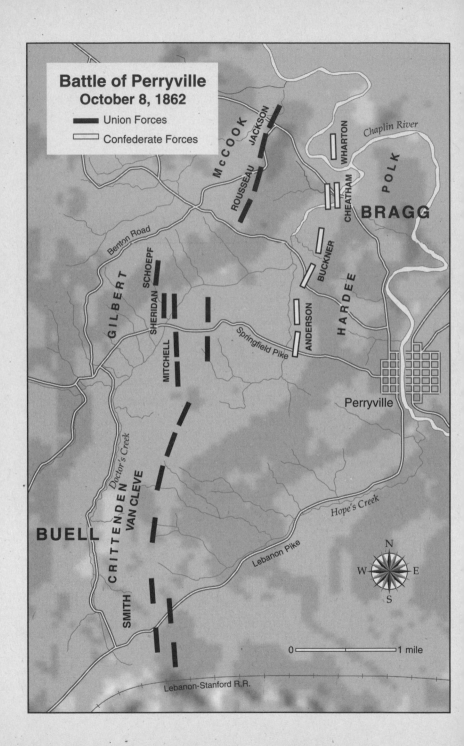

Battle of Perryville
October 8, 1862

■ Union Forces
□ Confederate Forces

McCOOK

JACKSON

WHARTON

Chaplin River

ROUSSEAU

CHEATHAM

POLK

BRAGG

Benton Road

BUCKNER

GILBERT

SCHOEPF

SHERIDAN

HARDEE

ANDERSON

MITCHELL

Springfield Pike

Perryville

Doctor's Creek

VAN CLEVE

CRITTENDEN

Hope's Creek

BUELL

N

W   E

S

Lebanon Pike

SMITH

0 ⊏———————————⊐ 1 mile

Lebanon-Stanford R.R.

CHAPTER FIVE

We are going to Kentucky," wrote Webb, "to try our skill in the cane brakes." So he had thought, some months back, but had gone to Arkansas instead. Yet it was only a matter of time before he was bound to feel the bluegrass under his feet. From the beginning, Lincoln had seen clearly that the war would be won or lost in the border states. "Kentucky gone," he declared, "we can not hold Missouri, nor, as I think, Maryland. These all against us, and the job on our hands is too large for us. We would as well consent to separation at once, including the surrender of this capital . . . I think to lose Kentucky is nearly the same as to lose the whole game." By its strategic location, Kentucky controlled the east-west flow of industrial products such as iron and coal along the Ohio River; gave access to Louisville, Cincinnati, and other towns of industrial might; and was the gateway to Tennessee, rich in mineral ores—iron, saltpeter, copper, lead—and a breadbasket of the south. Great rail and river roads also extended by way of Kentucky and Tennessee through Alabama and Mississippi all the way to the Gulf.

When the war began, Kentucky, though a slave state, had declared itself neutral, but that was sure to be short-lived. "We cannot escape history," Lincoln had said; nor could Kentucky. Before long those favoring secession had armed themselves by joining state guard units, those for the Union a rival militia called the Home Guards. In September 1861, the Confederates seized Columbus on the Mississippi; the Federals, in response, took

Louisville and Paducah—and the scrimmage for the state began. That November, secessionist delegates from sixty-eight counties convened to establish a provisional government, which declared itself for the south; in December, the star of Kentucky was added to the Confederate flag. Such an act, however, could be maintained only by force. The Rebels fortified Columbus and the "Iron Banks" above it, planted batteries along the water's edge, and established a five-hundred-mile defense line from the Mississippi River to Cumberland Gap. A Union plan was at once devised to outflank that line by way of the Tennessee and Cumberland Rivers, in the first instance, to drop below Columbus, surround it, and compel it to surrender by cutting off its supplies. The Rebels, however, preemptively occupied New Madrid and erected Forts Henry and Donelson with full-bastioned earthworks in a triangulated defense of all three river routes. But, as we have seen, those defenses failed to hold. The Mississippi had been opened from above and below, and after the fall of Fort Donelson, Grant, thanks to the Battle of Pea Ridge, was able to make his way down the Tennessee River without a Rebel army at his back. By June 19, the Federals were also digging in at Cumberland Gap.

Despite all these setbacks, the Confederates in the West were still full of fight. The deeper into Rebel territory the Union troops advanced, the more they were exposed to guerrilla operations and disruptions in their lines of communication and supply. Rebel raiders proved adept at such tactics, which tended to diminish, if not neutralize, some of the Federal gains. Moreover, by June two large Confederate armies were rapidly gearing up for a major counteroffensive into Maryland and Kentucky, the two critical remaining border states. In the East, the advance was to be led by Robert E. Lee, now in overall command; in the West, by Braxton Bragg.

The son of a famed commander of the Revolutionary War, Lee had served with distinction under Winfield Scott in the Mexican

War and as superintendent of West Point and was a cavalry colonel in west Texas when the war began. At Scott's urging, he was offered the field command of the Union armies, but declined, to become the foremost general of the south. As such, he was a reluctant champion. In 1856, he had written, "In this enlightened age, there are few, I believe, but will acknowledge that slavery as an institution is a moral and political evil in any country," and as late as January 1861 he declared, "I can anticipate no greater calamity for the country than a dissolution of the Union. It would be an accumulation of all the evils we complain of, and I am willing to sacrifice everything but honor for its preservation. Secession is nothing but revolution." In the end, however, a local and familial rather than national feeling swayed him, and so, in April, as the conflict began, he explained, "I had to meet the question whether I should take part against my native state. With all my devotion to the Union and the feeling of loyalty and duty of an American citizen, I have not been able to make up my mind to raise my hand against my relatives, my children, my home." That loyalty, though poignant, was tragic, and looked back to a time when one's country and state were the same. That time had now passed, or was passing. And Lee's failure to understand this did neither version of his country any good. Even so, he fought as well as anyone in the war.

After Pope had been bested, McClellan was recalled. Lee went on the offensive, drove McClellan from the Peninsula and prepared to cross the Potomac River into Maryland. His stunning victory at Second Bull Run had already opened the state to further conquest. And this he now prepared to make good. Meanwhile, in the West, Bragg's movements also augured well for Rebel arms. Bragg had entered the Confederate service in charge of the Gulf Coast from Pensacola to Mobile, and with a sterling military record behind him in the Seminole and Mexican Wars, he rose quickly from brigadier to major general. Soon after his promotion, he joined the war in the West under Albert Sidney Johnston and at Shiloh led the 2nd Corps. He was a shrewd if cantankerous man, adroit, industrious, able, and a wizard for detail. But he lacked imagination and, some critics aver, was "incapable of making crucial decisions once combat was joined." He also had a gift for making enemies. Even as a West Point plebe, he had been arrogant and harsh, and during the Mexican War, at the battle of Buena Vista, a colleague had tried to blow him up by placing a bomb under his cot.

Grant, who had known him, described him in his *Memoirs* as intelligent, well-informed, and "thoroughly upright," but "irascible" and obsessed with protocol. He told the following anecdote to illustrate the point:

> On one occasion, when stationed at a post of several companies, he himself was commanding one of the companies and at the same time acting as post quartermaster and commissary. As commander of the company he made a requisition upon the quartermaster himself for something he wanted. As quartermaster he declined to fill the requisition, and endorsed on the back of it his reasons for so doing. As company commander he responded to this, urging that his requisition called for nothing but what he was entitled to, and that it was the duty of the quartermaster to fill it. As quartermaster he still persisted that he was right. In this condition of affairs Bragg referred the whole matter to the commanding officer of the post. The latter, when he saw the nature of the matter referred, exclaimed: "My God, Mr. Bragg, you have quarreled with every officer in the army, and now you are quarreling with yourself!"

His first task was to rescue Beauregard's army from despair. After the evacuation of Corinth, Beauregard had withdrawn to Tupelo, and there, after moping about for two weeks, Beauregard suddenly announced that he was leaving to recuperate at an Alabama spa. Bragg took over, refurbished and roused the troops, and reorganized the army into two wings, one under Leonidas K. Polk, the other under William J. Hardee. Hardee was the author of a standard manual on tactics much consulted by both sides and had served as commandant at West Point; Polk was an artillery expert and West Point alumnus who, more notably, had enjoyed high clerical rank as the Episcopal Bishop of Louisiana for twenty years before the war. At the outbreak of fighting, he had exchanged his vestments for a star-studded tunic of gray, and had done so with an alacrity that surprised even his slaveholding friends. But Polk himself saw no conflict in his altered state. He was a slaver of Biblical conviction in the Alexander Stephens mode, and if his military talents fell short of his rank, Jefferson Davis had deemed the political power of his appointment worth the call.

In theory, Bragg had about 85,000 men at his general disposal, though half of them, in fact, were under independent commands: 46,000 were at Tupelo under his immediate direction; 21,000 under Kirby Smith at Knoxville; 2,000 at Chattanooga; and 16,000 at Vicksburg under Van Dorn. Smith was a dashing commander in the Van Dorn mode, whose brigade had helped rout the Union right at First Bull Run.

The Union general whom Bragg faced was Don Carlos Buell. Like Bragg a veteran of the Seminole and Mexican Wars, he was an aloof, almost forbidding man, with a solemn face, black eyes, and a beard cropped like a privet hedge with shears. Though short, he had a proud bearing and "always gave the impression that he was much taller and larger than he was." He also had immense physical strength in his arms, which he liked to demonstrate by clasping his wife about the waist and holding her in the air straight out in front of him. Over the years, he had developed a solid reputation as a daring and gallant soldier, but, like Bragg, was something of a disciplinarian and from his long stint as an adjutant general had "a fixed way of doing things." He also entertained a somewhat conservative view of the war. He was known to be ambivalent about slavery, had been raised by a slave nanny, and by marriage owned a handful of slaves himself. That southern savor, though it distressed some of his men, was thought to be advantageous for a campaign in a border state.

When the war broke out, Buell, a friend of McClellan's, had been called to Washington to help train the new recruits. Then, sent west, he occupied Nashville, helped Grant prevail at Shiloh, and joined in Halleck's advance on Corinth before embarking on the liberation of east Tennessee. In June, he set out to take the strategic railroad hub of Chattanooga, where the Western & Atlantic and the Memphis & Charleston railroads met. At their junction, they also formed the East Tennessee & Georgia line, which conveyed war matériel to Lee's army in the East. Just to the southwest, there was still another railhead of importance, at Stevenson, Alabama, where the Nashville & Chattanooga linked up with the Memphis & Charleston line. This reticulated network, with its constant transfer of goods of all kinds, had done much to keep the Confederate war effort alive. "To take and hold Chattanooga," Lincoln had declared, "is fully as important as the taking and holding of Richmond." Bragg, for his part, thought that "no greater disaster could befall" the Rebellion than its loss. And he was determined to see it didn't fall.

Buell got a head start and marched for Chattanooga from Corinth with about thirty-one thousand men on June 10. His progress, however, was slowed by Halleck's insistence that he rebuild and repair the Memphis & Charleston Railway as he went. This railway was supposed to serve as Buell's main line of communications and supply, but in fact it would have taken his whole force to guard it, and so this precautionary labor erased the advantage he had in getting his army in motion first. A drought set in, rivers fell, partisans dogged his footsteps, and the slow, ever more dejected shuffle of his army down the parched and dusty roads of northern Alabama into middle Tennessee enraged his superiors in Washington, who thought everything he did took too long.

Lincoln was convinced Buell had a case of the "slows." At the same time, the press got on his back. "Where is Buell?" complained the editor of the *Indianapolis Daily Journal*. "For all the country knows, he might as well be in the middle of Brazil." And in the end all his labor went for naught. No sooner was the track work done and a small force stationed at Murfreesboro to protect the crews needed to maintain it than Nathan Bedford Forrest, one of the best of the Rebel cavalry commanders, swooped down on the town, took fourteen hundred men prisoner, wrecked all the trestles in the area, and destroyed Buell's stockpiled supplies. Finally, in mid-July, two of Buell's divisions—one commanded by Thomas L. Crittenden, the other by Alexander McCook—came in sight of their objective; but just at this time, Bragg made his move. With astonishing speed, he managed to shift thirty thousand troops from Tupelo to Chattanooga, his artillery and wagon train coming overland across Alabama; his infantry, by rail through Alabama and Georgia, then up into Tennessee. It took him just two weeks to do this—Buell had been on the march for six—and it is said that troops had never been moved so far so fast before.

Bragg himself rode into Chattanooga on July 30, and the next day sat down with Kirby Smith to outline a joint campaign. Bragg had a large map of Kentucky and Tennessee on the wall, and the two conferred until the early morning hours of August 1. They parted with the understanding that Smith, proceeding from Knoxville, was to turn the Union position at Cumberland Gap, while Bragg, with a feint toward Nashville, would advance into Kentucky and in the process draw the Union armies out of Tennessee. In Kentucky, Smith and Bragg would then unite to confront Buell. That would allow Price and Van Dorn, in a separate action, to secure west Tennessee for the South.

Smith put his army in motion on August 13. One column with nine thousand men moved north to invest Cumberland Gap, then defended by a Federal force of about the same size; another, twelve thousand strong, crossed the Cumberland Mountains and marched through Barboursville to Richmond, Kentucky, where they overwhelmed a garrison of mostly green recruits. From Richmond, Smith advanced to Lexington, where he established his headquarters on September 2. Meanwhile, Rebel cavalry over-ran the Federal garrison at Gallatin, Tennessee, wrecking part of the railway there (a branch of Buell's line of supply). By then, Bragg himself had decamped from Chattanooga, crossed the Tennessee River, and begun marching for middle Tennessee. This was all more or less according to plan. As Bragg moved northward, keeping his army between Smith's and Buell's, Buell was obliged to give up on Chattanooga altogether and retreat through Tullahoma "to keep abreast of the Confederate move." Even so, there was now a real possibility that Bragg and Smith might unite to cut him off. Bragg marched to Sparta; Buell, in a parallel move, through Murfreesboro to Nashville, but from there he was obliged to fall back into Kentucky to prevent that state from falling into Rebel hands. The next two-step in this deadly minuet brought Bragg to Glascow, Buell to Bowling Green, the latter always taking care to follow the path of the Louisville & Nashville Railway, his line of supply. By then, Webb's unit had become part of the dance.

During Buell's abortive advance on Chattanooga, Webb had marched through the upper South in a holding pattern that nearly drove him up the wall. Long, seemingly aimless marches had alternated with equally aimless, long idle days in camp. After helping to pursue the Confederates to Booneville (after Corinth), his unit had been sent to Jacinto, Mississippi, where he remained for two months. "I would rather go [march] every day even if we only went 10 miles & back," he declared in a letter to his mother on July 11, "so they would make us believe we were going some place. I get so lazy laying in camp—I am sure to get the blues." His malaise increased as the temperature rose. The days seemed to pass by in a haze. "The boys are in their tents or shelters from the scorching rays of the sun, for I tell you it does scorch down here . . . Thermometer stands at 98 in the shade. We get up at 3 A.M., get breakfast & scrape & clean our tents & yards & ground & then drill an hour & a half—that brings us to 6 A.M. By that time it is so hot that we hunt the shade till evening when we have supper, drill and dress parade. This is all we do and are so lazy that we count it a killing job." Now and then the spell was broken by bursts of rain, but "then the dust gets shoe mouth deep . . . I think this country must be like the Sand Prairie. It is dry enough to plough an hour after the rain . . . I suppose we will remain here this winter, but can't tell. We really know nothing about it, no difference what the rumor may be." He wanted more men to join up, to speed the war along. "How many more men can old Coles Co. turn out?" he asked his mother. "Tell Dave Adams [a cousin] this is a good business & that he had better go. He is footloose & every man who can ought to go. They are all needed & the sooner they go the better."

These last words reached unintended ears. Webb's brother, John ("footloose" like his cousin), read them and took their exhortation to heart. A deep, fraternal feeling also moved him: he missed Webb greatly and if his willingness to serve could bring Webb home the sooner, how could he not go? And so, on July 22, Webb received an unwanted letter from him announcing his intention to enlist. That made Webb think twice about everyone coming in. On August 2 he replied, "I am just off picket duty . . . With regard to your going into the army. I know that somebody must go; but I can hardly consent to let you go. You are my only brother & somehow I have forebodings for you. I am strong &

tough you know & can stand it. And then it seems as if it would not be right to leave grandfather & grandmother alone. Soldiering is hard work & dangerous by reason of exposure." But not wanting to slight John's manhood or be a hypocrite, he added with a kind of stoic strength, "Still the country must be saved. I guess you may exercise your own judgment about coming. Hope we will both get through all right." What else could he say? To change the subject (awkwardly perhaps), he closed with a bit of gossip: "Tell the girls I am all right so far—I hear that you are hugging a Miss Haddock. Write soon & tell me the news of home."

Webb worried about the letter after he sent it, and on the 15th, as his unit passed through Iuka, sent John a simple note to get things back on an even keel:

> *Iuka, Miss., Aug. 15, 1862*
>
> Dear Brother:
>   We got our pay today & I send you twenty dollars. All quiet on the Potomac as far as I know. Health is good among us. The weather is extremely warm. We are in the pleasantest camp we have ever been in. I am getting more than fat. I weigh more than 200 lbs.
>
>   Your Brother,
>   Webb.

That pleasant lull was about to end. There had recently been a skirmish at Bay Springs, and a week after his "all quiet" note was sent, his unit was thrust into the contest between Buell and Bragg.

> *Across the River from East Port, Tenn, Aug. 21, 1862*
>
> Dear Mother:
>   I was glad to hear from you once more. I should have answered immediately, but we marched. We came here yesterday & will remain perhaps another day. The rest of the division came down & is crossing over . . . We are headed for some-

where. You were mistaken about Joe Neal. He has not returned
to his regt. & I think he never will.

You think the time long. It has grown into a year. I expected
to be at home in three months, when I left, but think now it will
take three years anyway. The first three months seemed longer
than all the time seems now. Time goes very fast when we are
on the move. I. D. is well. Health among the soldiers is good.
There is hardly a sick man in the whole division of eight regt. I
saw Leroy Willison & Role Bostick this morning [friends from
home in other regiments]. They are well. They send regards to
grandfather & [grand]mother. Bragg is reported in our vicinity
with a large army. We may have a fight one of these days.

Webb.

Time was speeding up.

Murfreesboro, Tenn., Sept. 1, 1862

Dear Mother:

Just as I expected. We were headed somewhere. We left East
Port on the 23 ult. & came via Florence, Lawrenceburg, Spring
Hill & Franklin to this place. This is a beautiful country, &
seems to have been a flourishing country. There are marks of
progress. But everything is at a stand still now except war. That
is progressing. The report here today is that Pope was driven
back, but that finally he has defeated the reb, they losing twice
as many as we, & that they are retreating, & the army after
them commanded by Gen. Sigel. If he does not bring them to
time, it is no use for any other man to try.

It is rumored that our forces have gained a victory at Baton
Rouge & that Buell has gained a victory at Chattanooga, taking
7000 prisoners. It is too good to be true. [It was.] There is also a
rumor that we are on our way to Cumberland Gap to help
[General William] Nelson dress [down] Kirby Smith [Smith
had already beaten Nelson at Richmond, Kentucky]—[Gener-
als William] Rosecrans & Sherman are said to be after Price at
Tupola, & the remainder of the army of the Miss. is making
every exertion to take in [Frank Crawford] Armstrong [a cav-

alry commander under Price]. Such a general move ought to be made & if it were the Southern confederacy would soon go up & the war end.

We started early this morning & have marched 20 miles already today. This is the 7th day in succession. We are all well.

Truly yours,
Webb.

Such a "general move" as Webb yearned for was still two years off and awaited the reorganization of the army under Grant. Other hopes for swift progress were also dashed. Price occupied Iuka soon after he passed through, and on the evening of September 1, Webb's unit had to retreat from Murfreesboro to Nashville with part of Buell's main force. By the time Webb got to Nashville at 10 o'clock the next morning he had marched thirty miles straight. That meant, in fact, that he had marched from Franklin some fifty miles altogether "in a little more than a day." Five days later, on September 7, he sat down to tell his mother about it in a brief note ("writ[ing] short," as he put it, because "preaching [is] in 15 minutes. I want to attend"). No sooner did he write this than service was cancelled and the troops were ordered across the river to Louisville as fast as they could go. "Don't know or care where we will be by next Sabbath, so [long as] I am well."

Instead of Louisville, Webb's unit went with Buell to Bowling Green. Meanwhile, at Glascow Bragg tried to rally Rebel feeling in the state. On September 13, he issued a resounding proclamation in which he promised to help free the people of Kentucky "from the tyranny of a despotic ruler" and appealed for their broad support. "If you prefer Federal rule, show it by your frowns and we shall return whence we came," he offered grandly, if insincerely. Otherwise, he hoped they would "choose rather to come within the folds of our brotherhood," "cheer us with the smiles of your women," and redeem their "heritage of liberty" from disgrace. As these words went forth, he sent a brigade to Cave City, ten miles to the west, to cut the railroad leading north from Bowling Green. After slicing up the tracks, that brigade then continued on to Munfordville, where a bridge spanning the Green River was held by Union Colonel John T. Wilder, later famed as the head of a mounted infantry brigade. At Munfordville, Wilder beat back two stiff assaults and when asked to surrender "to avoid further bloodshed" replied, "If you want to avoid further bloodshed keep out of the range of my guns."

Up to that moment, everything had been going Bragg's way. But his failure to take this Union outpost threatened to dampen troop morale. So he brought his entire army up to subdue it and ringed it with his guns. Faced with annihilation, Wilder surrendered, but only after haggling past midnight over the terms. At 6 A.M., his small garrison marched proudly out "with all the honors of war, drums beating and colors flying," and, as agreed, were at once paroled.

Wilder had been trying to buy Buell time. Bragg was now squarely across the latter's supply line, so Buell advanced to Munfordville to confront him, as he really had no other choice. For a few days the two camps faced each other, and there, by all rights, a battle should have been fought. But neither found any advantage by which to strike. At length, Bragg withdrew northeast to Bardstown, which left the road to Louisville open to the Federals, who marched to the city as fast as they could.

If Buell had escaped, there was little in this to give his men heart. It was not escape they wanted. In nine months of marching, they had done almost no fighting, and their mood was dark. That of Buell was darker still. "His dress was that of a brigadier instead of a major general," wrote one eyewitness. "He wore a shabby hat, dusty coat, and had neither belt, sash or sword about him . . . Though accompanied by his staff, he was not engaged in conversation with any of them, but rode silently and slowly along."

Buell found Louisville in a panic akin to a state of siege. Bragg's perceived threat to Union strongholds on the Ohio River had alarmed the whole Midwest, and the governors of Indiana, Illinois, and Ohio had taken a number of emergency measures in response to it, even as they appealed to the government for help. That summer, when Bragg crossed into Kentucky, they had also, with some foresight, mounted a great recruitment drive that brought in thousands of new recruits. Their influx was timely, because after the Union debacle at Second Bull Run and Lee's invasion of Maryland, few if any troops from the East could be spared. In Coles County, the pressure, or fervor, to enlist reached its height in August when, according to the *Mattoon Independent Gazette*, "The brave men of this district are coming nobly to the rescue of an imperiled country. By the hundreds and the thousands they are volunteering—coming from the workshops, from stores, from their half-harvested grain—from the pulpit, the bar, and the studio—men of brains, money-men, the best men in the country—and are falling into the ranks, proud of being volunteer *privates* in the Army of the Union, rather than have it said that Illinois' quota of soldiers were *drafted* into the field. To arms! Fall in!"

One of those to fall in was Webb's brother, John. An ardent soul, he could scarcely resist the government's near-frantic appeals. Despite Webb's fearful warnings, he had enrolled in the 123rd Illinois Volunteer Infantry Regiment, organized at Mattoon by Colonel James Monroe, and as a member of Company K was mustered into service at Camp Terry (Mattoon) on September 6, 1862. With him came a stepbrother, John W. Moore—"Little Johnny," as Webb called him—who must have lied about his age, for he was just fifteen. On the 19th both boys were loaded into boxcars, transported to Louisville, and at once put to work on the fortifications then being prepared against Bragg.

Camp B near Louisville, K. [Undated.]

Dear Mother,

It is with pleasure that I take my pen in hand to write you a few lines to tell you that I am well. I would have written sooner but I was on guard on Sunday. On Monday I was breaking mules. Tuesday we all was throwing up breastworks. The secesh is [with]in 90 miles of us but we are ready for them. We have all our things. We quit our work about sundown, got supper, then it was night . . .

John Baker.

Both Louisville and Cincinnati across the Ohio River were expecting an attack any day and could not dig their trenches or throw up earthworks fast enough. Cincinnati's defense had been entrusted to Lew Wallace, a veteran of Fort Donelson and Shiloh, but today chiefly remembered as the author of *Ben-Hur.* Louisville was defended by William "Bull" Nelson, a large, tempestuous man, who had been the first to cross the Tennessee River at Shiloh to reinforce Grant. In the Union counterattack, he had beaten stragglers over the head with his sword, shouting, "Damn your souls, if you won't fight, get out of the way, and let men come here who will." At Louisville, he was ready to destroy the city, if necessary, in order to save it, and had made arrangements if the Rebels took it to set it on fire and bombard it from the Indiana shore. Almost no one could stand up to his temper, but one dark day it brought him into a fatal collision with Jefferson C. Davis, the Union general who had led a division at Pea Ridge.

Nelson had asked Davis to help prepare the city for attack, but then accused him of not doing all he could. Davis demanded a retraction, and in a subsequent encounter, Nelson rashly called him "a damned puppy" and struck him in the face. Davis grabbed a pistol and shot him through the heart. There could hardly be any doubt that Davis was guilty of murder, however much provoked, and he was promptly indicted—but never tried: his talent, apparently, was deemed too great to spare. Released on bail, he continued to serve in the Western theater, often with distinction, and became Webb's division commander when Buell's army was revamped.

At Louisville, the Union troops refreshed themselves, gained strength, sang patriotic songs like "John Brown's Body," and began to look forward to a new campaign. The feared assault by Bragg had not materialized, and the legions of raw recruits that had come in to defend the port were now impatiently incorporated into the army's swelling ranks. Not far away in Bardstown, Bragg's troops were in the best of spirits, too. All day long their camp rang out with "Lorena," a ballad that had become almost the anthem of their march:

> *The years creep slowly by, Lorena,*
> *   The snow is on the grass again,*
> *The sun's low down the sky, Lorena,*
> *   The frost gleams where the flowers have been.*
> *But the heart throbs on as warmly now*
> *   As when the summer days were nigh*
> *Oh! the sun can never dip so low*
> *   Adown affection's cloudless sky.*

If Bragg had stopped just short of Louisville, which he still hoped to take, he also knew that he had chased Buell in. Lincoln and his general in chief, Halleck, knew it too, and ordered General George H. Thomas to take over the command. Thomas conferred with Buell and decided to decline the appointment on the grounds that it is unwise to replace a general on the eve of his own campaign. The orders to relieve Buell were thereupon suspended—but not revoked. Over the next few weeks, they would hang like a sword of Damocles above his head.

Bragg had expected Buell to take some time to get his army together. In the interim, Bragg disposed his forces in a wide strategic arc to hem him in: 22,500 troops under Polk were posted at Bardstown, thirty-five miles to the southeast; 10,000 more were strung through Lexington, Harrodsburg, and Frankfort. So Bragg was surprised when on October 1 Buell led his new Army of the Ohio, as it was called—some sixty thousand strong—out of Louisville to challenge his hold on the state. Advancing southeast over a sixty-mile front, Buell's army was divided into three corps, led by Generals Thomas W. Crittenden, Charles C. Gilbert, and Alexander M. McCook. McCook commanded the left, Gilbert the center, and Crittenden, accompanied by General Thomas, a kind of supra corps commander, in this instance, the right. The weather was fair and morale once more high. The men marched out to the cheerful sound of fife and drum, their sabers and bayonets flashing and gleaming in the sun. Buell's army was mighty by any measure, even if part of it was green, and Webb and his brother now belonged to the selfsame host. Webb's unit was attached to the 32nd Brigade, 9th Division, of Gilbert's corps; John's to the 33rd Brigade, 10th Division, of McCook's. Though at Louisville they had had a chance to visit only once due to their divided encampments, now they could almost see each other in the great parade.

Bragg and Smith considered together also disposed of a sizable force, but they had expected it to be far larger than it was. During the early summer, John Hunt Morgan, a Rebel raider operating in Kentucky, had depicted the state as ripe for the taking on the grounds that many of its people were keen to fight for the South. He thought only a show of force and determination was needed, as proof that the South was ready to stake its claim; then recruits in large numbers would flock to the cause. Confederate officials believed him, and Bragg brought with him wagons loaded with rifles to arm some thirty thousand volunteers. But in the end, few had joined. "Our prospects are not what I expected," he wrote Jefferson Davis. "Enthusiasm runs high, but exhausts itself in words." An embittered Kirby Smith more harshly disparaged Kentuckians as too attached to their ample farms, "fat cattle," and prosperity to care how freedom fared. Worse, "bushwhackers had sniped at his columns" in the Kentucky hills.

Bragg turned to conscription. To do so legally, he went to the state capital of Frankfort to install a pro-Confederate regime. On the morning of October 4, with considerable fanfare, he led Richard C. Hawes, a doddering ex-official and his personal choice for governor, from his quarters under military escort through the streets to the Kentucky House of Representatives, where a Confederate flag had been raised above the dome. Hawes had barely begun to speak, however, when the rumble of Federal artillery could be heard on the town's outskirts. Soon couriers brought word that a Union army was drawing near. Hawes cut short his remarks and departed. By the time the sun had set, the new Confederate government had come and gone.

Bragg was not in as much danger as he feared. The two Union divisions then approaching were actually a feint. Buell's main army was heading toward Bardstown, expecting, ultimately, to confront Bragg there. For his part, Bragg wasn't sure what Buell was up to, but, after his initial fright, thought an attack on Frankfort might be one he could win. "Should it be a real attack," he wrote to Polk at Bardstown, "we have them . . . With Smith in front and our gallant army on the flank [Hardee near Harrodsburg] I see no hope for Buell if he is rash enough to come out. I only fear it is not true."

Over the next few days, both armies groped for the true position of the other, but despite much tactical tacking back and forth and an admonition from Hardee to Bragg that his forces were "too much scattered" to strike anywhere with strength, the ground of battle would ultimately be determined less by military considerations than by an elemental need.

Kentucky was in the throes of a drought. It lasted all summer and into the fall, and as the troops plodded along the chalk dirt roads, they were tormented by an unrelenting thirst. The earth was parched and blistered. Leaves had dried up on the trees, and "all the grass had withered and turned gray. The procession of men and animals stirred up blinding clouds of limestone dust, which every breeze sent whirling through the camps." Many of the creek and stream beds they came upon were dry, or had "tired-looking threads of water in them"; others had not a trace of dampness but lay seared with fissures and cracks. Wherever water was found, men pushed, scrambled, and even fought "for a few muddy drops." What water there was often was contaminated by dead matter and other waste. "I never saw men suffer for water as we have," wrote one soldier. "It is horrible to think what we have been compelled to drink!" Hogs seem always to have wallowed in it; one morning, soldiers found to their disgust that they had filled their canteens the night before from a pond that contained a dead mule.

Thus it was that the little hamlet of Perryville in central Kentucky, traversed by a still-flowing river and laced by creeks and streams, drew generals from both armies as surely as if each held a dowsing rod trembling in his grip.

Three roads converged on the town—Springfield, Mackville, and Lebanon, named for the towns to which they led—and on October 6 the Rebels arrived first when Hardee tramped in with two divisions along the Springfield Road from the west. Though he had planned to continue north, he was struck by the presence of water and at the same time disturbed and puzzled by the strength of the enemy on his heels. He thought, just as Bragg did, that most of the Union force was near Frankfort. But he could not square this with the way he was being pressed. Hardee asked Polk to reinforce him, and Polk came himself from Bardstown with one division, taking charge. Writing to Bragg, he explained, "I have directed General Hardee to ascertain, if possible, the strength of the enemy which may be covered by his advance. I cannot think it large." In fact, the Union force converging on Perryville was three corps strong, between fifty-five and sixty thousand men. Buell's plan had been to keep the Rebels guessing about his line of march, to prevent Bragg and Kirby Smith from linking up. And this he had successfully done.

On the 7th, the Federals began to arrive. On the left, moving in by the Mackville Road from the north, was McCook, accompanied by Thomas; on the right, Crittenden from the south; in the center, Gilbert from the west. Gilbert's vanguard, which included Webb's unit, "kept up a running fight with a large force of Rebel cavalry, which stubbornly contested its advance." The skirmishing became intense, and Buell himself rode forward to assess it. On the way, he came upon stragglers foraging in a garden and paused to rebuke them. One of the soldiers grabbed the bridle of his horse and gave it an angry jerk, causing the horse to rear and fall backwards, bruising one of Buell's legs. Lamed as a result, Buell spent the rest of the day in an ambulance wagon being wheeled back and forth.

Facing what he supposed to be Bragg's entire army, not just the sixteen thousand men who were there, Buell pored over area maps with his staff. He wasn't quite sure where the Rebels had drawn their line, but established his own, north to south, about three miles from the town. Meanwhile, the Rebels occupied the town itself and disposed their forces in a roughly opposite formation under Hardee's practiced eye. As evening fell, he posted two brigades on a ridge above a stream called Doctor's Creek to prevent the Federals from getting at the pools of water that it held. Well back from this forward position, he planted his batteries on a range of low wooded hills overlooking and completely commanding a stretch of open ground lying immediately at the foot of the range. His infantry was massed behind and around his artillery, and his cavalry ready to charge down the easy slopes and "sweep every living thing from the level ground below. This was his trap, and into this he expected the advanced positions of the Union army to fall."

If Buell mistakenly supposed he was confronting Bragg's entire army, Bragg was equally wrong in supposing that only a wing of Buell's army was there and that most of the Union force was still converging on Frankfort to the north. Out of their blundering confusion emerged one of the terrible battles of the war.

The first clash occurred over Doctor's Creek. Gilbert wanted to drive the Confederates back from the heights above it and chose Philip Sheridan, one of his division commanders, to do it. Sheridan had recently been promoted to brigadier general for his role in the taking of Corinth, and his star was on the rise. Abraham Lincoln once comically described him as "a brown, chunky little chap, with a long body, short legs, not enough neck to hang him, and such long arms that if his ankles itch he can scratch them without stooping." A fighter by nature—even at West Point, from which he had been suspended for threatening another cadet with a bayonet—he eagerly assumed charge. Just before dawn on October 8, one of his brigades seized the high ground, and despite a prolonged attempt by the Rebels to regain it, by late morning he had secured the water for his men.

This might have proved an auspicious beginning to a long day's fight, but Buell decided to postpone the general attack he had planned because McCook and Crittenden had been delayed in coming in. As he waited for them to fill out their lines—and the sun climbed ever higher in the sky—he assumed the Rebels would also not attempt any major action until the following day. Bragg, on the other hand, supposing Polk and Hardee to be facing only a part of the Union force, had already ordered an attack. And he meant to see it through. At nearby Harrodsburg, he waited impatiently all morning for the tell tale sounds of battle, but at length, hearing none, hurried to Perryville to ascertain what had gone awry. By then his colleagues had divined "the great disparity of forces" between the two camps and had decided, as they explained, to adopt "the defensive-offensive, to await the movements of the enemy, and to be guided by events."

Bragg insisted that an attack be mounted at once. A little past noon it began, in echelon from right to left, against the Union left. In the heart of that left stood Webb's brother in the brigade of General William Rufus Terrill, who had fought at Shiloh and other engagements and who, it so happened, was also the West Point cadet whom Sheridan had onced threatened with a bayonet. Just two days before they had met and shaken hands to efface the grudge. Terrill's own division commander was General James S. Jackson, who had just ordered Terrill to move the 123rd Illinois to the large Open Knob or hill above the Mackville Road. As John's regiment came up on the rise, it was accompanied by an eight-gun battery managed by a tenacious artillery lieutenant by the name of Charles Parsons. John and the others were arrayed in formation to defend these guns. The sky was clear, the sun shining brightly overhead. In the distance a handful of Rebels could be seen on horseback, "evidently taking a survey of the field." They looked toward the Union position, then abruptly disappeared. A few minutes later, exactly where they had been, there emerged from a clump of trees the head of a column of men. As they came out, one soldier afterwards recalled, "their bayonets glistened, and I knew they were coming for us."

The Federals, though surprised, were well and strongly placed, for the Confederate left extended only to the center left of their own line. As a result, the first Rebel assault, launched by Daniel S. Donelson, head of a brigade, found itself in a crossfire, as Parsons's battery swiveled and tore into its flank. But as that brigade fell back, two others advanced, one in support of Donelson; the other, led by George Maney, the best of Bragg's brigade commanders, to contest the Open Knob and take Parsons's battery by storm. The 123rd was still shuffling into place when Maney's brigade, concealed till then in a wooded patch of ground, seemed to come out of nowhere and sweep down the opposite hill. The Federals knelt and loaded, their fingers fumbling with the new percussion pouches they had just been issued and the cartridge boxes tied to their belts. Reinforcements were rushed forward from the rear. Parsons wheeled his guns about and began firing, but the Rebels kept on. Behind them others could now be seen massing. Seeing no other way they could be stopped, Terrill suddenly ordered the 123rd to fix its bayonets and charge.

At the time, this unit was possibly the least trained Union regiment ever to take the field. Its men had drilled in companies only a couple of times, and as a regiment only once. Every man in it, in fact, including the officers, except for Colonel Monroe, was a raw recruit. It has been said that volunteers are superior to regulars "in skirmishes and irregular warfare . . . which call for individual action and chivalrous daring, but inferior in those stern evolutions when . . . an army becomes an unthinking machine, moved by another's will." The bayonet charge of the 123rd at Perryville stands as preeminent proof of this maxim, the more so because, for lack of any drill, the men had no idea what kind of machine they were supposed to be.

In front of them the ground was clear for a hundred yards until, at the bottom of the hill, it came to a high rail fence; as the men advanced, the timed and staggered fire from Maney's veterans repeatedly ripped into their ranks. The men of the 123rd managed but a single volley, then turned in terror and tried to claw their way back up the slope. Moments later, "their thinned and butchered" remnants scrambled over the crest and continued a broken retreat down the other side.

Others took their place, as fighting on the Open Knob continued, but now the Rebels brought forward heavy guns of their own. Minute by minute the crest of the hill began to pile up with bodies of the fallen. Then four more Rebel regiments, yelling at the top of their lungs, started over the rail fence at the base of the hill. Terrill tried yet again what had already failed, and had another regiment, the 105th Ohio, fix bayonets for a charge; meanwhile, "the rest of the blue line remained hunkered down on the knob, pouring volleys of iron and steel into the attacking line." At that moment the Confederates could have walked without touching ground on the mingled dead and wounded that matted the entire slope from the fence line to the top. Once more they surged forward to get at Parsons's guns, and this time "the exhausted Federal defenders broke." Terrill ordered the Union line back "to a skirt of woods at the western foot of the hill, about fifty yards to the rear," and there he tried to rally his broken men around another rail fence. But he couldn't hold that line either and withdrew through a cornfield. The Rebels chased him up another hill until, near a country lane called Benton Road, he was able to gather the remnants of his command along a ridge under the protection of two new batteries of guns. Meanwhile, behind him, the entire Union left had almost crumbled. In four and half hours of heavy fighting casualties on both side were high. Only a lack of sheer numbers prevented the Rebels from prevailing, even in the face of fierce cannonades. Again and again, the Rebels struggled to the top of the ridge, where Terrill's men and a fresh brigade were standing, as the fighting became hand-to-hand. "It was a life to life and death to death grapple," wrote one soldier. "The sun was poised above us, a great red ball sinking slowly in the west." As it touched the horizon, it seemed to suffuse the plain with blood. Just at that moment, the Rebels gave up on their attempt to carry the defense works and withdrew. They did not have to draw back far. Claiming the land between, they firmly entrenched themselves on the Open Knob where the 123rd had made its first and fatal stand.

The Federals were aghast. The night before, General Jackson

and his two brigade commanders, Terrill and Colonel George Webster, had ruefully discussed the chances of any particular individual being killed by enemy fire. They had decided that, according to "the doctrine of probabilities," the chances were slight, and to give the troops heart had conveyed this to the men. Twenty-four hours later, all three were dead: Jackson had fallen with a bullet through the lungs, Webster after a cannonball carried away a thigh, Terrill when a piece of shrapnel tore open his chest.

Yet this was a battle that Buell's army should have won. Almost all the action of the day had taken place on the Union left. Gilbert, in the center, with twenty thousand men at his disposal, had allowed himself to be paralyzed more or less by a tenth that number, not knowing the true Confederate strength. On the Union right, Crittenden, with twenty-two thousand, had been deceived by a clever deployment of Rebel cavalry into believing that a large Confederate force was in his front. Only Sheridan's division, posted west of Perryville across the Springfield Road, had been fully engaged and had fought off the onslaught of two Confederate brigades. Other units had waited in vain for some command. Webb's regiment, for example, and the whole 9th Division to which it belonged, had been held that day in restive reserve. His division commander, General Robert B. Mitchell, had been furious to be so idled and chafed to join the fray. Indeed, the night before, he told Buell he thought he could take Perryville all by himself, if only Buell would let him. With unbecoming scorn, Buell had brushed him aside.

But it was Buell who lacked the proper enterprise. That day, the Federals did so poorly because there had been no overall direction on the Union side; that in turn was because Buell had been blissfully unaware that a great battle was taking place. For most of the morning he had been convalescing behind the lines in his tent, on his back, reading a book. About noon, just before the battle started, his staff officers had "all drifted back to join him for a midday meal." As one writer tartly put it: "Their synchronized stomachs served notice of emptiness at the same hour and they returned to headquarters, not one having sufficient curiosity or sense of responsibility to remain and keep an eye on developments." By the time Buell knew that a battle was going on it was late in the afternoon. At 4 P.M. a member of McCook's staff dashed in to report that the Union left was in a fight for its life. "I was astonished," Buell wrote. "Not a sound of musketry had been heard." Apparently, an "acoustic shadow" or still zone, created by a quirk of topography and wind, had "virtually deadened the sounds of battle" nearby. One member of Buell's staff, dispatched in search of Gilbert, remembered that his horse had carried him "from stillness into the uproar of battle" at a single bound. "Just one turn from a lonely bridle path through the woods," he later testified, "brought me face to face with the bloody struggle of thousands of men."

It had been a confused day all around. At times, the two armies, not always easily distinguishable by their dress, had blurred or blended together: one Union colonel, for example, had mistaken Polk for McCook, and coming up to him had announced that he had come to his aid. Polk asked him for the name of his unit, and when he heard it declared, "There is some mistake. You are my prisoner."

Almost the reverse happened later that day. As dusk fell, Polk thought he saw one Confederate unit firing into the ranks of another, and riding up to its colonel demanded what "he meant by shooting his own friends." The colonel replied, "I don't think there can be any mistake about it; I am sure they are the enemy!" "Enemy!" cried Polk. "Why, I have only just left them myself. Cease firing, sir; what is your name?" The colonel identified himself, then asked, "Pray, sir, who are you?" Polk realized he was in the midst of Union troops and that his only hope was "to brazen it out." He shook his fist in the colonel's face, and said, "I'll soon show you who I am, sir; cease firing, sir, at once." Then he wheeled his horse about and, with his back "screwed up" at the thought of being hit by a hail of fire, cantered slowly away. When he got to a small copse, he dug in his spurs and sped back to his own lines.

The firing on both sides ceased at dark. "The sun was declining in a cloudless sky," wrote one eyewitness, "rank, red and fiery in the West, while almost simultaneously the full moon, its counterpart in bloody mien, rose opposite . . . Gradually the fire slackened, the moon rose higher and lit up the ghastly faces of the dead, until at 8 o'clock, all was the stillness of death." One young officer, trying to make sense of what had happened, encountered an aide to General Jackson and learned of the latter's painful fate. He was told of the awful carnage among the 123rd—which in fifteen minutes had lost a quarter of its men—and sought to discover how General Terrill himself had fared. He remembered the day almost exactly six months before when he and Terrill had gone up to Pittsburg Landing on a small steamer to join Grant at Shiloh on the battle's second day. They had sat together on the deck, and "as the first streak of daylight came, Terrill . . . had recited a line about the beauty of the dawn . . . I asked about Terrill now . . . and was told he had been carried to the rear to die." He asked, too, about Charles Parsons, whom he had known at West Point, where he had seen him knocked down seven times in a fight with a bigger man, "without ever a thought of quitting so long as he could get up." He was told that, true to form, Parsons had stood by his guns until "he had to be dragged away." His battery had been wrecked, and "no one then knew where he was. And so the news came in."

In his official report, General McCook described the battle of Perryville as "the bloodiest battle of modern times, for the number of troops engaged on our side." Bragg, in his own account, coincidentally agreed. "For the time engaged," he wrote, "it was the severest and most desperately contested engagement within my knowledge," Shiloh included. The war correspondent for the *Cincinnati Gazette* reported simply, "The severest action of the war (in proportion to the numbers engaged) has just taken place." Perhaps it was. In a war of such carnage, the truth of such pronouncements is impossible to gauge. But the whole spectacle presented by the battlefield, wrote one Union soldier, "was enough to make angels weep."

Casualties had been heavy. Almost all the units involved on either side had lost much of their original strength, and nearly every building in and around the village and every farmhouse for ten miles around was converted into a hospital ward. As at Pea Ridge, neither side had an adequate number of medics or supplies, but the situation for the Federals was worse. Buell had almost no regular army surgeons with him, no regularly organized ambulance and field hospital plan, and had left most of the medical and hospital wagons behind. He hadn't even bothered to bring hospital tents. His negligence in this respect would long remain a Federal disgrace.

That night, recalled one soldier, "the moaning and sighing of the wounded and dying was so heartrending" as to cause "any man to oppose war." Limbs and body parts of all kinds were strewn about, and in places the dead were stacked like cordwood in the yards. "Some lay with their tongues swelled out of their mouths, others with their hands stuck out as if surprised, with an expression of amazement on their faces." A number of the Confederate dead were also found to be black and swollen, giving rise to the rumor that they had been fed on gunpowder and whiskey before battle to fire them up for the fight. Not much hope was held out for those with serious wounds. "It seemed the climax of impotence," wrote one observer, "to see a surgeon peering wisely into a hole through the small of a man's back that you could put an elephant's head in."

Buell hoped to redeem himself somehow by a counterattack at dawn and told Thomas and Crittenden to have their divisions ready at the left and center of the line. But Bragg now realized that the entire Federal army was in front of him, and during the night fell back to Harrodsburg, where Kirby Smith's army and another division joined him on October 10. That gave him considerable strength, and when Buell followed, Smith urged Bragg to fight. "For God's sake, General, let us fight Buell here," he told him, to which Bragg reportedly replied, "I will do it," but did not. Three days later, to prevent a flanking movement by Buell, he abandoned Kentucky altogether and with Knoxville as his goal, headed for Cumberland Gap. Buell chased him for another sixty-five miles but failed to bring him to bay.

Meanwhile, both sides began to tally up their losses. The Federals, in final possession of the field, scoured it for their dead and wounded. Webb's brother had not been with his unit at nightfall on the 8th, and Webb searched for him in anguish across the bloody ground.

Perryville Battle Ground, Oct. 11, 1862

Oh Mother; How can I say it! But I must!! John is dead!!! He was killed on the battlefield on the 8th inst. in one of the hottest engagements of the war—he was shot in two places. The balls must have struck him at the same instant—one entered his left side at the waistband & passing through his heart came out under his right arm. The other struck him in the neck under the jaw & near the jugular vein & passed up into his brain. Either of the balls would have killed him instantly. He evidently never moved after he fell, nor at all only to fall for his arms were as if he had been holding his gun to shoot. I suppose he was at the time the balls struck him. I was on the right of the battle field & he on the left. I did not know that he was on the field at all till the next day. There was only a skirmish on the right—but on the left it was very hot. Crocket Neal [a friend from home] was killed half a mile from the line of battle in the retreat. I suppose a stray ball must have struck him. It went into the back of his head & did not pass through. He fell on his face & apparently never moved. Anthony Cox [another friend] was killed. Anthony was shot through both legs just above the knees. The legs were both broken. He was not killed instantly, but doubtless soon bled to death. He must have suffered. He attempted to crawl off the field—he got back about 8 or 10 feet from where he fell. There was an agony look on his face. There were two others of the company killed—I do not know them—Robert Eardsley, John Jones & Calvin Moore were wounded, & some other of the company whom I do not know. I had permission from Capt. Taggert & helped to bury the boys & marked the place. I send you a lock of John's hair. Everything was taken from his pockets but his Testament. John died like a man & a soldier at his post & in the front rank. Would I had died in his stead—my only, my true & noble hearted brother. What a great vicarious sacrifice our homes & country are costing. How many noble hearted brothers. I can't write more. God bless & sustain you in this great bereavement. I sent Bige Neal a lock of Crocket's hair.

Truly your son,
Webb.

Webb buried his brother where he found him and placed above the spot a simple cross. But he did not want that to be his resting place. He hoped, devoutly, that sometime later that fall, as the days grew colder, John's body might be safely taken home. "I am very lonesome," he wrote his mother two days later. "While John was living though I only saw him once in a whole year, I was not so lonesome. But now he is gone. I feel as if you & Mr. Moore must come & see I. D. & me when we get into camp." He thought if the Federals could only catch up to Bragg they would "clean him out entirely . . . & that the war might close." But he doubted it would be.

Meanwhile, Webb's mother wanted to learn everything she could about John's last hours. From Nashville, Webb wrote her on

November 13: "John Jenkins [an acquaintance from home] was the last to speak to John. They were standing together in the front rank & did not hear the order to fall back. The company was back 50 yards when Jenkins told John to come on. John replied he would give them one more load. He was sober & thoughtful on the day of battle more than usual so the boys said." He had also been one of the few to stand his ground.

Once in East Tennessee, Bragg was ordered to report to Richmond on October 23. "At once the dogs of detraction were let loose upon me," he wrote his wife, "and the venal press has decided I should be removed from my command." But Jefferson Davis stood by him, despite the urgings of many that he be replaced. For his part, though he had won the battle by default, Buell was sacked on October 24 for allowing Bragg to escape. The sword above his head had dropped. A new department, that of the Cumberland, was thereupon created with General William S. Rosecrans at its head.

Webb looked on all this with an indifferent eye. "I am resigned to my fate whatever it may be," he wrote. "There is no prospect of the war ending—I wish there would be a general move & that the rebellion would be crushed out—it seems to me that it could be done." But his own, more pressing concern, one that he could partly control, was to see to his brother's remains. "I . . . believe now that the weather is so cool John might be taken home," he wrote his mother from Bowling Green on November 4. "If Mr. Moore will do it I will pay for it." Later that fall it was done, and John was reinterred in Hurricane Cemetery, Hutton, Coles County, not far from the family farm.

CHAPTER SIX

The Battle of Perryville—the principal battle of the war in Kentucky—was an almost accidental clash. But its consequence was large. Bragg had chosen the wrong time and place to attack, and though he did better than he should have under the circumstances, Kentucky slipped from his grasp. As James McPherson has noted, the battles at Antietam and Perryville together saved Maryland and Kentucky for the Union, "forestalled European mediation and recognition of the Confederacy, perhaps prevented a Democratic victory in the northern elections of 1862 that might have inhibited the government's ability to carry on the war, and set the stage for the Emancipation Proclamation, which enlarged the scope and purpose of the conflict."

At Antietam, the Army of the Potomac had checked Lee's attempt to carry the war into the North. In early September, as Bragg was entering Kentucky, Lee crossed into Maryland by the fords on the Potomac near Leesburg, camped briefly near Frederick, and had just begun his advance when he learned, to his dismay, that a copy of his Special Orders, No. 191, found wrapped around three cigars, had come into Mc-Clellan's hands. These orders described the routes, objectives, and times of arrival for his several commands. That ought to have placed him at McClellan's mercy, but the latter failed to take prompt advantage of his luck. Lee hastily withdrew through Turner's Gap in South Mountain, a spur of the Blue Ridge range, but geography was against him, and on September 17 McClellan appeared to trap him at Antietam Creek, where stupendous carnage ensued. Both armies were nearly ruined, but Lee escaped the outright destruction that ought to have been his fate.

McClellan's victory therefore served him personally no better than Buell's. He had not so much prevailed as endured, and his failure to eliminate Lee's army weighed heavily on Northern morale. That morale had begun to falter as Lincoln struggled to maintain the national will to fight. Indeed, as the weary and costly stalemate in the East dragged on, a great many Northerners had come to favor some conditional recognition of Southern independence, or a negotiated peace. Various foreign powers, chiefly England and France, also waited in the wings. Although the Northern blockade of Southern ports had failed to arouse the ire of European nations, at least to the extent the South had hoped, there was acute concern that England and France might eventually find some pretext to intervene. The immediate fear was that England would recognize the Confederacy as an independent power. Sir William Gladstone, then Chancellor of the Exchequer, did so in fact in an unofficial speech to a large audience at Newcastle in October 1862. "We may have our own opinions about slavery," he said, "we may be for or against the South; but there is no doubt that Jefferson Davis and other leaders of the South have made an army; they are making, it appears, a navy; and they have made, what is more than either—they have made a nation." British Prime Minister Lord Palmerston would not go so far, but he would have been only too happy to have declared it true.

Just at this juncture, Lincoln announced his intention of setting free by his military authority all the slaves in Rebel states.

Lincoln's thinking on emancipation had evolved. In the beginning, as we have seen, he had refused to agree to the extension of slavery but had also pledged not to challenge it where it existed. In the spring of 1862, he came up with a plan for gradual emancipation involving a monetary payment to slaveholders in areas within the Union fold; but that met resistance, and the scheme was given up. Meanwhile, some Union generals, notably Frémont and Hunter, had taken it upon themselves to issue emancipation decrees in territory they controlled. To the bitter disappointment of his abolitionist friends, Lincoln revoked such edicts, and in a famous letter to Horace Greeley of the *New York Tribune*, made it clear that he was prepared to preserve the Union at almost any price. "I would save the Union," he declared. "If there be those who would not save the Union unless they could at the same time *save* Slavery, I do not agree with them. If there be those who would not save the Union unless they could at the same time *destroy* Slavery, I do not agree with them. My paramount object in this struggle *is* to save the Union, and it is *not* either to save or destroy Slavery. If I could save the Union without freeing *any* slave I would do it; and if I could do it freeing *all* the slaves I would do it; and if I could do it by freeing some and leaving others alone, I would also do that."

Three slave states—Maryland, Delaware, and Kentucky—had remained loyal, and a fourth, Missouri, had been won for the Union by war. Kentucky had also been fought over from one end to the other, and the last thing Lincoln wanted was to drive any of these states from his camp. But the movement for a general emancipation had also begun to build. Legislation in support of it had recently been sponsored in Congress, and on June 19, 1862, Lincoln himself signed a bill that abolished slavery in the territories, in nullification of the Kansas–Nebraska Act. A month later, Congress passed a confiscation bill that granted freedom to any slave who reached Union lines. Meanwhile, Lincoln's Cabinet secretly approved an even more sweeping decree, but Lincoln decided to postpone announcing it until a Federal victory could lend it strength. Antietam was not quite the victory he had hoped for, but he decided it would do, and five days later the Emancipation Proclamation was set forth in its preliminary form.

By then, emancipation had also become a practical war aim. It gave the North a moral and ideological advantage on the international stage, especially among the English working class; threatened to wreck the Confederate economy; imperiled the strength of Confederate armies (in theory), as slave labor allowed the South to send more white troops to the front; and opened the door to the enlistment of blacks in the armies of the North. In fact, the War Department had already quietly sanctioned the recruitment of five thousand runaway slaves from islands off the South Carolina coast. Eventually, 185,000 blacks, organized into 166 regiments, would serve on the Union side.

Yet strategy alone does not wholly account for Lincoln's act. As "the tide of blood rose frightfully in the cup," Lincoln became convinced that slavery was such a horrendous evil in itself that it alone could explain by way of divine retribution the wholesale carnage taking place. "If we shall suppose," he said,

> that American slavery is one of those offences which, in the providence of God, must needs come, but which, having continued through His appointed time, He now wills to remove, and that He gives to both North and South this terrible war, as the woe due to those by whom the offence came, shall we discern therein any departure from those divine attributes which the believers in a living God ascribe to Him? Fondly do we hope, fervently do we pray, that this mighty scourge of war may speedily pass away. Yet if God wills that it continue until

all the wealth piled by the bondman's two hundred and fifty years of unrequited toil shall be sunk, and until every drop of blood drawn with the lash shall be paid by another drawn with the sword, as was said three thousand years ago, so still it must be said, the judgments of the Lord are true and righteous altogether.

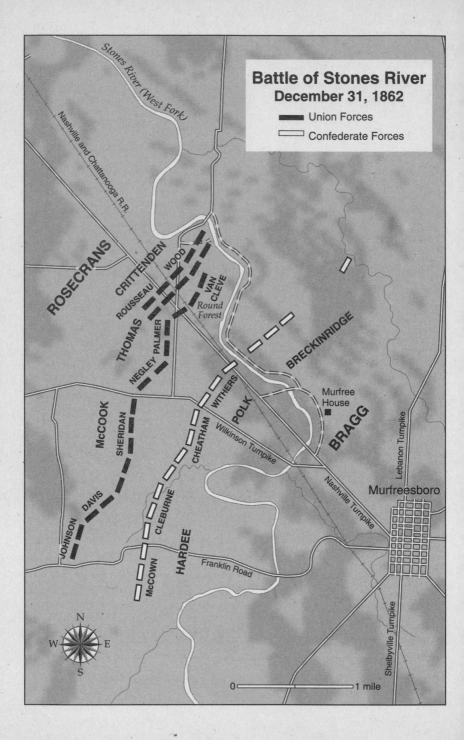

Battle of Stones River
December 31, 1862

Union Forces
Confederate Forces

Stones River (West Fork)

Nashville and Chattanooga R.R.

ROSECRANS

CRITTENDEN

WOOD

ROUSSEAU

THOMAS

VAN CLEVE

Round Forest

NEGLEY PALMER

BRECKINRIDGE

WITHERS

POLK

CHEATHAM

Murfree House

BRAGG

McCOOK

SHERIDAN

Wilkinson Turnpike

Murfreesboro

DAVIS

CLEBURNE

Nashville Turnpike

Lebanon Turnpike

JOHNSON

McCOWN

HARDEE

Franklin Road

Shelbyville Turnpike

N
W E
S

0   1 mile

S till there was no apparent end to the war in sight. Seven weeks after Antietam, McClellan was again relieved of command, replaced by Ambrose Burnside, a modest man with great mutton-chop whiskers afterwards known as sideburns. Burnside had commanded a brigade at First Bull Run and a wing at Antietam, but he was best known for his successful amphibious assault on North Carolina coastal installations early in the war. However, an overall command was quite beyond his competence, as he himself well knew, and his first and only offensive, aimed at Richmond, was a disaster. His assault on Lee's fortified positions at Fredericksburg, Virginia, on December 13, 1862, resulted in such wholesale slaughter that it stands as "one of the worst defeats the U.S. Army has ever experienced, on its own or foreign soil."

Lincoln looked to the West, where Grant was trying to work out an approach to the reduction of Vicksburg, and Chattanooga still beckoned as a prize.

After being driven out of Kentucky, Bragg withdrew his army to Murfreesboro in central Tennessee; there, as he prepared to go into winter quarters, he remained poised to respond to the next Federal move. He did not have to wait long. General William S. Rosecrans, "the hero of Iuka and Corinth" (so called from two recent battles, in which he had bested Price and Van Dorn) had taken over for Buell and at once began to assess the forces in his charge.

He found them in a shambles. Since Perryville, there had been over seven thousand desertions, and a third of the troops, for one reason or another, were absent from the ranks. The remnant was composed in part of raw levies, who had to be drilled and equipped. In early November, he established his headquarters at Nashville, not far from Bragg's lines, and acted energetically to reconstitute and reinvigorate his command. He secured his lines of communications; brought forward supplies; set pioneer brigades to building and repairing bridges, roads, and tracks; and was often up past midnight toiling to see that the needs of his men were met. He would brook no excuse when they were not. "Everywhere in the Army of the Cumberland," as the army was now called, "the men sensed that Rosecrans was for them. The food seemed to improve; the mail and pay, both important to a soldier's life, came more on time." Even dietary luxuries, like pickles, pepper, and potatoes, suddenly appeared on their plates. The postal system was also entrusted to the direction of a police detective, who ferreted out negligence, corruption, and abuse. When a barefoot soldier complained he couldn't get shoes, Rosecrans exhorted him in a way that only showed his concern: "Can't get shoes! Why? Go to your captain and demand what you need! Go to him every day till you get it. Bore him for it! Bore him in his quarters! Bore him at meal-time! Bore him in bed! Bore him; bore him; bore him; don't let him rest. Let the captains bore their colonels; let colonels bore their brigadiers; brigadiers their division generals; division generals their corps commanders; and let the corps commanders bore *me. I'll* see then if you don't get what you want. Bore, bore, bore, until you get every thing you are entitled to."

All that, however, took a little time. In a letter to his mother on November 4 from Bowling Green, Webb wrote that the back pay promised to the men had not come through, and that his own regiment, at least, had yet to get its tents. In fact, "we have had no tents since we left Miss.," which meant he had been sleeping out in the open for two months.

When Rosecrans decamped to Nashville from Bowling Green later that same day, Webb's unit went with him as part of the 3rd Brigade, 1st Division, Right Wing, 14th Army Corps. Discipline among the rank and file, precarious in Buell's last day, had been reestablished, but nerves were still frayed and violence sometimes flared. Webb recounts a striking incident in camp:

Nashville, Tenn., Dec. 2, 1862

Dear Mother:

 We are just in from a five days scout down the river. We marched in the roads 130 miles. We had a pleasant time as far as weather & country is concerned except last night—it rained all night & we had no shelter for we took no tents. However, we built large fires with rails—they burn first rate. On the scout we had plenty of fresh pork, mutton, turkey, chicken, & whiskey. We fatted up a good deal. Everything went first rate except the whiskey. It raised a row as usual & one of our boys (Mike Caton, an Irish boy, a good soldier when sober) shot Capt. [Charles A.] Clark of Co. A who was trying to put him under guard. The Capt. told the corporal (John West) to take Mike's gun from him. John could not do it, was afraid to do it & well he might be. The Capt. took it himself knocking Mike down with the butt of a gun. Clark rode to the front & saw the Maj. as to what should be done with Caton & then rode again to the rear & asked of West [where the man was]. At that moment Mike having got his gun again fired & shot the whole top of Clark's head off. Mike is now being court marshaled. I reckon he will be shot. He is a good soldier when sober, but he killed a good capt., one of our best. [Caton, in fact, escaped his predicted fate. Records indicate that he was discharged at the end of his three years' term.] The Nashville Union of today reports the Rebels at Murfreesboro 100,000 strong. That is but 30 miles from here. Our forces are moving out that way. A heavy battle is pending. We are going out tomorrow—I don't care how soon the battle comes. I guess we can clean them out. We shall not stay here this winter. I don't know when you will get to come. I guess you will have to start when you get ready & keep coming till you catch us. I reckon we will stay close along the railroad. I. D. is well & so am I. Have only had one letter from you since the Perryville battle. Write often.

Truly,
Webb.

At Nashville, Rosecrans was 183 miles from his Louisville base, to which he was linked by a single line of track. This line had been poorly built, constructed for commercial, not military, purposes, and "crumbled under the stress and pounding" of the special traffic it now had to bear. Though the railroad was ostensibly in Union hands, Rebels were also constantly uprooting sections of it, interdicting provisions, and derailing trains. By December, however, most of the trains were running through, and Rosecrans seemed within reach of his stated goal, which was to fully supply his troops before they marched. To Washington, all this seemed to be taking too long, and Halleck began to prod him to speed things up. "The President is very impatient at your long stay in Nashville," Halleck wrote him at the beginning of December. "Twice have I been asked to designate some one else to command your army. If you remain one more week I cannot prevent your removal . . . The Government demands action, and, if you cannot respond to that demand, some one else will be tried." Rosecrans retorted, as if between clenched teeth, "I have lost no time . . . If my superiors have lost confidence in me they had better at once put some one in my place and let the future test the propriety of the change. I have but one more word to add, which is, that I need no other stimulus to make me do my duty than the knowledge of what it is. To threats of removal or the like I must be permitted to say that I am insensible." He continued his preparations for three more weeks, rounded up five thousand mules for his pack trains, held daily drills and reviews, garrisoned Nashville, posted detachments along his line of supply, and after laying up a thirty days' stock of provisions, prepared to set out with about forty-five thousand men. These were divided into three corps, under Crittenden, Thomas, and McCook. The best of the three by far was Thomas, who was also second in command.

A former West Point instructor and cavalry major before the war, George H. Thomas, like Lee, was a Virginian, but unlike Lee had refused to cast his lot with his state. At the outbreak of fighting, he was made a brigadier of volunteers; won a notable victory in Kentucky at Mill Springs, the first break in the Confederate left flank; and, as noted, had been Lincoln's choice to replace Buell before the Kentucky campaign. With typical self-effacement he had declined the honor, to the detriment of his subsequent career. Rosecrans admired him greatly—had done so, indeed, since their West Point days—and likened his character to that of George Washington, beyond which one could hardly go in praise. Some students of the war consider him the best of the Union generals, if overshadowed by Sherman and Grant. But he was not the sort to advance his own case. A quiet, dignified, and extremely modest man, he was a brigadier for months before he wore the star and earned his rank as a major general well before the double star adorned his trim.

Bragg seems to have expected Rosecrans to take his army back into Kentucky, but it was the latter's plan to make a fight for middle Tennessee. Rosecrans set the time for his own advance as the day after Christmas, and on Christmas night met with his general staff. As they departed, he took each commander by the hand and said, "Spread out your skirmishers far and wide! Expose their nests! Keep fighting! Good night."

December 26 dawned with storm clouds overhead and a heavy mist drifted slowly through the camp. Then the clouds broke and the rain came down in sheets. Through the din, reveille rolled like muffled thunder through the tents. By 6 the soldiers were up and at their breakfast; by 7, they were tramping across the rain-drenched fields. Thomas led the center, McCook the right, Crittenden the left. "We had to carry our blankets, pup tents & all our clothes," Webb wrote his mother during a pause in the march; also "three days rations & 100 rounds, a pretty good load when the roads are good, & a big one when the rain is pouring down & the mud half knee deep." About noon, the clouds parted before a stiff northwest wind and the sun came out in all its sudden glory to brighten the air of the gloomy winter day. There was scarcely time, however, to bask in its benediction. Rifle fire could be heard in the distance and now and then the boom of a heavy gun. Already rebel "nests" were being "stirred up," and the men were kept at the ready as they toiled all day across the broken ground. Toward nightfall, "we had a heavy skirmish," wrote Webb. "We took one piece of artillery & 10 prisoners. Just in the evening," he added, "a ball struck John Hawkins [an acquaintance from home] square on the belt buckle. It made him grunt, but was so far spent that it [did] no further damage, but dropped at his feet. He picked it up & is around every day now bragging that he is bullet proof." That night the men bivouacked in the wide, soft fields; as they settled down, a heavy storm broke over them again and battered them in their tents. Over the course of the next two days, the Federal columns slowly felt their way forward through constant mist and rain. "Another division passed us in the night & were skirmishing all day yesterday," Webb wrote on the 28th as he huddled in a field tent after a march of twenty-five miles. "They took 6 pieces of artillery. As usual it rained all day."

The artillery wagons sank up to their axles in the muddy fields; the men were drenched to the skin. At 3 o'clock the next morning they were roused and, teeth chattering, fell into line. Up ahead, Bragg arranged his troops for battle, and the Federals cautiously pushed through the cedar thickets toward his lines. Meanwhile, they were harried by Rebel cavalry under Joseph Wheeler, "who contested every ridge and ford." No one doubted that the battle would soon be joined. "If Gen. Bragg tries us on at Murfreesboro," Webb predicted, "I expect we will go into them tomorrow. If he falls back I reckon we will follow to Chattanooga where we expect to have a roaring fight. Wherever the fight comes I hope we will not make a Fredericksburg of it," meaning a bloody mess like Burnside's awful debacle of three weeks before.

For the past two months, Bragg's army had been arrayed in a great arc centered at Murfreesboro to cover all routes to Chattanooga to the south. But as soon as Rosecrans marched, Bragg called in his troops and entrenched them astride Stones River, near the Nashville Pike. His position there shadowed the Nashville & Chattanooga Railroad and sought to take advantage of the surrounding terrain, which was marked by irregular outcroppings of rock, with thick glades of red cedar interspersed with open farms. Most of his troops lay under the cover of the woods, but his line also extended across the river and occupied both banks. In the meantime, he sent Joseph Wheeler, his cavalry commander, on a number of raids to try to sap the Union strength. In one spectacular strike on the 30th, Wheeler made a complete circuit of the Union force and destroyed a supply train of over three hundred wagons and captured eight hundred men. "The turnpike as far as the eye could reach," recalled one Federal soldier, "was filled with burning wagons" and littered "with empty valises and trunks, knapsacks, broken guns, and all the indescribable debris of a captured and rifled army train."

That evening, Rosecrans moved his own army into line opposite Bragg's. Its left, under Crittenden, rested on Stones River; its right under McCook, on a wooded ridge, fronting open ground; its center, under Thomas, was posted on a rolling slope. The farthest brigade on the right was drawn back nearly at right angles to the main line and readied for any flanking movement the enemy might try. To the back of the Union position lay "half-burned clearings," cedar thickets, and a patchwork quilt of forest and cultivated fields.

Both commanders then proceeded to develop identical battle plans, each designed to pin his opponent against the river by enveloping his right flank. Bragg assigned his attack to Hardee; Rosecrans, his to Crittenden, who was to launch an assault just after daybreak, fording the river to take a strategic hill. Thomas was then to push forward and roll up the Rebel side. For both of these actions to succeed, McCook had to hold his own position firmly if assailed. His was the pivot on which the whole maneuver was to turn. That night, Rosecrans reportedly met with McCook in a wagon in the woods to review the next day's plans. As they talked, they sat on some rough plank boards, a single candle between them, stuck in the socket of a bayonet. The point of the bayonet had been driven into the floor. Rosecrans wanted a clear assurance from McCook that he could hold his ground for at least three hours. McCook assured him that he could. But even as they talked, Bragg was massing his forces for a predawn attack that McCook could not withstand.

As the troops that night pitched their tents on the cold wet ground, musicians of both armies began playing patriotic songs. First came "Yankee Doodle," then, in quaint response, a spirited rendition of "Dixie," as the brave and unbrave together tried to calm their common fears. At length, the gentle melody of "Home Sweet Home" floated mournfully up from someone's violin. Musicians North and South then took it up together, and soon the voices of their legions swelled the chorus of the song.

Rosecrans rose early and, a devout Catholic, celebrated High Mass in his tent. Having thus "committed himself and his army to the God of battles," he stepped out into the cold morning air. His officers, with their overcoats on, had already gathered around newly kindled fires. Colonel Julius P. Garesche, his Catholic chief of staff, sat apart under a tree reading *The Imitation of Christ*. As they waited for Crittenden to begin the battle on their left, the Confederates attacked on their right. Unseen, they emerged from the cover of the cedars and were almost on top of the Federals before they knew an assault was on. Four brigades were in the forefront of the attacking line; more were gathering behind. "In five minutes," writes Bruce Catton, "one of the most desperate battles of the war was in full blast. McCook's position was hopelessly swamped, hit from the flank and in front by seemingly limitless numbers . . . Men in reserve behind him hardly heard the crash of battle before fugitives from the front came scampering through their camps, spreading panic in their flight."

Webb was eating a breakfast of hoecake and fat pork when the first Rebel yell thrummed dreadfully against his ear. It seemed impossibly close given the way the lines were drawn, yet units to his left were already crumbling as the onslaught gathered speed. His own unit was ensconced in a stand of cedars on a ridge behind a fence. A little after 7, the Confederates came after it across an open field. The brunt of their charge drove it back into the woods, but then for over an hour the battle ebbed and flowed. Twice the 25th Illinois regained the fence, the second time with a bayonet charge. But all around them men were fleeing, and as their own ammunition began to run out they took with them what wounded they could and joined the retreating tide.

Three-fifths of Bragg's army had now joined the attack, and by 10 A.M. the Confederate wheeling movement reached the Union center as McCook's entire corps was forced back nearly to the Nashville Pike. But there, near a bend in Stones River, stood a wooded knoll known as the Round Forest—in part afterwards as "Hell's Half Acre"—where the Federals under Thomas regrouped to make a stand. Every available brigade was called in to hold the line, drawn almost at right angles to the first, and six batteries were planted on the crest. Bragg now mounted an attack on this rise. His gunners fired up the pike and, as they got the range, waves of Rebel infantry emerged from the woods. Rosecrans rode forward with his staff to exhort and direct the men, and time and again exposed himself to Rebel fire. A cannonball struck the road a short distance off, bounding away. A second struck nearer. A third, "with a swift, rushing sound, swept past him in a line" and beheaded his chief of staff. As the afternoon wore on, Bragg hurled up to ten brigades against the Union defenders but could not dislodge them or break their line. At length, toward evening, he gave up trying, and, in the face of his own high casualties, withdrew.

Even though Bragg had failed to turn the Union right completely, the Federals had not fared well. Rosecrans had had to abandon his own plan of attack; his right had been bent back and nearly destroyed and his communications with Nashville cut by cavalry to his rear. Supplies were running low. Seven brigadier generals and twenty colonels were dead or missing, and 20 percent of his artillery had fallen into Rebel hands. Moreover, though Bragg had been denied victory, he had not been beaten either, nor was there any indication he meant to withdraw. In fact, he fully expected Rosecrans to try to retreat to Nashville if he could, and that evening cabled Richmond, "God has granted us a happy New Year." At a late-night conference with his own corps commanders, Rosecrans discussed the options, including a fighting withdrawal down the Nashville Pike. Thomas said simply, "This army can't retreat," and no one dared challenge his resolve.

The next day, the first of the new year, there was only tentative contact: an artillery duel in the morning, followed by skirmishing along the line. That night, however, Rosecrans greatly improved his position when he sent a division across the river to occupy a patch of high ground. That enabled him to enfilade the Rebel right. On January 2 Bragg tried to reclaim the hill, but in a ferocious fight, in which the Federals were at first pressed back to the stream, the Rebels were smashed by cannon massed nearby on a commanding rise.

On the 3rd, Bragg yielded up the field. As he retreated to Tulla-homa, forty miles to the south, he cabled Richmond: "We have re-tired from Murfreesboro in perfect order. All our stores are saved," which was simply an attempt to put the best face on things. It had been an equal encounter between more or less equal numbers, in the end a slugging match. Both sides had lost about a quarter of their army, between nine thousand and ten thousand men. But it was the Federals who had held. When Lincoln learned of Bragg's retreat, he wrote Rosecrans, "God bless you, and all with you. Please tender to all, and accept for yourself, a nation's gratitude for your and their skill, endurance, and dauntless courage." Later, when Rosecrans had fallen on hard times, Lin-coln would tell him, "You gave us a hard-earned victory [at Stones River] which, had there been a defeat instead, the nation could hardly have lived over." Which was mighty praise indeed.

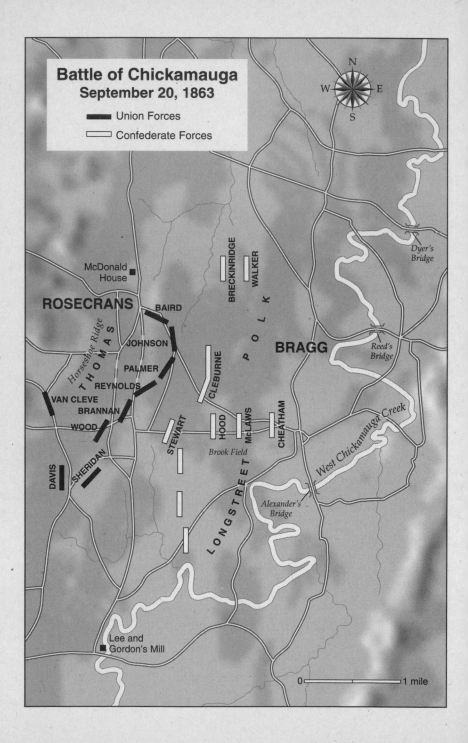

Battle of Chickamauga
September 20, 1863

Union Forces
Confederate Forces

N
W — E
S

Dyer's
Bridge

McDonald
House

ROSECRANS

BAIRD

BRECKINRIDGE

WALKER

P
O
L
K

BRAGG

Reed's
Bridge

JOHNSON

Horseshoe Ridge

T
H
O
M
A
S

PALMER

CLEBURNE

REYNOLDS

VAN CLEVE

BRANNAN

WOOD

STEWART

HOOD

McLAWS

CHEATHAM

West Chickamauga Creek

Brook Field

DAVIS

SHERIDAN

L
O
N
G
S
T
R
E
E
T

Alexander's
Bridge

Lee and
Gordon's Mill

0 ————————————— 1 mile

CHAPTER EIGHT

In the aftermath of the battle, the men foraged and skirmished and waited for the next big fight. It rained for several days, then a light snow began to fall. "Rebs seem to be prowling over the country in every direction," Webb wrote on January 19. Bragg had reportedly been reinforced at nearby Shelbyville, "with 40,000 [new men], we are receiving reinforcements & there may be a battle. If we don't go to the rebs they will come to us." Either way, he didn't mind.

For Webb, Stones River had been just another battle—an inconclusive battle in a long and inconclusive war. Though he had been in the midst of the action and his own regiment had lost ninety-six, he was remarkably matter of fact about it in his letter home. "There was a hard fight here," Webb reported on January 10, "a heavy loss but Rosecrans gained the victory & the rebs. are gone. McCook was driven back 2 miles by the massed force of the enemy on our right before we were reinforced. The secesh got our knapsacks & blankets. I have been having the chills. Am well now. I am better satisfied now that John's remains are at home." His mother hoped to visit him at Murfreesboro, where Rosecrans's army was encamped, but he advised her against it, as he expected to be on the move. "We are likely to follow the enemy right up," he told her, "& I hope we will keep at it till the job is done—don't like to waste so much time. I don't mind fighting for my country if we will only do it but I hate to lay round while the work remains to be done."

On the 19th, as he stood on picket duty four miles south of camp, a Rebel appeared with a flag of truce and a sealed dispatch addressed to Rosecrans. Perhaps it had to do with a prisoner exchange; it was not for Webb to ask. On the 31st, his regiment began a three days' march through mud, rain, and snow to Franklin, where they hoped to take on Nathan Bedford Forrest, the Rebel cavalry commander, who was wreaking havoc on their lines of supply. Almost every major bridge and trestle on the Louisville & Nashville Railroad had been damaged, cars burned, engines destroyed. In one place, "a tunnel had been choked with rubbish to a distance of 800 feet." Forrest sped up to Harpeth Shoals on the Cumberland River, and Union troops pursued. There, it was wishfully reported, he had "got decently cleaned out & himself mortally wounded & taken prisoner"—which wasn't so. Meanwhile, General Jefferson C. Davis had turned the command of his division over to one of his colonels and taken a cavalry brigade up to try to cut off Forrest's retreat. "We are in readiness to go to his support if he needs us," Webb wrote his mother. "If you hear of a fight near Franklin now you may know we are in it."

Around Murfreesboro the skirmishing was chronic, as the opposing armies scoured the countryside for food. The Union troops, on half rations, were soon at risk of scurvy, and even officers regarded onions and potatoes as luxury fare. Webb seems to have accepted his plight, as usual without much complaint; military and political issues were uppermost in his mind. "One of our parties killed 10 rebs the other day & got 80 prisoners," Webb reported, as well as "several wagons & 300 cavalry saddles & accoutrements . . . No set battle is expected till we get to Chattanooga, but every inch of ground between here & there will be contested so our advance will be slow but I think sure." Meanwhile, a few weeks before, he had written, "I wish we could move soon & talk less—Somehow I hope the war will close before another summer passes—I don't know how the settlement is to come but somehow

I look for it to come." Like many others, he also expected the manpower advantage of the North to tell and put great hope in the new draft act. "How do the fellows up north like the conscription bill?" Webb asked his mother. "The soldiers like it I tell you. Hope those braggy fellows at home will all get pulled in." Lincoln had also just signed a bill to authorize back pay. "The talk is that we will get 4 months soon. It will not be before we need it."

Both developments gave the soldiers heart, but there was another kind of trouble in the ranks. The Emancipation Proclamation, when first announced, set off celebrations in many Northern cities, but it had not been greeted with complete enthusiasm by the troops. "[It] has stirred things up considerable," reported Webb. "Some of the boys are very bitter about it. They say that they did not come to war to free niggers, but I guess this will bring the South to a compromise. Anyway, I hope the war will soon be over." Though primarily a Unionist, he didn't object to the Proclamation itself as an executive act; indeed, as we know, he had accepted the possibility of it a year before. But it incited others to near rebellion all that spring. "There has been a good deal of deserting since," Webb confessed to his mother in early March, "but I guess it will stop now—I understand that the law is to be executed to the limit on deserters, & that means death—for my part I would as soon die any other way as to be set up against a stump & shot at." At the same time, he questioned the Proclamation's practicality and timing, as he returned to the subject again:

Murfreesboro, Tenn., March 16, 1863

Dear Mother:

Yours of the 5th inst. was here [when] we got in. We have been on a ten days' scout. Nothing of importance transpired while we were gone. We got a drenching for 36 hrs. but it is clear & warm now. This is really a summer day. The trees are putting forth their leaves & the earth will soon be covered again with verdure. Already the grass is about good enough for cattle to live grazing. I would rather be here than at home till [the] war is over. I don't understand how loyal men can remain at home. I am sorry there is so much division in the North. The Proclamation serves a good purpose, as an excuse for some rebel sympathizers in the north. It can't do the slave much good till he gets inside of our lines. I suppose it will be hard on him till after that. The boys many of them don't like the idea of making soldiers of negroes. But after all they will do to shoot at as well as anybody if we could only think so.

Truly yours,
Webb.

Blacks, indeed, served admirably. On many a battlefield, as Lincoln's secretary of war, Edwin M. Stanton, would report, "they proved themselves to be among the bravest, performing deeds of daring and shedding their blood with heroism unsurpassed."

Meanwhile, Webb had now spent quite a bit of time in Tennessee and was strongly drawn to the land. Though parts of it were "devastated, & like a ruin," he still thought it "the prettiest country" he had ever seen. He liked the climate ("it is as warm as a May day today," he exulted during a brief winter thaw) and imagined he might come to live there after the war. "The few people who are left," he added, "are very friendly, & of refined manners. They are most all secesh. They say they never will submit to the usurpation of their rights. But I guess they will" (letter of February 8, 1863).

It seemed they must. "The enemy is in force in front of us," Webb wrote his mother on March 25. "We have ⅓ of the army on picket all the time now I guess & the rest are under orders to be ready to march with three days rations at a moments warning. It looks as if we were going to have a fight. Let it come."

News, some of it confused, came in from the Eastern front.

After the Federal defeat at Fredericksburg, Burnside had been replaced by Joseph Hooker, a dashing corps commander known to the rank and file as "Fighting Joe." A veteran of the Mexican and Seminole Wars, he had fought well in the Peninsular Campaign under McClellan, but he was a hard-drinking, boastful man, and his nickname actually derived from a copyediting error in an article telegraphed to newspapers, not from the martial ardor he had shown. Nevertheless, it stuck, and that helped him in his task. Over the next few months he took the Army of the Potomac in hand, reorganized and enlarged it, and restored its spirit and strength. At the end of April 1863, he advanced to Chancellorsville in an attempt to outflank Lee's left. "The enemy must either ingloriously fly," he informed his troops, "or come out from behind his defenses and give us battle on our own ground, where certain destruction awaits him." Later that night, he actually announced, "The rebel army is now the legitimate property of the Army of the Potomac. They may as well pack up their haversacks and make for Richmond."

They did no such thing. Lee divided his army and sent most of it through a dark ground called the Wilderness to attack Hooker's right. The forest cover was thick, mostly pine and black oak, with a dense undergrowth tangled with vines. Though vastly outnumbered, Lee fought with more skill, and in every part of the five-day engagement beat Hooker's army in detail. On May 5, the baffled Union commander withdrew his forces back across the Rappahannock in defeat.

In Webb's camp, the men were "jubilant over the fact authentic that Charleston, S.C., the mother of secession," had fallen (though in fact it had not); but learned the truth about the Federal debacle at Chancellorsville. "We are disappointed to some extent," he told his mother on May 19, "though not so much perhaps as we would have been if the Potomac army had never been beaten before, but anyway we expected something of Fighting Joe, & we got something, i.e. a good drubbing. We should have liked it better if the result had been different but we are not here to complain. I guess Burnside & Hooker are not the men to handle great armies. They are good fighters directed, but not to direct." Such has been the judgment of history, too.

But for the armies of the South, a purely defensive war held out almost no hope for their aspirations, for, as one historian notes, "sooner or later Lee's army would be forced back on Richmond, and there meet its end." Grant was now at the gates of Vicksburg, a Gibraltar-like stronghold on the lower Mississippi, and Bragg was hard put to keep Rosecrans from advancing farther in east Tennessee. Lee therefore opted to strike north again, in a reprise of his Maryland campaign. This time, however, his goal was not to gain a border state, now recognized as hopeless, but, by his very boldness, to increase political dissension in the North, wreck supply routes, and help other Confederate armies survive by forcing Lincoln to draw troops from all quarters to protect the capital and other sites. In a row with the War Department, Hooker quarreled over how to meet Lee's threat and was thereupon replaced by George Gordon Meade, a seasoned general who had shown courage and ability in a number of battles, including Antietam and Second Bull Run.

Early in June Lee began his advance. He moved north by way of the Shenandoah and Cumberland Valleys, crossed the Maryland state line, entered a small valley surrounded by low hills just across the state line in Pennsylvania, and there met Meade at the town of Gettysburg. Both armies established defensible positions on various ridges and hills (among them, Cemetery Ridge, Culp's Hill, Oak Hill, and McPherson's Ridge), and after two days of incomplete but costly encounters, tore into each other with terrific force. At Cemetery Ridge, the heart of the contest on that day, thousands upon thousands on both sides fell, with the Rebels leaving nineteen battle flags behind them on the field as they withdrew. Lee escaped once more back into Virginia, but he had failed to achieve any of his aims. And on the very next day, July 4, Vicksburg fell.

Meanwhile, toward the end of June, Rosecrans began his march on Bragg. At Murfreesboro, he had done what he could to get his army into shape, and after appealing in vain to the War Department for a cavalry contingent, created one himself out of an infantry brigade. The men were mounted and armed with the new Spencer repeating rifles, which from a single loading could fire six copper rimfire .52 caliber slugs. Under Colonel John T. Wilder, this cavalry would go on to fight in Tennessee, Alabama, Georgia, the Carolinas, and Virginia and win fame and glory as Wilder's "Lightning Brigade." The 123rd Illinois was a part of it, and had Webb's brother lived, he would have belonged to its heroic tale.

Bragg was strongly entrenched at Shelbyville, twenty-five miles to the south, and at Tullahoma, on a branch of the Nashville line. His extreme right lay at McMinnville, his left near Franklin; Chattanooga was his base. Rosecrans's plan was to turn his right flank. To do this, he made a feint toward Shelbyville while moving his main force toward Manchester and the Cumberland Mountain gaps. As always, it rained at the setting out, and Webb's regiment slogged along the Shelbyville Pike. In his haversack, he had one week's supply of bacon and meat "on hoof" and twelve days' supply of coffee, sugar, salt, and bread.

Manchester, Tenn., June 30, 1863

Dear Mother:

Your kind letter of the 12 came to hand yesterday. It was so welcome. We are finally out of Murfreesboro as you see. We left there on the 24 & have been making slow progress. We are in 13 miles of Tullahoma, the advance of the army is reported 8 miles beyond that. We have to repair the railroad as we go in order to get supplies . . . this is the 7th day [we have been out]. It has rained every one of the six preceding days & looks as if it would today. It is very muddy. We are going 5 or 6 miles a day.

We are fighting for every step we gain. The fighting is only skirmishing, but it makes slow marching.

Wilder's Brig. is in the advance . . . One of our boys has word that there is a company of rebs. organized in Hutton Township & a regt in Coles County. I wonder if it is so. I hope every one of them will be drafted into our army & sent to the very front. I hope this may find you well.

Truly your affectionate son,
Webb.

The Union feint worked beautifully, and before Bragg could prevent it, Rosecrans was threatening Bragg's line of retreat. The latter fell back behind his fortifications at Tullahoma, but by a second turning movement, Rosecrans forced him out. Bragg now started for Chattanooga and Rosecrans briefly pursued, as vigorously as the rough roads and swollen streams would allow. Lincoln wrote to urge him on. "If we can hold Chattanooga and East Tennessee," he told him, "I think the Rebellion must dwindle and die." Rosecrans then paused to consider how this might best be done. Between him and Bragg's army, now in Chattanooga, lay the broad Tennessee River and the high plateaus and gorges of the Cumberland range. That range, a spur of the Appalachians, stretched through Tennessee into northern Georgia and was as difficult terrain as the Federals would face in the war. Its heights included Sand, Raccoon, and Pigeon mountains, Missionary Ridge, and the crest of Lookout Mountain beyond the wide valley of Lookout Creek.

Meanwhile, the swift, almost bloodless eviction of Bragg from his whole fortified line in just nine days ought to have prompted rejoicing in the North. But it was eclipsed by the Federal victories at Gettysburg and Vicksburg, with which it happened to coincide. No one in Washington seemed to appreciate what Rosecrans had done. On July 7, he heard from Secretary of War Stanton: "Lee's army overthrown; Grant victorious. You and your noble army now have the chance to give the finishing blow to the rebellion. Will you neglect the chance?" Rosecrans, irate, replied, "You do not appear to observe the fact that this noble army has driven the Rebels from Middle Tennessee. I beg in behalf of this army that the War Department may not overlook so great an event because it is not written in letters of blood."

As he pondered his next move, Rosecrans spread out his army along the northwestern base of the Cumberland Range, with camps at McMinnville, Tullahoma, Dechard, and Winchester. Chattanooga lay to the southeast. As part of the 3rd Brigade, 1st Division, 20th Army Corps, Webb was posted at Winchester, where letters reached him again in early July. As always, he was eager for simple news from Hutton and had recently told his mother how he and other Huttonites had peppered one Tom Temple, "taken prisoner at Stones River" and "just in from home," with questions "till he was nearly tired out. It does us so much good to see one from home who has seen the folks" (letter of March 25, 1863). But most of his mother's letters at this time were of a different cast and seem to have upset him, either with talk of personal troubles or civil unrest. He was deeply alarmed, for example, by her reports of all the "discord & contention," faltering resolve, and even subversion on the home front. He began to wonder if war might soon rend the North from within. "The northern people," he warned her in a letter on July 12, "do not know what war is" and would be "blind . . . to invite civil war into their homes . . . Suppose a busy army of 20,000 should camp on Mr. Moore's farm. [Webb's stepfather had a substantial estate.] In the morning there would not be a chick or pig or cow [left]. The potatoes & onions & all eatables in the house would be gone. The fences would all be burned. If they stayed a week in the neighborhood the whole community would be . . . utterly devastated—no pen, let alone mine, can describe the horrors of civil war."

The whole question of slavery came up again. "I am not an abolitionist," he wrote candidly, "though I would rather be one than to be a secessionist. I never advised anyone to desert. I would not advise any man to dishonor himself & disgrace his friends." Above all, he was loyal to the Union. If emancipation helped to preserve it, that was all right with him. That same sense of honor or allegiance to something larger than himself also gave him a capacity to empathize with war-ravaged victims in the South. Since John's death, Webb's mother had been almost inconsolable, and he sought to comfort her the only way he knew how. "Please Ma," he wrote, "don't be despondent. Your trouble is hard, I know, but not so hard as some. I met a widow here who had 5 sons. All went into the southern army. Three of them have been killed, & the other two are at Vicksburg."

As always, Webb tended to minimize his own afflictions by making his letters as cheerful as he could.

Winchester, Tenn., Aug. 1, 1863

Dear Mother:

I did not write you last week, but I seldom fail, & I wrote Mary [his twenty-three-year old stepsister] last week, so you will hear & I reckon that will do. Our company is still on pious duty here & having the best kind of time—I have gotten acquainted with several families. The people are sociable & intelligent & very obliging to the soldiers, in spite of the insults that they are exposed to from drunken, worthless fellows, who, if they ever had any breeding, sense, or humanity, have lost all traces of it since they left home. This town is very healthy & beautifully situated. It has been favored with large schools. There has been as high [many] as 600 young ladies here at school at one time. I have gotten acquainted with a Mr. & Mrs. Merritt here who are very kind to me. The Regt. expects to stay here.

Truly your son,
Webb.

That was not to be. A few days later, orders came down for his regiment to draw ten days' rations and prepare to march. "The indications are that we are to go to . . . Chattanooga. I hate dreadfully to leave here," he admitted. "The Dixie gals are awful nice." Perhaps others were beginning to feel too comfortable, too, for the previous Thursday there had been "a grand Division meeting" to rev up the troops. Several chaplains and then General Davis had spoken. "[Davis] made a few appropriate remarks & then said he was no speaker, but that if he was on charley & we were on our way to Chattanooga & Bragg was between us & that town, he would know how to talk. We cheered him heartily." Then General McCook "was repeatedly called & finally stood up to say that he could not talk, but promised us the advance, the post of honor as we go."

By "us" Webb meant his brigade, which was made up of four regiments, including the 25th. Proud as he was of this, he would not have been unhappy to linger where he was, or, as he put it, "guard the train, or some nice town." Meanwhile, "somebody went through the regt. after pay day" and took all the money, including Webb's, that he could find. "I think I know who did it," he wrote, "but am not certain . . . it is too bad." Webb lost $50; that was four months' pay. Every penny he had saved to send his mother was gone. But now something else was getting under his skin. "We hear that there is a great excitement at home over the draft, & that the Copperheads [Peace Democrats] are drilling to resist it. [I] hear that six hundred drilled in Mattoon. Is it true?"

Nothing could have enraged the troops more. There was a large antiwar movement in the North, and though most of it was principled—and stirred by issues that move any free people to debate—the Copperheads, or some among them, belonged to one of its subversive wings. For various reasons, it was not always easy to distinguish who they were. In both North and South, there was justifiable concern that the war's prosecution might give rise to despotic regimes. Jefferson Davis ruled almost by fiat; Lincoln, to a lesser degree, had assumed semidictatorial powers. It has been said that he wielded more power than any Anglo-American since Cromwell, and, indeed, some of his measures alarmed even those who agreed with his aims. He had authorized the summary arrest of "suspected persons," had suspended the writ of habeas corpus for those charged with "disloyal" acts, had banned the circulation of certain newspapers, such as the *Chicago Times*, for their dissenting views, and had introduced the draft. The draft was considered draconian, because it meant that any able-bodied male between the ages of twenty and forty-five could be selected for compulsory service at the turn of a wheel. Few were exempted—unless they could find a substitute or pay a commutation fee. That favored the rich, of course, and provoked the poor. *"Inter arma silent leges,"* Cicero had written: Laws must sleep when a nation struggles for its life. That may be, but without someone of the wisest forbearance—a Washington (or a Lincoln) at the helm—tyranny is apt to result.

The South had been driven to conscription first. It had less manpower to draw on—about a fourth of that of the North—and as the meatgrinder tactics of the war ground on, the Confederate army began to admit old men and boys, robbing, in Grant's words, both the cradle and the grave. Once enrolled, soldiers had to remain for the duration, and by the war's end, an estimated eight hundred thousand, or four-fifths of the South's eligible white males, had served. That was hard on the whole population. But the North, too, was finding the cost too much to bear. Whereas antiwar sentiment was suppressed in the South, in the North it grew. For the most part, Republicans stood fast behind Lincoln, though some might grumble; the Democratic opposition took various forms. Those who favored a negotiated peace were known as Peace Democrats or, less kindly, Copperheads, after the venomous snake. Some rejected the epithet as a slander; others took pride in the name and wore on their lapels the goddess Liberty cut from copper pennies, to give it a patriotic twist. Their slogan was, "The Constitution as it is and the Union as it was." They saw the war as a failure, creating unbridgeable hatred between the sections and futilely spilling blood.

The more militant Copperheads were of a different stripe. Though often mingled with the moderates, they were a seditious "third column" in the Union's midst. Many belonged to a secret society known as the Knights of the Golden Circle (later, the Order of American Knights and the Sons of Liberty), established satellite "lodges" or "castles" in various towns and cities, and, sometimes under the guise of constitutional concerns, fomented opposition to the war. But their real agenda was threefold: the perpetuation of slavery, its extension into Central and South America, and military victory for the South.

Unrest in the North culminated in the antidraft riots of 1863. On July 14, two days after the first drawing in New York, crowds of workmen, most belonging to the Irish poor, poured into the streets shouting "Down with the rich men" and "We'll hang Horace Greeley on a sour apple tree." As the mob surged up Third Avenue, it tore down lampposts, ransacked mansions, and, coming to the induction center, ripped up the census lists and smashed the lottery wheel. Then the building itself was set on fire. Before long, the violence turned into a race riot, and over the next few days mobs attacked blacks at random, looted the Second Avenue Armory, destroyed the offices of Greeley's pro-war *Tribune*, and razed a black orphanage to the ground. For two days control of the city remained in the vandals' hands until Federal troops, straight from the Gettysburg carnage, arrived to restore elected rule. Sharpshooters were perched on rooftops; cannon swept the streets. When it was all over, a thousand lay dead.

Disorder erupted elsewhere throughout the North and Midwest, including Coles County, where the Knights of the Golden Circle had a lodge. There Copperheads built up a hidden cache of arms that included a small cannon and even met for military drill. They made threats against local Republicans, provoked fights with soldiers on leave, and in some cases ominously marked the houses of their opponents with a circled K, the emblem of their clan. In Paradise, Charleston, Mattoon, and other towns there were various reprisal killings, followed, in March 1864, by the so-called Charleston Riot that left twenty-one dead and wounded, most of them Union troops.

All that spring and into the summer, Rosecrans, according to his own meticulous fashion, prepared for his march on Bragg. His plan was to cross the Tennessee River below Chattanooga and turn the Confederate left, intercepting Bragg's communications, than take the town from the rear. On August 16 he began his advance, with Crittenden on the left, Thomas in the center, and McCook on the right. Altogether, he had an army of about sixty thousand men advancing on a fifty-mile front. To deceive Bragg as to his point of crossing, he made a feint with one corps along the river to the north. Webb was with McCook as they made their way through a mountain pass:

> *Camp near Stevenson, Alabama, Aug. 25, 1863*
> Dear Mother:
>   We left Winchester on the 17 & came out to the mountains 7 miles. On the 18 we climbed to the top of the mountain 2 miles & on the 19 helped the wagons up & marched on the mountain 10 miles. It was a hard day's work. We did not get to camp till 12 at night. Be sure we were all tired, & glad when our days work was done. On the 20th we helped the wagons down—we fastened ropes to them & let them down the steep places by hand while the teamsters got down with the mules. Sundown found us in camp in the valley close to a splendid

spring. After feasting on sow belly & hardtack with plenty of green corn & green apples & a good bath, I never slept better in my life. On the 21 we went into camp at 10 o'clock in a regular gutter up Alabama swamp where the mosquitoes are nearly as big as horse flies, & where nobody ever lived but mosquitoes. Here we are in this swamp today & will stay here till we march. We are 23 miles from Stevenson 25 miles from Chattannooga on the Memphis & Charlestown Railroad. I. D. & all are well.

Truly your son,
Webb.

The feint succeeded, enabling Rosecrans to bring his army across the river on a pontoon bridge. The crossing was led by Colonel Hans Christian Heg, who had raised a Wisconsin regiment of immigrant Norwegians at the outbreak of the war. He was Webb's brigade commander. In keeping with McCook's promise, the 25th Illinois was in the vanguard of the crossing, just before dawn on August 29. It is generally considered one of the great strategic moments of the war. Webb describes the scene:

Camp in Front, Alabama, Sept. 1, 1863

Dear Mother:

Sure enough we stayed in that swamp till we marched. We left camp with a pontoon train & came to the river 4 miles & camped for the night, our brigade in advance. Gen. McCook kept his word. There were 4 regts. in the brigade [the 8th Kansas, the 15th Wisconsin, the 35th Illinois, and the 25th Illinois]. Early Saturday morning we were divided into companies of 25 each & loaded into the pontoons with 100 rounds & our guns loaded, & at the command of the general all the boats pulled for the south shore of the Tennessee where we expected a battle for the rebs were in sight & a few shots were fired. It looked like risky business going out into the river in those boats facing the enemy. There was a sure thing that nobody could run. The river is 800 yards wide. It was a beautiful site to see the boats in line of battle nearly a mile long pulling together regularly. It looked too many for the few rebels on the south shore for they took at once to the bushes. We all landed together. Gen. McCook went over with us making his promise good that he would give us the advance & go with us. We guarded the southern shore while the Pioneer Brigade put down the Pontoon Bridge. The first to come over the bridge were Rosecrans, Davis, [James Scott] Negley, Sheridan, [James A.] Garfield [later president of the United States] & their staffs. Part of the second brigade [of his division] came over & relieved us & we marched out to the foot of Sand Mountain & we went into camp. We rested Sunday & on Monday we came up & went into [our present] camp [in the front] . . . The rest of the Division came up last night. Today Gen. [Richard W.] Johnson's Division [also part of McCook's Corps] is crossing. We are about 6 miles from the river. McCook complimented us highly for our efficiency in throwing across the Pontoon Bridge. Another week will show us new things perhaps. The boys are all well.

Truly yours,
Webb.

Once again, the Federals got behind Bragg before he knew it and threatened to surround him completely and cut him off from his line of supply. As they hastened through two passes south of Lookout Mountain, the Rebels were forced from their positions on the heights. "The broad Tennessee below us," wrote one Union soldier, "seemed like a ribbon of silver; beyond rose the Cumberlands, which we had crossed. The valley on both sides was alive with the moving armies of the Union, while almost the entire transportation of the army filled the roads and fields along the Tennessee . . . No one could survey the grand scene on that bright autumn day unmoved, unimpressed with its grandeur and of the meaning conveyed by the presence of that mighty host."

Bragg was duly impressed himself, called in his outlying detachments, and evacuated Chattanooga on September 8. He crossed into Georgia and regrouped just below Pigeon Mountain, fifteen miles to the south. As the Rebels departed, the Army of the Cumberland marched in. In just twenty-three days, with little loss of life, it had marched three hundred miles, crossed three mountain ranges with ridges up to twenty-four hundred feet in height, and forded one of the mighty rivers of the West—all in the face of the foe. Well might Rosecrans argue, if only with a fleeting hurrah, that he could do more with strategy than other commanders with their huge expense of lives.

> *Camp between Sand Mountain & Lookout, Sept. 15, 1863*
> Dear Mother:
>   We are here in Alabama & 30 miles south of Chattanooga. Bragg has skedaddled & left us in undisputed possession of the mountains . . . Rosecrans is in Chattanooga with his headquarters. As soon as the Railroad is repaired to Chattanooga we intend to make Bragg hunt his hole. We are all well & in fine spirits. We are full of good rumors. I am sorry to hear that an early frost has spoiled the corn. Hope it is not as bad as you think. Some of the boys have had letters about Copperheads. Tell me the names of those Copperheads. I think they ought to be rode on a rail.
>
>   Truly,
>   Webb.

Had Rosecrans stopped at Chattanooga and consolidated his hold on the town, he would today be remembered as one of the masters of the war. Instead, he mistook Bragg's orderly withdrawal for headlong retreat, rashly broke up his force, ordered McCook's corps to push south to try to cut Bragg off and Crittenden to chase him along the railroad to Ringgold and Dalton with Wilder's mounted infantry brigade. Thomas, who considered the idea of chasing Bragg imprudent, was ordered to proceed eastward through Lookout Mountain by Stevens' and Cooper's Gaps.

As the separate Union columns, scattered over a forty-mile

front, filed through mountain passes into the north Georgia hills, Bragg almost succeeded in luring two of them to their demise. Failing that, he drew his army together along the banks of a creek called Chickamauga, a Cherokee word meaning "River of Death." Rosecrans belatedly realized the danger his army was in and managed to bring its diverse elements together before they could be caught in detail. Crittenden, commanding the Federal left, arrived first on the afternoon of September 18; Thomas brought up the center during the night; McCook, the right the following day.

Bragg was on the east side of the creek, the Federals on the west, some ways back from the bank, where they had gone into line. There they had to hold the roads back to Chattanooga, which lay through two gaps in Missionary Ridge. There was skirmishing between the armies all day on the 18th; their forces were in motion through the night; and by morning, Bragg had managed to move almost his entire infantry across the creek to the Union side. But neither army knew the exact position of the other, and some of the division commanders were not even sure where in the woods their own men were. In this manner, the battle lines formed. Bragg's target was the Federal left under Crittenden at a place called Lee and Gordon's Mill. But overnight that left had been extended, with Thomas marching around Crittenden to the north. In this way, he could better cover the two roads through the gaps, by posting troops between the ridge and the fords. Meanwhile, Bragg was expecting nine brigades of reinforcements from Virginia under Lee's principal lieutenant, James Longstreet. On the morning of the 19th, three arrived under John Bell Hood, giving Bragg the larger force. Once the others came in, he would have seventy thousand men.

The fate of Chattanooga was once more in the scales.

Early on the 19th, Thomas sent a reconnaissance toward one of the crossings, where it came up against the dismounted cavalry of Nathan Bedford Forrest, and the fighting began. At about the same time, a Confederate reconnaissance had been groping for any soft spots in the Union left. Thomas outflanked this party with a division of his own, and the contest spread. The Federals were outflanked in turn, more and more units were drawn in, and by midafternoon the greater portions of both armies, including Webb's unit in the 3rd Brigade, 1st Division of McCook's corps, moving up from the right, were engaged along a three-mile line.

The struggle continued until sundown, and at the end of the day, a day of hard but inconclusive jousting, the Federals still held the Chattanooga roads, but the Confederates had gained some ground. It was a restless night. Medics worked through it, tending to the wounded, though the cries of those they could not reach pierced the darkness between the camps. Pioneer brigades worked at breastworks and other barricades and entrenchments; divisions on both sides were marched and countermarched into new positions to fill gaps in their lines. Rosecrans withdrew his right from Lee and Gordon's Mill to Missionary Ridge and shortened his lines by more than a mile, as he turned his army toward the south. Meanwhile, "a sharp fire was kept up between the pickets, and, ever and anon, the booming of a cannon, startling us in our troubled slumber, reminded us of the carnage of the past day and the coming horrors" of the next.

There was gloom on the Union side. Bragg had been further reinforced, with six more brigades under Longstreet, so that his army now outnumbered the Federals by ten thousand men. It was clear he would again try to turn the Federal left, to drive it back, rout it, and seize the mountain gaps.

Rosecrans consulted with his officers late into the night, then, "as was his habit," kept them "a bit longer to socialize." He asked McCook to regale the assembled generals with a rendition of "The Hebrew Maiden's Lament," a plaintive, popular ballad that his baritone voice seemed to run through like a dirge. "As the wind whistled through the puncheons of the tiny cabin and the telegraph clicked its accompaniment," writes one historian, McCook came to the final verse: "Dearest youth whose care-worn image,/ Graven in my heart will be,/ Ah thou seest not the bitter,/ Bitter tears I shed for thee." The generals then "quietly filed out of the cabin and returned to their commands."

The following morning fog drifted up from the creek and hung low over both camps. At dawn, Bragg attacked as expected, hurling his troops in echelon from left to right down the Union line. Despite the ferocity of his assault, the Federals held their first positions and the battle was largely a stalemate until about noon. Then, as his center came under attack, Rosecrans mistakenly thought one of his divisions was out of position and ordered another to march out of line to fill the gap. That created a half-mile divide for the Rebels to charge through. Under Longstreet, twenty-three thousand men did just that. The Federal divisions on either side "were slammed out of place," writes one historian, "like doors swung back on their hinges and shattered by the blow. The whole right wing was taken on its left flank, completely torn away from the rest of the army, and swept off the field in utter and hopeless rout." Five of its brigades were also cut off completely from the rest of the command.

The headquarters of Rosecrans was overrun, and assuming the worst, he withdrew to Chattanooga with most of the other commanders to supervise its defense. Overwrought at the debacle, it is said, he could barely stand. Yet all this time, Thomas had remained on the field. In spite of the enveloping chaos, he had managed to hold his wing together on the Union left, and retreating back a mile to Snodgrass Hill, a wooded knoll on Horseshoe Ridge, he rallied fleeing troops, established a defensible position on the western slope, and there, as the "Rock of Chickamauga,"

he withstood for several hours a dozen assaults by four Confederate divisions, until twilight at last allowed him to withdraw to
Chattanooga through Missionary Ridge.

As at the Round Forest nine months before, Thomas had saved
the army from destruction—though this time not from defeat. In
two days of fighting, each side had lost between sixteen thousand
and seventeen thousand men. But the Confederates had won the
day. Bragg reported to Richmond: "It has pleased Almighty God
to reward the valor and endurance of our troops, by giving to our
arms a complete victory over the enemy's superior numbers.
[They were actually inferior.] Homage is due and is rendered unto
Him who giveth not the battle to the strong." Addressing his
troops, he said, "Your commander acknowledges his obligations,
and promises to you in advance the country's gratitude. But your
task is not ended. We must drop a soldier's tear upon the graves of
the noble men who have fallen by our sides and move forward."
Just one tear? There was cold comfort in comfort so coldly stated.
Another general, haunted by the carnage, would later ask himself,
with more feeling: "Are you the same man who once stood gazing
down on the faces of the dead on that awful battlefield? The soldiers lying there—they stare at you with their eyes wide open. Is
this the same world?"

The wounded at Chickamauga fared badly, but those on the
Union side worse. Corps hospitals had been placed at Crawfish
Springs to take advantage of its ample supply of water for dressings, but that was three miles to the south and separated from the
army's base by Missionary Ridge. Chattanooga was twelve miles
north. Although most of the wounded were taken to Chattanooga, others were dragged all the way back to Murfreesboro,
three hundred miles to the north, over rough mountain roads in
an ambulance train. The journey was a hard one, but those who
survived it probably fared better in the end.

That's where Webb ended up.

General Hospital No. 1 Ward A, Murfreesboro, Tenn.,
September 27, 1863.

Dear Mother,

This is my first opportunity to write you since the battle. I hope it will reach you before you get the details so you will not be uneasy about me. I received a wound in the left arm, the ball ranging upwards through the deltoid muscle to lodge in the shoulder near the joint. The surgeon is going to cut it out next week perhaps. The wound is already sloughing & doing well. Think I will join the company in a month. I was wounded in Saturday's engagement [i.e., on the 19th] together with Hogan, Wesley, Williams, Goodrich, Hawkins, Hatmaker, Myers, McClain, Hendy, H. Beevers, Wallace, & Red Cartwright. There is some others reported but I don't recollect their names. Out of 33 who went into the battle, only 13 stacked arms. Several of the boys are lost from the company, perhaps killed. I was pretty near the last man wounded on Saturday. I saw I. D. just as I was leaving the field. He had not received a scratch but they had shot his hat away & he was bareheaded & laughing. On Sunday the Division had another hard engagement & was driven from the field. The company only stacked six guns that night. Tom Denricks & I. D. were still with the company & unhurt. Bill Beevers was supposed to be wounded & have fallen into the hands of the enemy. Don't know certain . . . Henry Beevers [Bill's brother] is here. He is wounded in the leg. You will get a description of the battle from those whose business it is to describe it in the papers & in the reports of the officers. Send me a Charleston Ledger [the hometown newspaper] please.

Webb.

Webb's injury was more severe than he let on, and it kept him in the hospital for almost four months. The bullet that had struck him, as before at Pea Ridge, was a minié ball, which expanded on impact, smashed the tissue it tore through, and splintered bone. The prospects for Webb keeping his arm were not very good. As one Union doctor tactfully put it, "The minie ball striking bone does not permit much debate about amputation." Webb was liquored up, anesthetized with ether, and some morphine was rubbed into his wound. The wound was probed, loose pieces of bone and tissue removed, and a wad of lint used to plug it up. Afterwards, he was given some quinine to help fortify his system while the wound sloughed and healed. In the end, remarkably, his arm was spared, though the surgeon had failed to dig the bullet out. Webb would carry "an ounce of Rebel lead," as he put it, in his shoulder for the rest of his life.

CHAPTER NINE

At Chattanooga, the defeated Union army took over the defense works recently established by Bragg and built new ones, as Bragg's army occupied the surrounding hills. The Federals were now under siege. In an ironic twist, the army that had taken the offensive to get possession of the town "had been beaten and driven back into it, and was there besieged by the very army it had maneuvered out." Bragg arrayed his troops along Lookout Mountain and Missionary Ridge, erected ramparts, blockhouses, and other fortifications up the slopes, dug rifle pits along their base, brought forward heavy guns, and extended his pickets down the south bank of the river, nearly to Bridgeport, Alabama, a Union base of supplies. He thereby cut the Federals off from all river and rail routes. That left but one sixty-mile-long connected line of wagon roads open to the rear.

The beleaguered Federal army was in a fearful state. The Rebel positions looked directly down on the Union lines, and "our whole camp," recalled one officer, "was clearly in view. By daylight our troops could be counted, our reveille heard, our roll-call noted, our scanty meals of half rations seen—the last without envy. And we were not only heard and seen, but the enemy's signal-flag on Lookout Mountain talked, over our heads, with the signal-flag of Missionary Ridge."

In early October the rains set in, and soon the wagon roads over the Cumberlands became almost impassable, stalling supplies. The dirt roads broke down under the heavy traffic, the animals slipped and fell. Some of the hills along the route were so steep, wrote one Union general, "that a heavy wagon was almost a load going up." Without adequate forage, the animals began to die. Before long, "their very bones seemed to rattle within their drawn hides." By October 19, the Federals were losing some twenty animals a day, "in addition to the usual mortality rate." Over the next two months, more than ten thousand mules and horses perished in the near-futile effort to keep the army supplied. Confederate cavalry also destroyed hundreds of other wagons that might have gotten through. Rations for the men were repeatedly reduced, and soldiers often lived for days on such harsh fare as unripened fruit, parched corn, and even seed corn from the dirt where the horses had been fed. Some gathered acorns for roasting; others skinned and ate rats. It began to look as if the Union army might have to surrender, as famine stared it in the face.

At Murfreesboro, Webb was spared this ordeal directly, but he was scarcely out of harm's way. The town had been turned into a major Union depot for military stores, and the railway there and its bridges were a large strategic prize. Bragg was determined to destroy them and gave the task to Joseph Wheeler, who fell on the town on October 5 to lay it waste. Wheeler had first struck the Union supply route at a place called Anderson's Crossroads in the Sequatchie Valley, where he had wrecked or captured three hundred supply wagons and killed a thousand mules. Part of his contingent had then continued on to McMinneville, taking six hundred Union soldiers, along with $2 million worth of goods and munitions. Murfreesboro came next.

Murfreesboro, Tenn, Oct. 6, 1863

Dear Mother:

I resume my seat this morning to again address you. I wrote you immediately after my arrival here but lest it should not reach you & you would become uneasy about me I will write again. I never enjoyed better health than at present & my arm is getting well fast. If I havc no bad luck I will join the reg in two weeks. There is no news from the front [but] Forrest's rebel cavalry [under Wheeler] 10,000 strong succeeded in crossing the river & made a raid in Tenn as far up as here, cutting the telegraph & tearing up the railroad. They threatened this place all day yesterday. Everything was moved into the fortifications & skirmishing all day not half mile from town. We expected an old fashioned twist this morning. All the boys that stopped here when I did drew guns & ammunition & took our places behind the fort—some with one good leg & some with one good arm. The chaplain of our hospital was our capt. You would have laughed to have seen us there. They called us the Quinine Brigade. But just at night 15,000 of our cavalry from Chattanooga, Wilder's Brigade included, made their appearance & rebs skeddadled in the direction of Shelbyville & our fellows have gone in pursuit this morning. The train will be running to the front in a day or two. I saw the 123rd this morning. Johnny [Moore] & Dave is fat as pigs . . . Just tell all the folks you see they wished me to send word for them, said they did not know when they would get [home] . . . As the mail is going out in a few moments I will close for if I don't get this started today you will not get it Friday.

Give my love to all. Write me soon & believe me as ever your affectionate son,

Webb.

Webb probably owed his life to Colonel George Crook, who reached Murfreesboro with a column of Federal cavalry just ahead of Wheeler and turned him south. In retreat, Wheeler sacked Shelbyville and destroyed a bridge over Stones River, but failed to disable the Nashville Railway, as he had hoped. In the end, his command was cut up in several engagements and driven out of Tennessee. Some of the fighting had been fierce, at Farmington, for example, on the 7th, when the war once more struck home.

Murfreesboro, Tenn. Oct. 11, 1863

Dear Mother:

.... Our cavalry & Wilder's Brigade of mounted infantry had a sharp engagement of an hour & a half resulting in the capture of 20 pieces of artillery & 300 prisoners. Not, however, without a loss on our side. Col. [James] Monroe with several of his boys were killed. Among them, Johnny Moore, but I know the sad intelligence will have reached you before you get this. Poor little Johnny. On the morning before the battle, as the reg passed through here, I talked with him & he seemed to be so glad to see me & was so pleasant & in such high spirits. I cannot realize the fact that I will never see him again. If I could only have been there to have marked the place where he lays. It is only 36 miles from here & Lieut. Easton told me the place would be easily found. If I stay here this week I shall look hard for Mr. Moore [who would be coming for his son's body], but I am so lonesome I shall leave for the reg if I can get away. I know the boys must be lonesome. So many of us away & my arm is almost well. The soreness is all gone & will soon be healed up. From the best information I can get from the front, there will not be any more fighting at Chattanooga soon, if there is at all. I saw Major McIlvain of the 35th Ill belonging to the third brigade. He said that all was quiet & they had settled down to fortifying & the general opinion of military men [is] that there would be no fighting soon. I believe it will be like the siege of Corinth. About the time we are ready to strike, the rebs will leave. As we are going to have preaching & the chaplain is already to begin, I will close hoping this will find you all well as it leaves me ...

Truly your son,
Webb.

In addition to the three hundred prisoners taken, Wheeler had lost 250. Wilder lost ninety-three killed or wounded, of these, thirteen had been slain. Not long afterwards, Webb had a little more news about "little Johnny's" death. "I saw Dave Adam & Capt. Wiley yesterday enroute to Nashville for fresh horses ... [for] this last raid has killed nearly all their horses. In speaking of

John, they said he was killed by a ball passing through his head from the flank while among the foremost in a charge shouting for victory. They seem to feel nearly as bad as if he was their own brother. He was the company's pet & always ready to do his part. If Mr. Moore & Uncle Adams [Webb's Uncle Elijah] wishes to visit the army it will be useless for them to come at present for a citizen can go no farther south than Stevenson. As soon as they can go through I will write."

John W. ("Johnny") Moore was just sixteen when he fell, the youngest horse soldier in Wilder's famed brigade.

The desperate situation at Chattanooga soon led to a shake-up in the command. From the beginning of the war, the Union Army had been a kind of hydra-headed monster, made up of several semi-independent departments, without unified direction in the field. This was partially corrected on October 18, when Edwin M. Stanton, the secretary of war, met with Grant at Indianapolis en route to Louisville. Grant later recalled, "The Secretary handed me two orders, saying that I might take my choice of them. The two were identical in all but one particular." Both created the Military Division of the Mississippi and placed under his command all the territory and all the Union armies in it south of the Ohio River and east of the Mississippi. "One order," however, "left the department commanders as they were, while the other relieved Rosecrans and assigned Thomas in his place. I accepted the latter." Grant telegraphed Thomas from Louisville just before midnight on the 19th: "Hold Chattanooga at all hazards. I will be there as soon as possible." Thomas replied: "I will hold the town till we starve." Meanwhile, reinforcements (the 11th and 12th Corps from Army of the Potomac, numbering twenty-three thousand men) had been dispatched under Joseph Hooker to help secure the railway from Bridgeport to Nashville to the west.

Although Rosecrans was a brilliant general—as a strategist,

some say, the most brilliant of the war—his defeat at Chickamauga had changed him. In Lincoln's words, he appeared
"stunned and confused, like a duck hit on the head." At Chattanooga, in the midst of his army's deprived and imperiled state,
he spent a rather large amount of time working on a report that he
hoped would clear his name. That was not what his army needed
as it strove to hold on.

Grant arrived at Chattanooga on the evening of the 23rd, took
charge at once, and approved a plan, already devised, to seize a
ferry landing downriver out of range of Confederate guns and
open a new and much shorter supply route to the town. This was
accordingly done by a daring night maneuver; reinforcements
were dispatched to protect it; and it was dubbed the "Cracker
Line" for the hardtack (and other foodstuffs) that now flowed
along it to the grateful troops. Connecting routes were also established by bridge and rail to increase the volume of the convoys
coming in. This entirely transformed the circumstances of the
siege. "Instead of looking down from secure fastnesses upon a
prize which was sure to fall into its hands," notes one historian,
"Bragg's army now found itself confronted by an enemy whose
growing strength would soon exceed its own." Sherman (by
Grant's appointment, now head of the Army of Tennessee) was
hurrying east from Memphis with part of the force that had taken
Vicksburg, and Grant himself boldly declared: "If the rebels give
us one more week's time I think all danger . . . will have passed."

Webb kept track of the news. "Gen. Sherman's corps of Grant's
Army four days ago was at Florence, Alabama," he reported on
November 2, "& by this time I expect he is at Stevenson. Gen.
Hooker with the 11th & part of the 12th corps has crossed the
river at Stevenson & driven the rebels off Lookout Mountain so
that communication is open via the river from Bridgeport to
Chattanooga so the boys will get more rations. They have been on
one third rations for some time . . . I think Sherman & Hooker

will cross the mountain the way we went & by so doing completely flank Bragg so he will be compelled to fall back on Atlanta without giving battle. I do not believe there will be another battle at Chattanooga. Everything seems to work in our favor."

Bragg, in fact, still held Lookout Mountain, though Hooker was in the valley below, and he hadn't the least notion of giving up what he judged an impregnable line.

The battle for Chattanooga would be fought.

Webb might have wished to be a part of it, but his ardor for battle had cooled as he began to relish his leisure time. His arm in any case had been slow in mending, and the surgeon refused to let him go. "I don't know how long I will stop here," Webb wrote. "They have put me on duty today & perhaps will keep me all winter as I can't get away till the surgeon sees fit to send me. I am not caring much. I have a good bed & warm room & plenty of grub & that is more than I would get at the front. Besides, I have lots of good books & plenty of time to read them. Then why should I not be contented to stop just as long as they have a mind to keep me? At present I am reading the history of ancient Greece & hardly know how to take time to drill! . . . I never enjoyed better health in my life. I weigh 210 lbs." The following Sunday, November 8, he attended church and heard "as good a sermon as I have heard since I have been in the service. But that is not all—there were three ladies came with [the minister] & did the singing. O! they were such good singers. Perhaps I thought so because it is the first singing I have heard at church since I left home. It waked a train of reflections on bygone days that is easier imagined than described. When you read this you will say that I am homesick, but I aver that such is not the case. Of course, I should like to be at home a few days, but don't expect I would stay long if I was there."

In the next letter, it was as if he already were at home. An old friend, Dave Adam, he told his mother, was up in his room "now disputing with me as to which [of us] belongs to the best fighting corps, old fashioned, you know, how we used to do." And he had some older-brotherly advice for his fourteen-year-old stepsister, who was making herself unpopular among former friends: "Tell Harriet that she should not tell tales out of school if she would have the good opinion of the [other] scholars. A still tongue makes a wise ear & a tattler is disliked by everybody." But the war thrust itself to the fore. By November 20, Webb learned that Sherman had reached Chattanooga with four divisions "& a battle is again anticipated in that region such as the world never saw."

It was about to begin. The right and most forward position of the Confederate line rested on a hill called Orchard Knob, a mile in front of the western base of Missionary Ridge. From there the line ran to the south and west across Chattanooga Valley. About noon on November 23, Union troops assembled on the wide plain opposite the knob, rushed it, and drove the Rebels off. They then entrenched their positions and brought up heavy guns. The following day, Grant ordered Hooker to take Lookout Mountain and sent Sherman to the north to attack the right flank of Bragg's line on Missionary Ridge. Hooker advanced with unexpected speed, but as the battle on the mountain raged, a thick fog concealed the action from view. Suddenly it lifted, revealing a Federal triumph on the heights. Meanwhile, Sherman, at the other end of the line, had crossed the Tennessee River to seize the northern tip of Missionary Ridge. This he did easily enough, but then to his shocked surprise found a wide ravine he hadn't known about between him and Bragg's entrenched position on high ground to the south. Behind that ground, called Tunnel Hill, stood another, still higher mountain fortified with breastworks and studded with heavy guns. And so, by the evening of the first day, Sherman had crossed the Tennessee River but had not turned Bragg's right; Hooker had carried Lookout Mountain in "the battle above the clouds"; and Thomas, to take advantage of the fall of Orchard

Knob, had drawn up the Army of the Cumberland on a wide plain facing Missionary Ridge.

That night, there was an almost total eclipse of the moon—viewed on both sides apparently as a bad omen for the Rebels—as each army prepared for a decisive clash on the following day. At daybreak, Hooker began an assault on the enemy left at Rossville Gap, Sherman tried to push southward past Tunnel Hill on the right, while Thomas, on instructions from Grant, waited for these two flanking movements to succeed before mounting his own attack. Hooker made progress, though he was delayed unexpectedly by blockaded roads and a wrecked bridge; Sherman, stoutly resisted, stalled. To draw enemy strength from Sherman's front, Grant now ordered Thomas to advance his four divisions to the base of Missionary Ridge. His men were then to stop and await orders. At half past 3, they started forward, all Army of the Cumberland troops, eager to avenge their defeat at Chickamauga two months before. Chickamauga rankled, but then Grant himself had seemed to disparage their fighting spirit, and that rankled them, too, from Thomas on down. Three lines of entrenchments were before them: one (the rifle pits) at the foot of the ridge, a second near the middle of the slope, the third and strongest on the crest. The ridge itself was four hundred feet high, steep, well-fortified, and broken by swales and ravines.

Rushing over and around a formidable abatis of felled trees, the men took the rifle pits with unexpected speed. Then, instead of stopping, as Grant had ordered, they kept on going, scrambling up the shot-swept slopes. As they worked their way steadily higher between the clumped brush and boulders arranged to block their path, their tenacity overwhelmed the astonished defenders. At times, the Federals seemed almost like mountain climbers on a precipice of rock, as they dug their bayonets into the ground like spikes to stabilize their climb. Suddenly, the ridge was carried in six places and Bragg's own headquarters almost overrun. Thirty-seven guns and two thousand Rebels were straightaway captured and Bragg's center, broken, driven from the field. Meanwhile, Hooker, with three divisions, had reached Rossville Gap, scattered the Confederate left, and turning northward had begun to advance along the ridge until his troops linked up with the right of Thomas's line. By the time darkness fell, Lookout Mountain, all the rifle pits in Chattanooga Valley, and the whole of Missionary Ridge were in Union hands. As the dead were gathered up, Thomas was asked by an army chaplain "whether or not they should be sorted and buried by state." "Mix 'em up," he replied. "I'm tired of States' Rights."

As Bragg's army retreated, the Federals followed. On the 26th, Bragg thought to make a stand at Ringgold, but then withdrew to Dalton. Five days later, at his own request, he was relieved of command. By then, Grant had sent part of his army to the relief of Ambrose Burnside at Knoxville, then under siege, and on December 4, the siege was raised.

The whole of east Tennessee was now under Union control, and Lincoln's devoutly cherished wish for the relief and protection of the loyal inhabitants had at last been achieved. On December 7, he appointed a day of national thanksgiving, and ten days later Congress unanimously passed a resolution of thanks to Grant's army and authorized that a commemorative medal be struck.

The Battle of Chattanooga had taken place on Webb's twenty-second birthday, and he was as pleased as if it had been a gift. "We have good news," he wrote on November 29, when Bragg was still being chased, "a dispatch today to the effect that we have fifteen thousand prisoners & have driven the rebs seven miles below Chickamauga, & are still pursuing them! . . . Bully for Grant. Reports say that Meade has crossed the Rapidan, perhaps so. & that [Major General Quincy A.] Gillmore has, ere this, made an assault on Charleston . . . Our prospect is bright at present." Webb continued: "I have left [General Hospital] No. 1 to nurse at No. 4 [Ward 2]." He thought he might get a brief furlough and hurry up to Hutton. "If I should slip in [for a few days] between now & Christmas, don't be surprised though you need not look for me unless you see me coming. But as strange things has happened."

He received the furlough he hoped for and was back by the first of the new year. "I was five days on the road," he wrote in his next letter home. "Had a very good time and pleasant journey . . . A great many are reenlisting. As I came through, I saw several entire regt that had reenlisted and were enroute for home to recruit. They were enthusiastic. One thing [is] certain," he added cheerfully, "they like soldiering better than I!" His mother had given him a couple of cakes to give to friends (one had gotten all "mashed up") and a pair of socks for I. D., which he sent on to Kaggerville, where the 25th Illinois then was. His stepfather had been hoping to get a pass to visit, but Webb thought it could only come by "recommend[ation] from the Governor or some prominent man in Illinois." In the meantime, he went to General Horatio Phillips Van Cleve, his post commander at Murfreesboro, to see if something could be arranged.

By mid-January, Webb had at last regained the use of his left arm, more or less (he never regained it completely), and was transferred to Stevenson, Alabama, en route to Chattanooga. "The railroad is repaired, so the trains run through," he wrote his mother on the 15th. "All that are able for duty and some that are not are being sent to their commands by order Gen. Thomas." Webb arrived at Chattanooga on the 20th and expected to be sent on to his regiment near Knoxville the following week. There were reports that Longstreet, reinforced, would try to retake the town. The 11th and 12th Corps had been ordered forward, and "the prospect for a battle," reported Webb, "is said to be good . . . If so the struggle will be sanguinary. Fellows from there report our forces driven in to the breastworks but don't know whether true or not." Knoxville, however, was secured, and Longstreet was actually on his way to rejoin Lee. Meanwhile, Webb had been detained at the Convalescent Camp. That was all right with him: "We have the finest weather, . . . as warm as summer and no storms. There is nine of our company here and we are having our own fun. Nothing to do and plenty to eat and a good shelter and we are not particular whether they send us to the regiment till after the fight" (letter of January 30, 1864).

Who can blame him? He had seen enough of this war to know that no rest from it could last.

CHAPTER TEN

The Union victory at Chattanooga opened the way for a full-scale invasion of the deep South. At the time, the South had only two organized armed bodies of any considerable strength left. These were Lee's Army of Northern Virginia and a combined force under General Joseph E. Johnston at Dalton, Georgia, composed of the Army of Mississippi and the Army of Tennessee. The great strategic front that Jefferson Davis had once drawn from Mississippi to Virginia had been sundered completely, and all that was left of what secession could claim was a relatively narrow strip of land "without seacoast or harbors, south of the Potomac and east of the Appalachian Range."

Just at this juncture, the several Union armies at last began to coordinate their might. In the past they had moved "like a team of balky horses," in Grant's complaint, in awkward disjunction, but now they were to work in concert as one. On March 3, 1864, Grant was summoned by telegraph to the War Office in Washington, and there on March 9, Lincoln, in the presence of his Cabinet, formally presented him with his new commission as lieutenant general and general in chief. In a brief statement, Lincoln commended Grant for what he had done—and what he expected him to do. In reply, Grant promised, with the help of Providence, not to disappoint his expectations. He kept his own counsel, but that was just as Lincoln wished. "Grant is the first general I've had," he said, "[who] hasn't told me what his plans are. I don't know, and I don't want to know. I'm glad to find a man who can go ahead without me." Grant did just that and, with Lincoln's ultimate approval, devised a plan to wear down by incessant battle what remained of the Southern force. It was the kind of general movement that Webb and other lowly soldiers had long yearned to see. Grant was to move on Lee and destroy him, taking Richmond if he could, while Sherman advanced on Atlanta, with Chattanooga as his base. Both men were to break up their opponent's interior lines, sever the rail and road links on which he depended, and oblige him to fight face to face. Grant intended to do this by a hammering force; Sherman, by a wide wheeling movement through the South that took advantage of all the army's western gains. In a letter to Sherman on April 4, Grant told him not only to press Johnston's army but "to break it up and to get into the interior of the enemy's country as far as you can, inflicting all the damage you can against their resources"—in short, to destroy his capacity to make war.

The Federals had already begun to probe Johnston's defenses, and by March troops were being rounded up for the big campaign. Webb was now back in the ranks, and in early March, writing from Tennessee, reported that he had just returned "from a reconnaissance in force" that had taken him forty miles northeast of Knoxville along the railroad in an effort to flush out remaining Rebel bands in the state. "We found no enemy though they are reported at Bulls Gap only twenty miles farther. Why we did not go farther I do not know."

Pockets of resistance remained stiff, for such rearguard actions were about all that could now delay the Federal advance. "We are under marching orders to be ready at a moments warning," Webb wrote his mother again from Morristown on the 15th. "We are only about 11 miles from the front and skirmishing is going on constantly. An engagement may be brought on at any hour." But, he added, to reassure her, "I do not think it likely . . . If there is, our Divis[ion] is in the reserve and will not be called into action unless we are like to lose the day . . . Grub is scarce enough you may believe though the prospect is good for it to be more plenty shortly as the railroad is in operation this far." A few days later, Webb's regiment was ordered to Strawberry Plains. "The rest of the Divis[ion]," he reported, "has gone farther up the river . . . We had the heaviest [snow] on the 22nd I have seen since I have been in the army. [Then] it snowed so it layed a foot deep all night, but it went off the next day. It snowed again last night and is raining today." During that cold, soggy interlude, he had been "cooped up" in a pup tent with a friend, and the two had imagined what they would write to their "ducks" (i.e., sweethearts) if they had any to write to. But "I haven't any, neither has he. Wish we had one a piece. I am sure we would spend an hour to the best advantage in writing them. Well, I have filled this sheet with bad sense and will quit for fear I make it worse."

Meanwhile, almost the whole of Chattanooga had been rebuilt and transformed into a massive supply depot and staging base. New bridges had been thrown over rivers and creeks, hundreds of miles of road and track had been repaired, and once-severed supply lines to the north restored. A ninety-mile military railroad, built and operated by Union troops, had also been forged to link Nashville to steamboat traffic on the Tennessee. Before long, writes one historian, "locomotives and freight cars, commandeered from all over the Union, were delivering a torrent of arms, animals and provisions" to the town. In the midst of this abundance, the men were put on short rations to further conserve supplies. The portly Webb was predictably annoyed. "I am pretty near mad this morning," he wrote on April 1, "have not had any breakfast and am not likely to get any till evening. About every fifth day we have to fast whether we will or not." On the other hand, his regiment had now been in the field so long there was some talk it might be discharged as early as June—three months, that is, before its term was up. "One thing I don't care," Webb confessed, "so they don't keep us another winter and I guess that will hardly be." But it soured him a bit to hear that two young men he knew back home had just gotten married at a time when recruiting was off. "Well, I don't care who gets married," he wrote, "hope they will all have good luck, but Hutton Township is getting behind. I don't like to hear that."

At the beginning of May, Grant's offensive began. At the time, Lee's army was dug in behind the Rapidan River and unassailable in front; Grant therefore had to turn one of its flanks. Lee's left was protected by field works, which reached to the spurs of the Blue Ridge Mountains; his right by entrenchments and a stream called Mine Run. Between the two armies stood the Wilderness, the same tract of land where Hooker had come to grief. Covered with a dense growth of scraggy pine, scrub oak, dwarf chestnut, and hazel, it was the hardest kind of ground to deploy in or advance through under fire. Grant had about 120,000 men, Lee about 73,000, but these were arrayed on the ground of his choice.

The contest began on May 5 as the two armies struck at each other through the woods. The fighting intensified and then continued with such ferocity over the course of two days that in places the woods caught fire. Lee's right flank was shattered, but Grant's right was also mauled. Neither army wanted to renew the engagement on the 7th, and by then Grant had lost over twenty thousand men. Lee's losses were likewise heavy, but unlike Grant's they could not be repaired. That was "the grim equation" on which Grant now relied. Instead of retreating, he advanced. The two clashed again at Spotsylvania Courthouse. Once more Union casualties were awful, but still Grant came on. Cold Harbor followed, where Grant had to carve his rifle pits in a malarial marsh and where, in his first brief assault, he lost seven thousand men in half an hour's time. By June 12 his losses exceeded fifty-four thousand, three times what Lee had sustained. But "it was Lee's army that was wearing out." Grant then worked his way round south of Richmond, to Petersburg, crossed the James River, and began a long investment of the town. He thereby managed to leave Washington unprotected, and the Rebel general Jubal Early swept through the Shenandoah Valley to its outskirts, filling the city with alarm. To close that route, the valley was ravaged by Sheridan so completely that, as he put it, "a crow would have to carry its own rations" through it on the fly.

Nor had Sherman neglected his part. Between him and Atlanta stood Johnston's army, ensconced behind a mountain screen at Dalton, thirty miles to the south; beyond Dalton lay a wide expanse of wild, rugged, hilly terrain, often thick with forest cover, extending for a hundred miles almost to the gates of Atlanta itself. All in all, "it was ideal country for a fighting retreat," and Johnston made the most of it, though heavily outnumbered and outgunned. Thomas was at Ringgold with the Army of the Cumberland, which formed the center and massive heart of the Union force. The Army of Tennessee, under Major General James B. McPherson, was on the right, the Army of Ohio, under Major General John M. Schofield, on the left. Webb's regiment belonged to the center as part of the 1st Brigade, 3rd Division, 4th Army Corps. His division commander was General Thomas J. Wood, the man who had inadvertently marched out of line at Chickamauga, allowing Longstreet to charge through. He had since redeemed himself at Missionary Ridge. Webb's corps commander was Major General Oliver H. Howard, a deeply religious man and Abolitionist, for whom Howard University in Washington would later be named. An artillery expert, Howard had fought at First Bull Run and in the Peninsular Campaign, where he had lost an arm at the Battle of Seven Pines; at Antietam; and then at Chancellorsville, where his troops were routed in Stonewall Jackson's famous flank attack. Subsequently, he had served with distinction at Gettysburg, Lookout Mountain, and

Missionary Ridge. Sherman considered him one of the best of his commanders, though Chancellorsville still haunted his career. When he received his new appointment in mid-April his divisions were somewhat scattered and his first task was to bring them in. This he did efficiently, near Cleveland, Tennessee, before proceeding to Ringgold, where the entire Union center was to assemble by May 1.

Cleveland, Tenn., April 16th, 1864

Dear Mother:

. . . After a march of ten days we again find ourselves with the Army of the Cumberland ready to participate in the contest that from the concentrated movements of the army is to come off soon. Ours, that is the 4th corps, commanded now by Gen. Howard of Chancellorsville notoriety is being concentrated at or in the vicinity of Cleveland 30 miles north of Dalton on the Knoxville and Dalton Rail Road and 30 miles east of Chattanooga. Whether there will be a battle or not I can't tell. Some say we are relieving Hookers 1st army corps off of the railroad so they can go back to the army of the Potomac where the great campaign is expected to open. For my part I have quit prophesizing and come to the conclusion that I know nothing about it and care less so I get plenty of grub. With regard to the Charleston [draft] riot [March 28], I hardly know what to say . . . but . . . if the reports that I have got are true, that every man engaged in the assault upon the soldiers is a traitor and ought to be hung as a criminal in the double capacity of murderer and traitor. But I can't think that I have true reports. Yet when I think of it I am vexed and have a notion to throw down my pen . . . Give my love to all.

Write me soon and believe me as ever your affectionate son,

Webb.

It was soon clear that a major troop movement was afoot. "We had general reviews by Gen. Howard, our Corps Commander, yesterday," wrote Webb on the 30th. "A very good sign of an advance and others equally as good that an advance is intended. We have been mustered for pay . . . If we stay here another week think we will get a little tobacco money." One of Webb's colonels, Richard H. Nodine, was still predicting that the regiment would be discharged in June, but that was still a month away, and "a month," Webb ruefully noted, "is a long time at this stage of the game . . . long enough for many a poor fellow to go to his long home. But our corps is [in] reserve and the engagement will be desperate if we are engaged." The Charleston draft riot still gnawed at his gut. "Politics is very little discussed here. The army, like the citizens, are divided though they do not carry things to such extremes." But he supposed tensions would rise if Lincoln were reelected because of the animosity some measures had inspired. (Webb's division, of course, was largely made up of ambivalent soldiers from south-central Illinois and the border states.)

Four days later, on May 4, Sherman began his march—the same day, by design, that the Army of the Potomac crossed the Rapidan to go after Lee. With an army one hundred thousand strong Sherman hoped to make short work of the defenders. Johnston's strategy, on the other hand, was to wear out Sherman's army by obliging it to make a series of grinding assaults. In so doing, he hoped to preserve his forces intact, hold Atlanta, and stall Sherman's progress long enough to affect the elections in the fall. Atlanta was now absolutely indispensable to the survival of the South. It was a large, industrial town, full of foundries, arsenals, and machine shops; cloth factories that turned out most of the uniforms for the Confederate army; and warehouses to feed it piled with grain. Railroads also radiated from the town in every direction; these not only brought in supplies but provided lines of communication with Lee.

Webb's regiment was at first held back with the 6th Ohio and assigned to garrison Cleveland. "This is a pretty town, half the size of Charleston [Illinois] and there is lots of pretty girls here," wrote Webb on May 9, "though I have not got acquainted with any yet . . . [We] have been busy putting up quarters, but . . . we are certain to have a good time this summer. Can go to town whenever we are not on duty." Meanwhile, he had heard that "a general engagement" near Dalton "will hardly be kept off longer than Monday, not more than till the middle of the week, no way."

At the outset, Sherman had adopted a plan proposed by Thomas to pin Johnston down to his entrenchments with his center and left, while Sherman's right, under McPherson, turned the Confederate left by pushing through Snake Creek Gap. That would allow the Federals "to cut in behind Johnston at Resaca," straddle the railroad above it, and trap half the Confederate force. On May 8, McPherson advanced through the gap unopposed, but Sherman, some would argue, failed to commit the full complement of troops needed for the maneuver to succeed, and when Johnston sent three divisions to oppose it, McPherson fell back to the entrance to the gorge.

So it began. Sherman went from one obstinate engagement to another as Johnston, withdrawing from one stronghold to the next, kept forcing him to halt, redeploy, reconnoiter, and entrench. Ever so slowly, Sherman pushed Johnston back past Rocky Face, Tunnel Hill, Resaca, and across the Oostanaula and Etowah Rivers, to Allatoona, New Hope Church, and Pickett's Mills. In each instance, Johnston was ultimately outflanked out of every position he held, but also succeeded in evading every attempt at envelopment Sherman tried. At length, their duel was brought to a final line of disconnected hills—Kennesaw Mountain, Lost Mountain, and Pine Mountain—north of Marietta, where Sherman was tempted to mount direct assaults. It had taken him over a month to reach that line at the painfully slow rate of a mile and a half a day. The whole campaign, complained Sherman, had turned into "one big Indian fight." He therefore decided to throw everything he had at Johnston's line. Webb became part of the mix, and on June 4 his regiment left for the front with a supply train of three thousand wagons and one thousand ambulance carts. On June 7, it joined its brigade and division near Marietta, and from that day till the end of July, Webb fought with the army to Atlanta's gates.

> *Camp in the field, June 8, 1864*
>
> Dear Mother:
>
> I embrace this opportunity of again writing you. We left Cleveland on the 31st of May being relieved by the second Ohio heavy artillery. We took the [railroad] cars and came to Kingston, from there we escorted a train through where we arrived last evening and joined our Brigade, our corps having been in advance all the time for the last month were relieved for a few days and what is left of them are enjoying themselves . . . though about one third have been killed or wounded. We have orders to march in the morning with nine days rations and sixty rounds of cartridges, so suppose we will take the front again. The rebel pickets are within two miles of camp. I hear them skirmishing with ours while I am writing, but the main force is said to be nine miles from here where they have the last but one [i.e., next to last] strong position this side of Atlanta, and they have none as strong as some they have left. We do not expect very hard fighting this side of Atlanta as we can easily flank their position and when we get to Atlanta, if they do not leave, we will starve them out . . .
>
> Your affectionate son,
> Webb.

It wouldn't be as easy as that. On the 10th, the Federals pushed Rebel skirmishers back as far as Pine Mountain and came up to within cannon range. During the night, they began preparations to besiege the enemy's breastworks, and over the next two days in a heavy downpour established their own fortified line. Behind Pine Mountain was the still more formidable Kennesaw, bristling with cannon and blocking their way to the Chattahoochee, the last broad river remaining in Sherman's path. Sherman was now about twenty-five miles from Atlanta itself. On June 13, Thomas worked two of his corps around the base of Pine Mountain toward the east and the next day extended his three-quarters of a mile on the left. Meanwhile, there had been a tremendous exchange of artillery fire, and that night the Rebels abandoned their advanced lines and withdrew within stronger works, running from Lost Mountain to Kennesaw. Early on the 15th, in the predawn hours, Webb, as part of Howard's corps, scrambled up Pine Mountain before advancing still farther to the south. Kennesaw was next, and during the night Howard connected two of his batteries by a fortified trench. The Rebels withdrew again from their own outer line, and on the morning of the 17th Howard's troops moved in. Toward nightfall, they also managed to drive enemy skirmishers across Mud Creek. On the following day, in a pouring rain, they bridged the creek and gained and entrenched a key ridge to the east. At dusk on the 18th, Webb squatted in a rifle pit, gnawing at some hardtack as he peered out at the enemy's position, almost within range of his gun. As he lifted his eyes, he could trace the Rebel artillery emplacements that bristled along the mountain crest as far as the southern spur.

On the 21st, his unit was among those ordered to seize and hold a strategic mound called the Bald Knob. The enemy had this patch of ground under their heavy guns, so Howard, with a consideration that endeared him to his men, attempted to pulverize the latter with an intense bombardment of his own before the Knob was rushed. He did so thoroughly, obliging the Rebels to retire, and the crest was secured. The Federals then advanced the right of their line some five hundred yards across an open field.

Directly in their front stood abatis and other entanglements. Slowly but surely, they extended their own trenches toward the base of the mountain as artillery pounded gun emplacements on the heights. That failed to dislodge the defenders, so on the 27th

Sherman ordered a direct assault. That proved costly and was re-
pulsed. But two days later, the Rebels withdrew to prevent their
left flank from being turned. Johnston's army now retreated six
miles to the north bank of the Chattahoochee, where his defenses
included a series of redoubts made of logs and packed earth up to
twelve feet thick. In between, he had planted "heavy siege guns
brought up from Mobile."

On July 5, with Wood's division, including Webb's regiment, in
the lead, the Rebels were pursued along the railroad as far as Vin-
ing's Station. From this point a road led to the east toward Atlanta,
crossing the Chattahoochee River by a pontoon bridge. As they
advanced, Wood's men encountered a brigade of dismounted cavalry, ensconced behind rail barricades along a ridge at right angles
to the road. They were ousted in a firefight, then Wood pushed
on to the river itself, where Webb and other members of his unit
were posted on the north side to hold the fords.

Two days later, the Federals scaled a high bluff overlooking the
Chattahoochee, and there before them at last lay "the domes and
minarets and spires of Atlanta glittering in the light." Generals
Sherman and Thomas came up and stood together in silence on
the heights. Then Thomas turned to a fellow officer and said,
"Send up a couple of guns and we'll throw some shells over there,"
pointing to a patch of forest cover on the river's south side. The
artillery came thundering up, and within fifteen minutes a Parrott
shell (an expanding projectile shot from a rifled cannon) went
screaming across the river from the top of the bluff.

Meanwhile, after crossing the Chattahoochee, Johnston
burned the great trestle bridge that spanned it, but Sherman's pioneer brigades were undaunted. His engineers, indeed, had done
wonders all along the march, repairing, building, and rebuilding
eleven bridges and over one hundred miles of track. The great
trestle bridge across the Chattahoochee was 780 feet long and 90
feet high, yet his specialty teams reconstructed it in just four and a

half days. No matter when or where a breach by the enemy was made, remarked Sherman afterwards, "the repair train seemed on the spot, and the damage repaired generally before I knew of the break . . . The locomotive whistle was heard in an advanced camp almost before the echoes of the skirmish-fire had ceased."

On July 17 Jefferson Davis, exasperated by Johnston's repeated retreats, panicked and replaced him with John Bell Hood. Hood was a superb commander at the division level and "a stand-up fighter," but not a strategist of any strength. His physical infirmities—a shattered left arm and a missing right leg—cast doubt on his ability to lead an army, and each morning he had to be strapped into the saddle by his aides. Above all, however, he was rash. He had been called in to do something dramatic and attack. This he prepared to do.

By July 17, all three Federal armies had crossed the Chattahoochee, and on the 18th they began their final advance. Hood took up a position on a ridge behind Peachtree Creek as Thomas's troops drew near. On the 20th, Webb's regiment was sent forward and deployed as skirmishers on the left, and at about 2 P.M. succeeded in crossing the creek under heavy fire. As more Federal columns came over, Hood's full assault began. The fighting spread and, with a vital railhead at stake, became desperate and continued unabated for two hours. Hood's gambit, not in and of itself ill-advised, cost him five thousand men, before he fell back on Atlanta. Then the battle for Atlanta itself began. On the 21st, Sherman began to bombard the heart of the town. Hood almost caught McPherson's corps off guard at Decatur, but again, his losses exceeded any gains. Then, to prevent Sherman from severing his last line of supply, the Macon & Western Railroad, he came out from behind his fortifications and launched a series of reckless assaults against the Union lines. "They'll only beat their brains out," remarked Sherman calmly, as Hood's men fell by the thousands before his obliterating fire.

CHAPTER ELEVEN

On August 1, 1864, with his regiment at the gates of Atlanta, Webb's service expired. Enrolled as a private, he was discharged as a corporal. He had been a brave and stalwart soldier and, despite his comparatively humble rank, had proved his worth as a man by any standard that counts. Though wearied and saddened by the war, he believed it had been fought to good purpose. He had thought so at the beginning, and he thought so at the end. But he had no taste for war itself. He would later write: "The tendency of war is to disorganize society, to arrest the wheels of civilization, to drag men down in the scale of manhood and to add to the sum of human misery." He had seen enough of that.

In the course of his three years' service, Webb had marched three thousand miles on foot; covered another seventeen hundred or so by boat and rail; fought in numerous battles; been wounded twice (three times, by the number of bullets that hit him); lost numerous friends and relations and, a sorrow that would never heal, his only and beloved brother, whom he had buried on the field. On the march to Atlanta, from June 7 onward, he had been engaged almost every day in some skirmish or other related to the campaign. When it was all over, the 25th Illinois had lost 232 men, or a third of its strength.

It had been a hard road. As the men prepared to entrain for their home state, Colonel W. H. Gibson of the 1st Brigade, 3rd Division, 4th Army Corps, to which the regiment was attached, addressed them with feeling for what they had done. He commended their endurance, "the cheerful manhood" with which they had "submitted to every hardship and overcome every difficulty," and thanked them for the "sacrifice and valor" with which they had fought. He spoke of the pride Illinois had in them and their devotion to duty, "having made history for all time and coming generations to admire." And he hoped, thanks in part to their service, that the country would soon emerge from its "gloom of blood." Orders were given for the troops to report at Camp Butler in Springfield, Illinois, and muster out. And so, on September 5, 1864, they did.

When Webb arrived, he found his mother waiting. She was standing almost alone at the camp's west portal, in a tiny cluster of others, her face immensely drawn. It seemed to him she had aged a hundred years.

The war was at last drawing down. Just four days before, Atlanta had fallen to Sherman's troops. The political impact was electric. All through that summer, Lincoln's prospects for reelection had seemed dim. In the last round of congressional elections the Republicans had suffered losses, and with Grant mired down before Petersburg and Atlanta still in Rebel hands, the war seemed stalled once more in mutual slaughter, without an end in sight. On July 11, the capital itself had been threatened by a Rebel raid, while tens of thousands of captured Union soldiers continued to rot in Southern camps. Congress, reflecting the public mood as well as its own agitation, asked the president to set aside a day for fasting, humiliation, and prayer.

As the fall campaign drew near, the Democrats exuded confidence, and at their national convention, which opened on August 29, Copperheads had the upper hand. In the Party platform they inserted a plank that declared the war a failure, called for a negotiated peace, and chose General George McClellan as their candidate, as he could not be tarnished by any of the recent disappointments in the field. McClellan, however, was a Unionist as well as a Democrat, supported the use of arms, and repudiated the Party's central plank. Meanwhile, news arrived of Admiral David Farragut's capture of Mobile, then of the fall of Atlanta, even as Sheridan began to enjoy a string of victories in his Shenandoah Valley campaign. Instead of an abject day of fasting, humiliation, and prayer, Lincoln proclaimed a day of Thanksgiving to be held throughout the land.

In November, McClellan was buried in a landslide after a campaign in which Lincoln also urged the adoption of the Thirteenth Amendment to the Constitution, aimed at eradicating slavery from the nation. He looked to the future, to a nation reconciled. "With malice towards none," he said in his Second Inaugural Address, "with charity for all; with firmness in the right, as God gives us to see the right, let us strive on to finish the work we are in; to bind up the nation's wounds." By then, Sherman had marched with terrible impunity from Atlanta to the sea, Thomas had crushed Hood at Nashville, and Grant had finally turned Lee's right flank. On April 9, the two old warriors met at Appomattox Court House to discuss the surrender terms. Grant was gracious and grand. The Army of Northern Virginia, though at his mercy, was at once paroled, its officers allowed to retain their sidearms, and those who owned their own horses—"They will need them for spring ploughing," Grant said—allowed to take them home. He also forbade the firing of salutes or any other demonstrations of the Union triumph, which would have made the defeat even harder to bear. "The war is over," he told his troops. "The Rebels are our countrymen again."

Lincoln could now have pushed any policy he pleased, but at his last Cabinet meeting, on April 14, 1865, his merciful disposition was also manifest. He would take no part, he said, in "hanging or killing" any Rebel leader, "even the worst . . . Enough lives have been sacrificed; we must extinguish our resentments if we expect harmony and union" to prevail. That evening, he went to Ford's Theater to see *Our American Cousin*, and while he was sitting in his box, "a ranting actor of melodrama," John Wilkes Booth, crept up behind him and shot him through the head. Booth then vaulted upon the stage and, brandishing a bloody dagger (with which he had also just stabbed one of Lincoln's aides), shouted "*Sic semper tyrannis*"—"Thus ever to tyrants"—and exited the scene.

Everyone struggled to find their bearings in the postwar world. Webb went home to his farm, where the work was as hard as it had ever been, and, though his heart wasn't in it, he kept at it for a couple of years. Then, after one especially long day behind the plow, his left arm aching unbearably from the strain, he gave it up and decided to return to school. He was intellectually hungry, a student by inclination, and had continued to read and study as much as he could. He lost—and found—himself in history. And the story of modern science among others drew him in. He marveled at the time "when the telescope first looked into the heavens and revealed undreamed of wonders," and as he put it, "the microscope first looked into a drop of water to reveal the myriad forms of life." He read about Harvey's discovery of the circulation of the blood, of the discovery of logarithms, "first used to measure the angles of the stars," and, not surprisingly, of the new antiseptic procedures established in the treatment of wounds. But it was political and religious history that held him most in thrall. With Protestant pride, he rejoiced in the fate of the Spanish Armada, was repelled by the Inquisition, and scorned the presumptions of a Renaissance pope who pretended to divide the discoverable world between the two great Catholic powers of Portugal and Spain. "By the interposition of the Pope," he tells us, the Portuguese "were limited to the Torrid Zone, as if they could be bettered by boiling." He wondered if the fate of French imperial ambitions in the New World had ultimately suffered because "there was upon them the unavenged blood of St. Bartholomew's Day." Webb, in truth, had something of the Puritan soldier in him, and like one of Cromwell's "Ironsides," had gone into battle with a copy of the *Soldier's Pocket Bible* in his boots.

It was the Puritan settlers, indeed, he most admired. "You can more easily prove the perseverance of the saints by these men than by the Bible," he wrote. "When they husked their first harvest of twenty acres of corn they met and thanked God and sung Psalms, and offered prayers. Then they built a church and beside it a schoolhouse, and then a college while they yet lived in log houses covered with clapboard roofs. The God who nourished Jacob when he was small, and Israel on the breast of Egypt, took this great country in his arms and carried it."

There was a natural eloquence in him that had begun to shine.

The more he reflected on the Civil War, the more he saw it in terms of the larger contest between tyranny and freedom—both in the world of his own day and reaching back in time. The epitome of that struggle, it seemed to him, was the Battle of Marathon, which had checked the expansion of the Persian Empire in 490 B.C. That empire had extended its authority "from the Aegean Sea to the Indus, and from the plains of Tartary to the cataracts of the Nile." Eventually, only Greece stood in her way. "Had Greece been conquered all would have been lost," he wrote, but Athens, "the first democracy of which we have any account," the first government "to assert the equality of men . . . marshaled her meager forces and sent them forth . . . demanding 'liberty or death.'" In his view, the "same love of human rights" that had "sustained the patriotic band on the plains of Marathon" had prompted the French Revolution, "commanded at Yorktown," emancipated the Russian serfs, and directed the course of the Civil War.

Webb decided he wanted to teach. In 1866, he applied for admission to Illinois State Normal University, a teachers' college founded a decade before near Bloomington. He wrote an essay titled "The Battle of Marathon" to demonstrate what he could do, was accepted, and enrolled that fall. At the time, the university consisted of one handsomely domed three-story building built on a hill between a cornfield and an abandoned spur of track. Its president was Richard Edwards, a learned man of Calvinist bent who believed in the operation of a divine intelligence in the control of human affairs. In addition to his other duties, Edwards gave a series of lectures on "The Heritage of Culture" that traced "the achievements of history through the character and precepts of great men." Under his direction, Webb embarked on an ambitious, five-year course of study that included English (including rhetoric), math (through trigonometry), science (natural philosophy, astronomy, geography, botany, zoology, and chemistry), philosophy (metaphysics and didactics), education (its history and methods), government (with an emphasis on the Constitution of the United States), history (ancient and modern), the arts (writing, drawing, and vocal music), and languages (Latin and French). Since State Normal was a teachers' college, graduating students also had to have at least two years of supervised teaching under their belts. Webb must have excelled overall, for upon his graduation in 1870, he was immediately taken into the faculty as principal of the Practice School. In subsequent years, he pursued his advanced studies at nearby Illinois Wesleyan, from which he eventually earned a doctorate in history. He married a fellow student, Martha Francis Henry, and started a family of his own.

If education was a passion for him, the ministry was in his blood. Both of his grandparents had been preachers—one Methodist, the other Baptist—and the first two churches in Hutton had been built by their hands. Webb himself had been raised in a moderately religious fashion, and during the war had regularly attended service in camp. But he seems not to have thought of the ministry until 1874, when he suddenly felt the call. He was admitted on trial to the Central Illinois Conference of the Methodist Church, assigned first to Lexington and afterwards to Watseka, Sheldon, Fairbury, Metamora, and other towns. In all of his early pastorates he organized Chautauqua reading circles, evidently believing with John Wesley that he should "press reading upon the people. They cannot grow in grace otherwise." Meanwhile, in 1876 the government, having judged him "disabled from obtaining his subsistence by manual labor" (Pension Certificate No. 145,169), granted him a pension of $12 a month.

Webb rose in the church, was made a presiding elder of the Streator District in 1885, and over the next fifteen years distinguished himself in the administration of Methodist schools, first, as the financial secretary of Illinois Wesleyan; then, as the president of two colleges: Chaddock, in Quincy, Illinois; and Missouri Wesleyan, in Cameron, Missouri (1898–1905). He had come a long way from the young soldier who had tried to learn some grammar on the march.

As a man of local prominence, he was often called on to make speeches on public occasions, on the Fourth of July, for example, or Memorial Day. In one Fourth of July address, delivered in 1896, he touchingly recalled his roots as he tied the day's observance to the land. "It seems providential," he said, "that this festive day should come at this season of the year . . . when the smaller cereals are ripening and being harvested, when a good estimate of what our prosperity is for the year can be made, at the time when men have an hour for rest between the finished cultivation and the gathering of small grain." In speaking of the war, he had no taste for platitudes. One Memorial Day, he told a large crowd: "Especially today we commemorate the dead. And yet I would also have you remember the sacrifices of those soldiers living . . . Many say we ought to forget the past; we ought not to stir up bad blood by services which keep alive the memory of our great fratricidal strife. What? Shall I tell my children that their father gave the three best years of his life to a foolish war? Shall I tell them, 'Your father had an only brother, John, possessed of almost every human virtue, who foolishly threw his life away?' Or, worse still, that Papa found his mangled form foremost in the front, where he had fallen, in battle, for nothing? God forbid! . . . Let us teach [our children] that the men who stayed at home and got rich on the spoils of war, while they talked loud about patriotism . . . are not to be compared in point of true manhood with the men whom they were willing to sacrifice." Moreover, he believed that because in the end the war had been fought for emancipation as well as the Union, that ought to be followed through. From a non-Abolitionist Unionist he had become an enemy to every kind of discrimination, and toward the end of his life even stood in the forefront of the women's suffrage movement, for, as he wrote, he could find no argument to justify the vote for men that wouldn't apply to women too.

Webb's health, impaired by the war, began to fail as he entered his sixties, and in November 1908 he suffered a crippling stroke. Seven months later, on June 20, 1909, he died. He was buried in Oakwood Cemetery in Metamora, Illinois. In a eulogy delivered at his funeral, Joseph Bell, a longtime friend and fellow pastor, said, "Dr. Baker impressed himself on the community in which he labored as a man who had a message in which he absolutely believed . . . His personal character was uncompromisingly honest, and . . . he went straight to the mark he had set, always higher up. He had that in his character which compelled men to believe in him . . . He was a most lovable, noble and manly man."

He also had a fine sense of humor about himself. The story goes that when he first began to court his future wife, he was a bit self-conscious about his weight, having always been a large man physically, even as a soldier in the ranks. One day, when they were at a student social together, the girls were asked to write a rhymed description of their escorts. He roared with laughter when he read:

All flesh is grass—so doth the good Book say—
And grass, when mown, is turned to hay.
When Father Time his scythe to you doth take,
My! What a haystack you will make.

The biblical wit and agrarian grandeur of these lines seem fit for his epitaph.

Postscript

S hortly after he died, a typescript of Webb's war letters was prepared by one of his children with a view to seeing them into
print. That project lapsed, but in September 1917, at the height of
the First World War, a handful of excerpts was anonymously pub-
lished in a sporting magazine called *The Outing* with the professed
hope that their patriotic spirit might stir fresh enlistment in the
ranks. Thereafter, all public knowledge of them dipped below the
horizon as copies of the typescript itself lay buried, a treasured
archive, in the desks of various relatives until in 1998 they came
into this author's hands. They ought to be a public possession and
are here appended in full. Such are the "mystic chords" that bind,
as by this book, "from every battlefield and patriot grave to every
living heart and hearthstone."

One man's remembrance of his great-grandfather's life.

— Benson (Baker) Bobrick
Memorial Day, 2002
Brattleboro, Vermont

PART TWO

The mystic chords of memory, stretching from every battlefield and patriot grave to every living heart and hearthstone, all over this broad land, will yet swell the chorus of the Union, when again touched, as surely they will be, by the better angels of our nature.
— ABRAHAM LINCOLN,
First Inaugural Address

The Civil War Letters of Benjamin W. ("Webb") Baker

COMPANY E, 25TH ILLINOIS
VOLUNTEER INFANTRY REGIMENT

The following letters are reproduced in their entirety, as handed down. A few of them were summarized or abridged by the transcriber; occasionally, a summary appears in the middle of a letter. In one instance, there are two slightly different versions of the same letter, which may indicate that Webb kept an earlier draft of the one he sent. The one surviving letter of Webb's brother, John A. Baker, is also reproduced at the end. Misspellings have been corrected; punctuation, where necessary, amended or supplied. Every once in a while an unintelligible or inscrutable phrase or sentence turns up and has been left as is.

St. Louis, Mo. Aug. 7, 1861

Dear Mother:

I suppose you would like to know why I did not come by home as per agreement—Time would not permit—the company started on Monday (the 4) & I could not return home if I went with it. We arrived at St. Louis late in the evening—got supper at 10 P.M. Capt. Adam's company had only 40 men & was not received so I joined Capt. Taggert's company on the 6th. Am well satisfied with the change.

St. Louis, Mo. Aug. 11, 1861

Dear Grandfather:

We arrived at St. Louis at dark on the fourth & went into camp in the Arsenal. I ask forgiveness for going contrary to your wishes in joining the army—I feel that I have only discharged a duty which as a good citizen I owe to my country, to my friends & to liberty. And now I ask your blessing as with my face to the enemy's land I go forward—as long as this arm has strength to wield a sword or handle a rifle; as long as these feet can carry me forward & these eyes can see to direct my steps I expect to march forward unless they submit to the Constitution & laws. I am already satisfied that a camp life is a hard one & would not advise any of my friends to join the army unless it becomes necessary. We have preaching every Sunday by Rev Mavear who was at Charleston last year—His text today Rev. 13:10 "they that take the sword shall die by the sword."

St. Louis, Mo. Aug. 18, 1861

My Dear Brother:

I will try to give you some of the particulars of soldier life so far as I have tried it. There are 800 on duty in our Regt. Health is good, with the exception of Diarrhea, which is some what inconvenient, though not bad sickness. We don't have more than half enough to eat. I was on guard two nights ago, armed with a pick handle. We drew our blankets yesterday—Had orders to march today at dinner—took down our tents & got all ready at the expense of our dinners. Were ready to march at 1 P.M. when the order came to pitch our tents as before. Drew our muskets about 10 P.M. under great excitement—as soon as the muskets were distributed, a double guard was put out. I was one of 150 that went from our Regt. At head quarters we received 10 rounds of cartridges after which we were posted at 12 P.M. in the Arsenal. We were disappointed, for there was no battle. Stood guard all night with out sleep.

Jefferson City, Mo., Sept. 17, 1861

Dear Mother:

I received yours of the 4th last evening. It has been here, perhaps, several days. We are just in from a ten day's scout. I am tired but send this that you may know I have not forgotten you. How could I forget a Mother that has been as good as you have been to me. I don't remember having said that Isaiah was coming home. I heard the Capt. say, however, that he, James Cartwright & several other boys who are not strong would be sent home. But I don't think any of them will come. Do not look for I. D. till you see him coming. We have plenty of peaches. We, almost, lived on peaches during our scout. I should like to be at your apple cuttings very much. News came since dark that Marshall's cavalry & 500 Irish troops were taken prisoners at Lexington. 80 miles up the river. Now if Gen. Price wants fun let him come down here. We took twelve horses in our scout. Mother can't you write once a week. I love to hear from home so well.

Your affectionate son,
Webb

Jefferson City, Mo., Sept. 21, 1861

Dear Mother:

I have received three letters from you written the last ten days. I gave you the particulars of both scouts. I am prepared to give you a true account of the battle of Lexington. Our boys gained the day. They lost 800 men while the secesh lost 4000. This is the news from Lexington last night at dark. It is all a mistake about Marshal's Cavalry being prisoners. We drew our uniforms this morning & expect to receive our money tomorrow. I am as fat as when I left home. We have plenty to eat such as it is. We have plenty of apples, peaches & cider when we pay for them. Ben Lamb is sick at the Hospital.

Yours with love,
Webb

Jefferson City, Mo., Sept. 24, 1861

My Dear Grandfather:

The money you sent was received for which I am grateful. We drew our uniforms yesterday. They consist of blue jacket & pants & a blue overcoat such as Doctor Lea wears. We have drawn no money yet. We have been expecting it tomorrow for several days. There is 4 months pay due us. It is not the fault of our company officers that we do not get it. We expect to leave here in the morning for Lexington. They have been fighting there for days. We have various reports with regard to their success. News came again to day that Marshall's cavalry are taken prisoners. We are going up 20,000 strong, with Sigel at our head to see the fun. Two companies went up the river, on the "War Eagle," scouting. They were fired on & Lieut. Buckner had his shoulder straps cut off lest he should be selected as an officer & popped over. When they returned he went to the same lady that sewed them on in the first place & told her to sew them on a little stronger.

Direct to Jefferson City as before.

Yours sincerely,

B. W. Baker

Otterville, Mo., Sept. 30, 1861

My Dear Mother:

I send you a line this morning which may be the last as we expect to fight before this reaches you. I am not quite well, but shall be better in a day or two. I am suffering with a hard cold. The prospect, as we think, is that there will be a hard battle in the vicinity of Lexington. It will be the last, perhaps, in this state this winter. If it is and I live I shall be at home some time in the winter if possible. Isaiah is well. Tell Hez & Annie that I should like to see them. Please write soon to

Your affectionate son,

B. W. Baker

Sedalia, Mo., Oct. 13, 1861

My Dear Brother:

Though I have not received a letter from you for a month, yet will I write you again. I wish you would send my watch by B. F. Lamb when he returns. When you write tell me whether any more of the boys have gone to war & whether you hug the girls any, & how the boys & girls get along on an average anyway. We left the Saline Bridge from where I wrote you last & moved up to Otterville 1½ miles. We were there just a week & then came here distance 14 miles. We came up on the cars, but had to walk & push a good part of the way. It took all day. It seems that we start every time on Sunday. We expect to leave here tomorrow, or next day, following after Price. He is now a good ways ahead of us, & I think he will keep ahead, but reports are here that our fleet has taken New Orleans. Isaiah got a letter today from one of his friends in Washington, who says that Gen. Scott has said that we shall all eat our Christmas dinners at home. I am as fat as ever I was, weigh 215 lbs. & think I am the best man in the Regt. Give my love to all.

Goodbye.

B. W. Baker

Warsaw, Mo., Oct. 19, 1861

My Dear Mother:

I wrote John last Sunday in the forenoon. In the afternoon I was detailed with a large number to go out & press teams, we were out two days in which time we pressed enough secesh teams to haul our baggage. We were three days marching to this place, two of which it rained, making it a little disagreeable under foot as well as over head, but we had lots of fun anyway. It is said that we are [with]in 40 miles of Price, who is fortifying. If so perhaps we will have some real fun in a few days. If he keeps on retreating, & we follow, the next time you hear from me I shall be in Arkansas. Hope we will winter in Texas this winter. It is reported that Gen. Lane has captured McCulloch with all his army. Hope it is so. Remember me to all.

Your affectionate son,

B. W. Baker

Springfield, Mo., Nov. 1, 1861

Dear Mother:

I was very glad to hear from home this morning. It is the first time since I left Otterville. We marched from Sedalia 120 miles. Our advance guard had a fight here with Gen. Price's rear guard. 14 of our men were wounded & 15 killed out right. It is said that 100 rebs were killed. I don't see how that could be since our men charged. I was on the battle field two days after the battle. The dead & wounded were taken care of, yet the ground was sprinkled with blood. How queer one feels on a battle field. The feeling is very much the same as that felt on a fourth of July occasion when one hears the fife & drum. Price's camp is only 40 miles from here & we expect to have an engagement in the next five days. So the Col. told us today in a speech, perhaps in two. I almost feel anxious to be in a battle & yet I am almost afraid. I feel very brave sometimes & think if I should be in an engagement, I never would leave the field alive unless the stars & stripes floated triumphant. I do not know how it may be. If there is a battle & I should fall, tell with pride & not with grief that I fell in defense of liberty. Pray that I may be a true soldier.

Yours affectionately,
B. W. Baker

Springfield, Mo., Nov. 3, 1861

Dear Mother:

An opportunity offers & I send you a line, which may be the last. We expect to be marched on to the battlefield before morning. I feel anxious to go. The news is that Gen. Lane is now fighting on the old battle ground where Lyon was killed. The place is 10 miles from here, on Wilson's Creek. The Col. told us on dress parade this evening to pack our knapsacks & be ready for we would be ordered out before morning. I feel very brave now & when we get there, if I don't get weak in the knees shall do some good fighting.

Yours sincerely,
B. W. Baker

Springfield, Mo., Nov. 5, 1861

Mr. E. Adams:

Dear Uncle:

I received your letter today & was glad to hear from home. So Kady is married. Good say I. Well, Uncle, we have traveled, almost all over the state of Missouri since I left home. We have been [with]in one day's march of a fight 5 or 6 times but have not got there yet, & guess we never will. Price escaped from Lexington & came to this place when we again came up with him after a toilsome march of 120 miles. Our advance guard consisting of 250 cavalry charged Price's rear guard & drove them out of town on the 28th of Oct. The report is that the rebels lost 100. The rangers lost 15 killed & 14 wounded. We got here the next day after marching 24 hours without sleep & but little to eat. We have been looking for a fight every day since till today. The news comes that Fremont is relieved by Gen. Hunter & the policy is changed. Fremont is thought unsound. Price is at Wilson's Creek 10 miles away. You know more of the movements than I do.

Respectfully yours,

B. W. Baker

Springfield, Mo., Nov. 11, 1861

My Dear Mother:

Yours of the 10th came the next day after I wrote you. That was a good day for letters. I had one from Albert, one from Uncle Elijah, one from John & one from Tom Gill. I visited the battlefield at Wilson's Creek, where Gen. Lyon was killed. Hats, shirts, coats & clothing of all kinds are scattered all over the ground. I saw the skull of one poor fellow who had been sent to his long home in a hurry by a ball entering just above the eye. Price has left the state and we expect to start for St. Louis in the morning. From St. Louis we go to Kentucky or Tennessee. The boys are all well except a few have the measles.

Ever your son,

B. W. Baker

Rolla, Mo., Dec. 8, 1861

My Dear Brother:

I got a letter from you & Dave this morning. Glad that you are getting along so nicely with the girls. Squeeze them some for me. I had the measles like sixty, but am all right now. I am very well satisfied with my position, but let me tell you there is nothing desirable in a soldier's life & I would advise all that are at home to stay there for the present because there are more here than there is a place for this winter. I don't expect I will get to come home till my time is up but I can't help it. How does Berket & Cady stand it? Does it make them look very lank?

Your affectionate brother,
Webb

Rolla, Mo., Dec 14, 1861

Dear Mother:

[Letter summarized by transcriber]: This letter is about the last day's march before reaching this camp—taking the measles—going to St. Louis—dying 5 a day—fare there & here—rumors of the camp—such as that we go to St. Louis to Kentucky to Washington—that we shall be discharged & others of like character.

Rolla, Mo., Dec. 16, 1861

Cousin Louisa:

I was very much surprised by your letter. I enjoyed it so much. I have been half over the state of Missouri since I left home, after "old Price" but the old fox is too cunning for our Dutch Gen. (Sigel) so we have given him up & are going to Kentucky to try our skill in the cane brakes. I have seen some pretty hard times, went hungry a good many days, slept many a night on the ground with a stone for a pillow & went some nights without sleep. But that is nothing for a soldier. We are as jovial a set of fellows as ever you saw. We don't look for easy times here— [Transcriber's note: Description of measles hospital.] Let me hear from you again soon.

Your cousin,
Webb

Rolla, Mo., Dec. 16, 1861

[Transcriber's summary]: Letter to Em Johnston. Minute description of guard duty length of beat, time of standing, pass, countersign, mounting of guard, how to get the countersign & c.

Rolla, Mo., Dec. 20, 1861

[Transcriber's summary]:
Letter to Mother:

Sent her a picture to demonstrate that I am in good health. Conclude not to go home Christmas—think if Eng[land] pitches in we will get to stay three years without any trouble. Smallpox in the Regt. Move away from the rest of the troops. Advise Mother not to come on uncertainties. Get the daily papers now—Lincoln going to free the "niggers"—don't believe it. Don't care if he does.

Rolla, Mo., Dec. 28, 1861

Dear Grandparents:

I have not received an answer to the last letter that I wrote to you but as the mail is somewhat uncertain I will write again. I reckon there is as merry a set of fellows here as ever you saw, what there is left of us. There is now but 300 able for duty out of 900 when we left Sedalia. There are new cases of smallpox every day. As fast as one gets well another is taken. No wonder there is sickness here for this is the poorest country in the world. Willow Creek is a Paradise compared to it. Our camp is in a ravine between two high rocky, shrubby hills, desolate beyond compare, & this is a fair specimen of this part of the state. Nobody ever did live here & nobody ever can, but Uncle Sam's boys & they would starve if he did not send them something to eat. We expect to stay here this winter, are building quarters that we may be comfortable. I hope to come home a few days sometime this winter.

With love to all I am
as ever your affectionate grandson,
Webb

Rolla, Mo., Dec. 31, 1861

Dear Mother:

I am glad to acknowledge the receipt of your kind letter. You ought not to indulge in your lonesome spells, they render you unhappy & everybody with whom you associate, at least to some extent. My happiest moments are spent in thinking of home & how I may surprise you by coming in unexpected. I may get to come home this winter though there is no such prospect now. The rumor is now that we shall start for Springfield in a few days, all that are able to go. I am booked as one, even though my health is not so good as it has been sometimes. The weather is pleasant & warm, & we are very comfortable in our new quarters. There is a great deal of solid comfort in the wild rough life of a soldier. It is true there are a great many hardships to be endured, but those I expected to find, & in them I find pleasure in the tendency they have to develop the unselfish in one's character. It seems to me that they develop the real characteristics of the highest type of manhood, yet the camp cannot be compared to home. Home [is] only valued when deprived of.

Yours,
Webb

Rolla, Mo., Jan. 13, 1862

[Transcriber's summary]: To Mother, telling how we live in our new quarters. Reviewing my studies with Spence, Brown's grammar and arithmetic & c. Smallpox in camp—a great deal of sickness—Regt. ought to be disbanded—[Lieutenant] Sallie at home recruiting—if boys don't want to see the elephant better stay at home—have all the war I want—

Rolla, Mo., Jan. 19, 1862

[Transcriber's summary]: To Mother. Account of camp life—supposition that we will remain here because of ill health of the regt. notwithstanding the rumor that we are to go. Mumps & smallpox bad—boys suffer in the cold—never so poor in my life but getting fat. Nearly all the Lalsbury boys sick but none bad.

Rolla, Mo., Jan. 26, 1862

[Transcriber's summary]: To Mother. Sabbath morning—acknowledge the receipt of a letter—very thankful for it. I. D. very well indeed—as fat as a buck but can't jump so far. Health generally improved—boys in fine spirits—drill three hours per day—most of the troops gone to Springfield to meet Price who is there with not to exceed 10,000 men—talk of our going—don't believe it—wish it were so—tired of camp—expect to be at home in a year from time of starting—prospect good—shan't come before—want to stay when I do come.

Rolla, Mo., Jan. 28, 1862

[Transcriber's summary]: To Brother John—Health of Regt. much improved—Marching order for Springfield in the morning—Price there with 10,000 men—certain of a battle inside of two weeks—very brave—fear for the boys because of the change from warm quarters to open air sleeping & living—hope for the best since the climate is somewhat warmer than in Illinois. Nothing more than a frost since New Year's. If we thrash Price be at home in June—surely by the 4th so as to have a big time at its celebration.

Rolla, Mo., Feb. 1, 1862

[Transcriber's summary]: To Uncle E. Adams. Beautiful morning—Snow two inches deep. Sublimity of landscape, standing on a hill where you have a view—winter warm—muddy—troops mired down between here & the Gasconade River—life pulled out of the mules—120 wagons mired down—35 Regt. Two weeks going to Lebanon 60 miles distant—rumored that we will start in a few days—doubt it if the mud continues. Great deal of sickness—health better than it was—boys spoiling for a fight—remarkably brave myself since there is no danger—have a great deal of fun—Sigel thinks if he has the 3rd Missouri & 25th Illinois he can whip two to one—Minear not dead—neither is his wife—Studying grammar with Spence—Minear referee—Spence a fine fellow—son of Baker Spence—send me Bullion's Grammer—Send this letter by Jim Lake whom you knew in Col.—He can tell you more than I can write.

Sharon, Mo., Feb. 7, 1862

Dear Mother:

Last Sunday the first for a long time that I have not written to you. Got orders to march Saturday night & Sunday morning took up our beds & walked—had to carry all our clothing & blankets—marched 12 miles—snowed all day—went into camp scraped the snow away—ground so rough we could not get the snow all away—pitched our tent & put up our stove—we have sheet iron stoves to warm the tent—make them comfortable while the fire lasts—stoves & tent soon cool when the fire is out—ate our suppers & went to bed—in the morning found that the warm stove had thawed the snow left in the tent & made it muddy—the fire going out it was so cold that it froze so that some of our blankets were frozen fast—marched 15 miles the next day—much of the same experience as that of the first day only did not snow. On the third day march started before daylight—crossed the Gasconade that day—camped as before after going 13 miles—rained that night—took the snow off—cold & froze up the next morning—next day marched 10 miles & went into camp—thawed all day & was very muddy—cut brush to sleep on to keep us out of the mud—rained nearly all night—started early next morning—mud shoe mouth deep—marched 11 miles & camped 1 mile south of Lebanon—froze hard last night & today is the coldest I have seen this winter—the boys are in fine spirits—we expect to do some brown fighting when we get to Springfield. Price is there with 20,000 men. We talk of giving them some blue pills & if they don't give me a dose I expect the scare will serve as well for physic. I. D. is writing.

Love to all, especially the girls,

Believe me ever your son,

Webb

Osage Springs, Ark., Feb. 23, 1862

Dear Mother:

Have not had an opportunity to write to you since we left Lebanon—We have been making forced marches in pursuit of Price, but did not catch him. He is largely reinforced since he got into this state. We are waiting for recruits & as soon as they come up we are going to follow him to the Gulf, or catch him. The boys are generally well & anxious to march. This is very good country—the climate nice & warm—I like it better than I do cold climates. [Transcriber's summary: Tell the story of going after milk, which happened on the day the letter is written.]

Benton Co., Ark., March 10, 1862
Camp on the Battlefield.

Dear Mother:

Through a well directed train of kind providence, I am again permitted to write you. I am well. The boys generally are well. Henry Beevers is gaining slowly. I don't believe he ever will get well till he gets in better spirits. We enjoyed the coveted privilege of going into a battle. We were in camp on a farm, five miles south of Bentonville. On the 5th. It was quite cold. The 37th suttler brought a barrel of whiskey to camp. A good many of the boys got drunk. On the morning of the 6th at 1 o'clock we marched. We were just off of a spree & in poor condition to march. Gen. Sigel got many curses for ordering us out so early. We thought there was no danger & we were very tired & sleepy. Every time we halted the boys tumbled down & went to sleep even though it was snowing hard. It quit snowing at daylight & the sun shone brightly all day. We got to our camp on Sugar Creek about 11 miles from Bentonville northwest, about 12 o'clock. We were stacking arms when the order came to about face & march at quick time to reinforce Sigel. The rebels drove him out of Bentonville. Though we were very tired we were rested [revived] by the excitement of a prospect of a battle. We soon got back 4 miles. We met Gen. Sigel & cheered him & then returned to camp. Slow time. We had nothing to eat all day & all day before because of our spree & so we were very hungry. The provisions what we had (flour alone) was in the wagons & did not reach us till 11 o'clock at night & it was twelve before we got anything to eat. Our teamster brought a keg of lard so we had shortening for our biscuit. We slept well the remainder of the night with our guns for pillows & the canopy for a tent. We were up early & got our breakfast & then provided two days rations of biscuits in our haversacks; ate our dinner & fell into line at command with one blanket each. We were glad to hear the command. We had listened all day to the continual rattle of musketry & roar of cannon & were anxious to join the fray. We spent the time from one o'clock till eight hunting a place to fight. Over hills & hollows, through brush & over fields we went from point to point. Once or twice we halted while our battery threw a few shell[s]. At eight, it being dark, we settled down for the night, on the picket line. Many of the boys had thrown off their blankets & consequently suffered for it was very cold. Part watched at a time & the rest slept cold or no cold for we had slept but little for three days & two nights. We remained in our place till 3 o'clock in the morning when we were relieved & taken to a place where we could build fires & warm ourselves. We remained there till eight o'clock. Prisoners that we took that morning said Price made them a speech before the battle began in which he told them that a half hour's fighting would give them the victory, that we were surrounded (& we were) & could not hold out long. At eight they opened the ball expecting to have the victory soon. In 15 minutes we were on the field supporting the artillery. There were 30 pieces of artillery about one hundred yards behind us firing as fast as they could. The rebels were firing at us with a large number also, the shot & shell rained thick around us, the air was full of blue streaks marking the track of shot & shell flying in both directions. For two hours the duel continued. The rebel guns were finally silenced & then we advanced in the face of the enemy at a double quick first east a quarter [mile] across a field & then north a quarter [mile] through thick brush. The rebel shell shot the tops off of the brush but fortunately overshot us. Their guns were again silenced & then we double quicked across the field a quarter [mile] farther, again the grape whistled over us, again they were silenced. We stripped to the canteen, fixed bayonets & again started on a bayonet charge into a hazel thicket. We advanced into the thicket about a hundred yards when the musketry opened on us at 70 yards. Such a rattling of musketry & such a whistling of bullets I do not want to hear again. Of course we did our best to return the compliment. For 15 minutes the rattling & whistling & shaking of brush continued & then the rebs skedaddled & the victory was ours, after a three days battle. Our regt., I have been speaking in this letter only of its movements, lost 4 killed & 20 wounded. Mike Waltrip of our company was killed. Enoch Frost was wounded in the wrist. His arm was broken. Two or three others were slightly wounded. I received a slight flesh wound on my back between the left shoulder blade & the backbone. I was on my knees with a cartridge in my teeth when the ball passed over my head or rather two balls, one cutting the skin right on the shoulder blade & the other took quite a large piece of flesh out between the shoulder blade & the backbone. I would rather the wound had been somewhere else. My back is so sore I can hardly write. Please send me some postage stamps. Write soon & often to your affectionate son,

B. W. Baker

Camp Wilfley, Benton Co., Arkansas, March 17, 1862
Dear Cousin Amos:

Your kind favor of Feb. 7 is just at hand. It was perused with pleasure. I was anxious to hear from home. Besides it gives me something to do. We are in Dixie, in a land of heathendom! We do not get any papers or anything else to read except now & then a letter from a friend up in God's land. This life is harder on me at present from the fact that I am not able to drill, or take part with the boys in their sports. My wound received in the late battle at Pea Ridge is the cause of my inability. Though the wound is doing well as could be expected & I am ready for another battle, whenever necessity calls for it, yet I am hardly well enough to do anything except from necessity. I do not desire to go into another battle but necessity causes us to do undesirable things sometimes. Battles are becoming more frequent now. I was out at the dress parade & listened to a long letter of praise & thanks for our conduct as a regt. in the battle. You have little conception of soldiers' feelings when he receives the approbation of an able general, one that is greatly beloved. After three days of cold March weather's hard fighting during which time we had little rest & little to eat & no time to warm; after the hardships of a winter campaign, covering a thousand miles march, in the midst of winter's exposures, over the rocks & hills of Mo. & Ark. After having been shut out from society & deprived of its luxuries; after having been exposed to all the dangers & diseases incident to a winter's campaign & battle, then to receive the approbation of our commander for having discharged every known duty, I tell you, it makes a fellow feel well. And the shouts of respect & confidence that go up from the various regts. as this approbation is read to them, ought to make the general feel well. Gen. Sigel says we shall pitch our tents on the banks of the Arkansas, ere two more weeks have passed. I expect to go with the regt. We are expecting a speedy peace. What is the prospect. We common soldiers know nothing. You at home know more of the situation than we do. Though we know we thrashed the rebs. at Pea Ridge. You will have to pay for this epistle for such a thing as a stamp was never known in this heathen land. The boys are generally well. Love to all, write soon. With kindest regards,

B. W. Baker

Camp Hoffman, Barry Co., Mo., March 21, 1862

Dear Mother:

My lame back is getting well as fast as could be expected; & I can use my gun well enough now, to give the secesh another turn, though I would rather compromise if it could be done honorably. We get no news here except now & then a rumor. We hear today that the whole number killed & wounded at Pea Ridge was 1,331. I suppose you have heard it long ago. We are waiting here in Southeast Mo. for the coming of Kansas troops, & for Grant to take Memphis, & then with his cooperation we expect to settle the mess shortly. That is the wind work at least. Ours is the crack regt. down here. What kind of reputation has it in the land of its nativity. Please send me a paper with the account of the battle in it. The last letter I got from you was dated Feb. 18. Got one from Weeden dated March 1st. The mail has been robbed from both ways by marauding bands. I sent a dollar for stamps did you get it? Did you get the letter that told of my big scare when I ran into the Texas battery? We have had real March weather for the last 24 hours. I am almost ashamed to read this letter, it is so poor. When a fellow has nothing to write he can write nothing.

Your affectionate son,
B. W. Baker

Camp Hoffman, Barry Co., Mo., March 28, 1862
Dear Mother:

It is rather discouraging. Every letter I get complains that you get no letters from me. I write every week. I get a letter once a month. The latest is from John dated March 12th. I received the socks you sent me today. Am very thankful. Was just out. Threw away my last yesterday. Clothing is scarce. We received our pay yesterday. We are camped 12 miles north of the battlefield. The boys are all in fine spirits. The rumor is that we are going to Little Rock as soon as Grant takes Memphis. But I was talking with Major Nodine yesterday & he says it is his opinion that we will never be in another engagement; & that he would sooner think that we would be ordered back to St. Louis. We are in fine spirits because we think that we will be at home by the middle of the summer. I think you will hear me bragging at a large rate by the time your apples are ripe. Don't then be down hearted. Look on the bright side. Don't borrow trouble. The secesh bullet has not been molded that is to kill me. A fellow stands a poor chance to get killed. We were exposed to secesh fire for four hours, & only three were killed & 17 wounded in our regt. My back is nearly well. I never felt better in my life. I am getting fat. The boys are all well. Now cheer up Mother, all will be well in a few weeks I hope.

Your affectionate son,
Webb

Camp Hoffman, Barry County, Mo., March 30, 1862
Dear Brother:

Yours of March 12 came duly to hand. Many thanks. The best letter I have received from you. The weather is warm & nice; it makes me feel like getting ready to go plowing. I never intend to plow any more. I shall learn to be a machinist when I am through with the army. Our orderly Sergeant is one & has told me about it. I would like to have you learn it, too. We have been on general inspection this morning. The sight of the army on a great field amid martial display is truly sublime, & yet it fills the mind with excitement & fully qualifies the soldier for deeds of rashness. Gen. Sigel is sick, & Gen. Curtis inspected the army. After returning to camp I went to church & heard Philip Minear preach a very interesting sermon on the birth of Christ. I got hold of, & have been reading the last few days, the life of Bonaparte & his Marshals. I got the book from the orderly. If what I have been reading is true, the opinion I had formed of the *Noble Chieftain* is very incorrect. Instead of being an ambitious tyrant, he was the noble defender of France. And a greater warrior or genius history gives no account of. My wound is nearly well. It would do me the most good in the world to be at home about this time. John, do tell if there is any prospect of closing this war. I am getting tired of this kind of life. If you will believe my racket there is no fun in this kind of life. We seldom hear from home & we get no papers. I don't know how long we will remain here. I presume not long. I don't know which way we will go when we leave. Give my best respects to the girls, & believe me your own brother,

Love to grandfather & grandmother,

B. W. Baker

P.S. Here is ten dollars. All I have saved since I came into the service.

B. W. Baker

Camp Hoffman, Barry Co., Apr. 4, 1962

Dear Mother:

I am well. Health is generally good. The boys are in fine spirits. They spend much of the time in playing ball, & other healthful plays. We have rumors that Price has gone to Miss. & that we shall follow. Hope it is so for then we can hear from home once & a while. I. D. is sick with a hard cold on the lungs caught doing the battle. He is getting better. Did John get the ten dollars I sent him? Send my long point notes to Wiles for collection. I send a little book with this letter. Please preserve it for me.

Your affectionate son,
Webb

Forsyth, Tany County, Mo., Apr. 11, 1862

Dear John:

We left camp Hoffman Apr. 5, came up to Cassville & thence eastward 9 miles where we camped. The next morning we marched up a hollow whose sides were precipitous rocks 3 or 400 feet high with but now & then a place it would be possible to climb out. The bottom was very narrow, wide enough for one wagon to pass, more or less. I began to think that we had all got into the narrow path way if it was very crooked & it certainly was. Almost noon we began to ascend the mountain. Took us till three o'clock to get to the top. There are beautiful pine forests here. Spruce, the tallest timber I ever saw. How they ever grew is more than I can tell. Some of them look like they come up out of solid rock. It took till night to get down the hill, we then camped on flat creek, about the size of [the] Hurricane [River]. We marched 25 miles without anything to eat. I slipped out to a house & got my supper. There are half dozen houses where we camped. The only houses we saw all day. When I got back the boys had got some meal & killed a hog, & had their suppers ready. Provisions are very scarce. We rested the next day & all went a fishing. The next day we marched 13 miles to Galena the county seat of Stone County. Here we crossed the James River. We made a bridge of wagons. Strung them across the river, took out the endgates, & laid in rails to splice them, letting them stand eight feet apart. It took 25 wagons to make the bridge. It took the troops all night to cross. To start with, in the morning we waded Flat Creek a little more than knee deep, & then as the day before we marched up hill & down, along deep ravines & over small creeks wading them. I think this has been the most interesting march that we have had. We expect to cross the river in the morning & go to Batesville; & then to Pocahontas to fight Price. Nothing certain about it. We hear that Island No. 10 is taken, & that Gen. Shields has gained a decisive victory at Winchester. Our news is only rumor. Have not heard from you for more than a month, or just a month. Did you get the ten dollars.

Love to grandfather & grandmother
—your affectionate brother,
Webb

[Transcriber's summary]: Wrote to Mother on the 12 of April a very similar letter. Talked about the same things. They are so alike that I will not copy here.

Forsyth, Mo., Apr. 20, 1862

Dear Brother:

We have been here since about the 11, waiting for it to stop raining. For four days it rained, not hard all the time but a good deal of the time, & it has rained a good deal since. It is raining today. I don't know when it will quit. We seem to be cut off from all communication & living on what we can forage. Keep writing, anyway. I will get a letter from you after while.

Truly your brother,
Webb

Forsyth, Taney Co., Mo., Apr. 21, 1862

Dear Mother:

I am well; all the boys are well but Brink Brandenberg. He is very sick with lung fever. Out of his head most of the time. He has been sick four days. I am going to stay with him tonight. Most of the troops have left here for Cape Girardeau they say. We are expecting to remain here for a while. We have had little to eat, & poor at that, corn meal & blue beef. We heard today of the capture of Island No. 10 & also of the victory at Pittsburg Landing; & more yet that McClellan had taken Richmond. These are only rumors, though with regard to the first two, I understand [General Samuel] Curtis has received official word from [General Henry] Halleck. We have no report yet from the Pea Ridge battle. Can't you send me a paper with it in. We have marching orders to go eastward as soon as the creeks are favorable. There has been a four days rain. This is a beautiful morning. Mother I have not received a letter from you since the one that came with the socks by the hand of Kress Walker. I write every week, to keep you in good spirits, if you do not get my letters it is not my fault. Did you get the dollar I sent for stamps?

Affectionately yours,
Webb

Camp Salem, Fulton Co., Arkansas, Apr. 30, 1862

Dear Mother:

I wrote you on the 21st from Forsyth, Mo. Today we muster for pay in the Suburbs of Salem, Fulton Co., Arkansas. Health is good & the boys in fine spirits. I. D. is getting so fat he can hardly see. Brandenberg died after eight days sickness. We marched from Forsyth seven days. We averaged 18 miles a day. The country is so rough the trains move slow & it takes all day to go a little distance. Expect to go southward tomorrow. The weather is very fine & we have lots of fun. Have had no letter from you or John since the 12th of March. A month seems a long time. I suppose it can't be helped.

Your affectionate son,
Webb

Camp near Batesville, Arkansas, May 5, 1862

Dear Brother:

I am on picket today & take this opportunity of writing. On picket we do not have to walk but sit still. As I write my mind goes back to our merry days at home. How much I used to enjoy your coming when I lived on the Sutton place. Do you remember those times, or are you so full of present pleasure that old times are forgotten. We were at Salem two days. We left there at 2½ A.M. May 2nd, & marched 25 miles. We did not get to bed till after dark. We rested finely till one when we were called out & started out again. We marched five miles before daylight. This is a pretty good country. Corn up & plowed once. Wheat is in head & there is a pretty good prospect for something to live on. Arkansas is a better country than Mo. We got to Batesville at dark marching 38 miles. I was very tired. We came out of the way 10 miles or more. Tom Devericks has just got back. He told me about your exhibition & how well you & Tishey Bensley did it. Send a letter in response to this.

Yours truly,
Webb

Love to grandfather & grandmother,

Webb

On the Tennessee River, May 23, 1862

Dear Bro. John:

I was glad of the few lines that you sent by Lieut. Salee—I had not heard from you before since we left Rolla—since that time we have traveled 900 miles over a very rough country. We have traveled all kinds of weather, at all times of night & under all kinds of circumstances. Yesterday we changed our mode of traveling—left Cape Girardeau at noon—left Cairo this morning—we will get to Fort Henry tonight & to Pittsburg Landing Sunday night if not hindered in any way. Expect we will have it hot down there—but the butternuts will have a good time when they run against the Pea Ridge boys. It is raining & the paper blots so I can't write any more now. Boys all well & in good spirits. Hope this will find you well. Please write soon to your affectionate brother,

Webb

P.S. I got my pay today, & for fear of not having a chance better than this, I send you $20.

Corinth, Miss., June 1, 1862

Dear Mother:

I should have written as soon as we got here but was hindered by reason of the fact that an order prevents mail from going out. We were four days coming from Cape Girardeau to the landing. We came on the steamboat Henry Clay. [Transcriber's note: That was the last trip the Henry Clay made. It sank before it got back.] We moved on to the line the next day & waited for three days momentously & anxiously expecting a battle. Now & then a shot kept us stirred up. The pickets were firing all the time. On the night of the 30th the firing ceased;

& the next day we found the rebs. gone—so we marched in & took possession, was not that home. They left tents camp equipage, guns & everything. We were told that they were on the point of starvation, but they have plenty of provisions left anyway in the camp. Pope is after them & the report says that he has many prisoners. I wish he would get all of them. I got the letter you sent by T. Devericks & one from John by Lieut. Salee—Give my love to all the pretty girls for I don't expect to see them soon.

Truly yours,
Webb

June 6, 1862

Dear Mother:

I have not received a letter from you since the Pea Ridge battle—I suppose it is not your fault. I. D. has written today. He is well. I have been down to the 38th Ill. to see Joe Neal. I should not have written today but we have orders to cook three days rations & so may be on the march & not have a chance to write soon again. We are having good times & plenty of fun. Tell Mary [Webb's stepsister] I am obliged for her long letter. Love to all.

Truly your son,
B. W. Baker

Jacinto, Miss., July 6, 1862

Dear Mother:

Since I wrote you last we have been out toward Memphis. We made a kind of circuit. We were out five days. We are constantly on the move. Though we do not go far, we keep going. The dust is shoe mouth deep. We got in on the 4th. I should have written immediately but have been quite sick with fever & ague & diarrhea—but am all right now & expect to march with the regt. at 3 P.M. The capt. says we are to go to Va. We hear that the Pea Ridge gen., I mean Gen. Sigel, made the grand charge at Richmond. We made Beauregard get out of Miss. & if the Pea Ridge boys go to Va., Jeff [Davis] will have to get from Richmond. Please Mother, send me a letter. It seems a long

time since I had one from you. I. D. is well, so is all the boys—
John's letters are so short—I wish he would write long ones.

With kindest regards to all,
B. W. Baker

Jacinto, July 11, 1862

Dear Mother:

When I wrote you before we were on the eve, so said the
capt., of starting to Va. May go yet though the prospect now is
that we will stay in camp. Most of the boys better satisfied. I
would rather go every day even if we only went 10 miles &
back, so they would make us believe we were going some
place. I get so lazy laying in camp—I am sure to get the blues.
Prof. Wilkerson of Marshal College is the chaplain of the 21
Regt. Leroy Willison & Rule Bostick are both in the regt.! All
well.

Truly yours,
Webb

Jacinto, July 20, 1862

Dear Mother:

This is Sabbath & in the afternoon the boys are in their tents
or shelters from the scorching rays of the sun, for I tell you it
does scorch down here. But it rained today & is cloudy & so not
so bad. It rains about three times a week & then the dust gets
shoe mouth deep between times. I think this country must be
like the Sand Prairie—it is dry enough to plough in an hour after the rain. We did not go to Va. after all, but simply took a
scout. I suppose we will remain here this winter, but can't tell.
We really know nothing about it, no difference what the rumor
may be. How many more men can old Coles Co. turn out? Tell
Dave Adams this is a good business & that he had better go. He
is footloose & every man who can ought to go. They are all
needed & the sooner they go the better. Boys all well. Love to
the girls.

Truly yours,
Webb

Jacinto, July 26, 1862

Dear Mother:

Glad to get your letter. You don't know how much I enjoyed it. You need not fear my joining the regulars. The time has passed when I can do it. If I could I would sometimes lock, but not now. My sickness as is usual was of short duration. My health is very good now. The weather is extremely hot. Thermometer stands at 98 in the shade. We get up at 3 A.M. get breakfast & scrape & clean our tents & yards & ground & then drill an hour & a half—that brings us to 6 A.M. By that time it is so hot that we hunt the shade till evening when we have supper, drill & dress parade. This is all we do & we are so lazy that we count it a killing job. I am sorry that we did not get to go to Richmond. I suppose we will remain here through the hot season unless it becomes extremely necessary to move. I. D. is well & the rest of the boys. Hope to hear from you soon.

Truly,
Webb

Jacinto, Miss., Aug. 2, 1862

Dear Bro. John:

I am just off of picket guard. Today is my rest day. We are on guard every other day. I will answer yours of the 22nd. With regard to your going into the army. I know that somebody must go; but I can hardly consent to let you go. You are my only brother & somehow I have forebodings for you. I am strong & tough you know & can stand it. And then it seems as if it would not be right to leave grandfather & grandmother alone. Soldiering is hard work & dangerous by reason of exposure. Still the country must be saved. I guess you may exercise your own judgment about coming. Hope we will both get through all right.

Tell the girls I am all right so far—I hear that you are hugging a Miss Haddock. Write soon & tell me the news of home.

Truly your brother,
Webb

Iuka, Miss., Aug. 15, 1862

Dear Brother:

We got our pay today & I send you twenty dollars. All quiet on the Potomac as far as I know. Health is good among us. The weather is extremely warm. We are in the pleasantest camp we have ever been in. I am getting more than fat. I weigh more than 200 lbs.

Your Brother,

Webb

Across the River from East Port, Tenn., Aug. 21, 1862

Dear Mother:

I was glad to hear from you once more. I should have answered immediately, but we marched. We came here yesterday & will remain perhaps another day. The rest of the division came down today & is crossing over from East Port. We are headed for somewhere. You were mistaken about Joe Neal. He has not returned to his regt. & I think he never will.

You think the time long. It has grown into a year. I expected to be at home in three months, when I left, but think now that it will take three years anyway. The first three months seemed longer than all the time seems now. Time goes very fast when we are on the move. I. D. is well. Health among the soldiers is good. There is hardly a sick man in the whole division of eight regt. I saw Leroy Willison & Role Bostick this morning. [Transcriber's note: They belong to the 21st Ills. Vol. or the 38th.] They are well. They send regards to grandfather & [grand]mother. Bragg is reported in our vicinity with a large army. We may have a fight one of these days.

Webb.

Murfreesboro, Tenn., Sept. 1, 1862

Dear Mother:

Just as I expected. We were headed somewhere. We left East Port on the 23 ult. & came up via Florence, Lawrenceburg, Spring Hill & Franklin to this place. This is a beautiful country, & seems to have been a flourishing country. There are marks of progress. But everything is at a stand still now except war. That is progressing. The report is here today that Pope was driven back, but that finally he has defeated the reb, they losing twice as many as we, & that they are retreating, & the army after them commanded by Gen. Sigel. If he does not bring them to time, it is no use for any other man to try.

It is rumored that our forces have gained a victory at Baton Rouge & that Buell has gained a victory at Chattanooga, taking 7000 prisoners. It is too good to be true. There is also a rumor that we are on our way to Cumberland Gap to help Nelson dress Kirby Smith—Rosecrans & Sherman are said to be after Price at Tupola, & the remainder of the army of the Miss. is making every exertion to take in Armstrong. Such a general move ought to be made & if it were the Southern confederacy would soon go up & the war end.

We started early this morning & have marched 20 miles already today. This is the 7th day in succession. We are all well.

Truly yours,
B. W. Baker

Nashville, Tenn., Sept. 7, 1862

Dear Mother:

This Sabbath morning gives me one more opportunity for writing to you. Inspection is just over. Preaching in 15 minutes. I want to attend & so will write short. Our supposed fight at Murfreesboro was a retreat to Nashville. We left M. on the evening of the first, after I wrote you last. We left at 5 P.M. & got to Nashville the next day at 10 o'clock—distance 30 miles making the distance from Franklin in a little more than a day 50 miles. I was very tired. It is said that there are 60,000 troops here. It is also said that a large force of rebs. under Bragg is close at hand & a battle imminent. All the country from here to Lawrenceburg is certainly as pretty as it can be, & we found plenty of corn, apples, peaches, melons, sweet potatoes, & everything else that is good on which we have lived. We are going across the river towards Louisville, instead of to preaching, so the Major just now said. We move as soon as the division now crossing is over. We are all well. Don't know or care where we will be by next Sabbath, so I am well.

Truly,
Webb

Perryville Battle Ground, Oct. 11, 1862

Oh, Mother; how can I say it! But I must!! John is dead!!! He was killed on the battlefield on the 8th inst. in one of the hottest engagements of the war—he was shot in two places. The balls must have struck him at the same instant—one entered his left side at the waistband & passing through his heart came out under his right arm. The other struck him in the neck under the jaw & near the jugular vein & passed up into his brain. Either of the balls would have killed him instantly. He evidently never moved after he fell, nor at all only to fall for his arms were as if he had been holding his gun to shoot. I suppose he was at the time the balls struck him. I was on the right of the battle field & he on the left. I did not know that he was on the field at all till the next day. There was only a skirmish on the right—but on the left it was very hot. Crocket Neal was killed a half mile from the line of battle in the retreat. I suppose a stray ball must have struck him. It went into the back of his head & did not pass through. He fell on his face & apparently never moved. Anthony Cox was killed. Anthony was shot through both legs just above the knees. The legs were both broken. He was not killed instantly, but doubtless soon bled to death. He must have suffered. He attempted to crawl off of the field—he got back about 8 or 10 feet from where he fell. There was an agony look on his face. There were two others of the company killed—I do not know them—Robert Eardsley, John Jones & Calvin Moore were wounded, & some other of the company whom I do not know. I had permission from Capt. Taggert & helped to bury the boys & marked the place. I send you a lock of John's hair. Everything was taken from his pockets but his Testament. John died like a man & a soldier at his post & in the front rank. Would I had died in his stead—my only, my true & noble hearted brother. What a great vicarious sacrifice our homes & country are costing. How many noble hearted brothers. I can't write more. God bless & sustain you in this great bereavement. I sent Bige Neal a lock of Crocket's hair.

Truly your son,

Webb

Oct. 13, 1862

Dear Mother:

I am very lonesome. While John was living though I only saw him once in a whole year, I was not lonesome. But now he is gone. I feel as if you & Mr. Moore must come & see I. D. & me when we get into camp. The boys of Capt. Wylie's company not mentioned in my last letter are well. Ham was left at Louisville sick—have not heard from him. It is reported that Bragg will make a stand at Richmond in this state (KY). If he does perhaps we will clean him out entirely, I wish it might be so & that the war might close but the prospect is poor it seems to me. We are having plenty to eat & easy marches now. I send this with I. D.

Love to all,
Webb

Bowling Green, Ky., Nov. 4, 1862

Dear Mother:

I am glad to be permitted to write you once more. We expected to get our pay while we were here, but no such good luck. We have not received our tents yet. We have had no tents since we left Miss. When Mr. Moore was with us it seemed hard we had no tent. I have been thinking about it since Mr. Moore left & believe now that the weather is so cool John might be taken home. If Mr. Moore will do it I will pay for it. Have not seen or heard from the 123rd since he left.

If we go into winter quarters I want you to come & see us for I don't expect to come home till my time is out.

I have written in a hurry, we leave in a few minutes for Nashville.

Truly your son,
Webb

Nashville, Nov. 13, 1862

Dear Mother:

Your long letter of the 31st ult. came yesterday & I was glad enough to get it, though I had heard from another source that you were well. John Jenkins was the last to speak to John. They were standing together in the front rank & did not hear the order to fall back. The company was back 50 yards when Jenkins told John to come on. John replied he would give them one more load. He was sober & thoughtful on the day of battle more than usual so the boys said, but so are all soldiers who have any sense. I am resigned to my fate whatever it may be. [Transcriber's note: The last sentence is not thoughtful.] Our tents came today. If we could stay here this winter, it would be a delightful place for you to visit us. There is no prospect of the war ending—I wish there would be a great general move & that the rebellion would be crushed out—it seems to me that it could be done.

We are all well.

Truly yours,
B. W. Baker

Nashville, Tenn., Dec. 2, 1862

Dear Mother:

We are just in from a five days scout down the river. We marched in the roads 130 miles. We had a pleasant time as far as weather & country is concerned except last night—it rained all night & we had no shelter for we took no tents. However, we built large fires with rails—they burn first rate. On the scout we had plenty of fresh pork, mutton, turkey & chicken & whiskey. We fatted up a good deal. Everything went first rate except the whiskey. It raised a row as usual & one of our boys (Mike Caton, an Irish boy, a good soldier when sober) shot Capt. Clark of Co. A. who was trying to put him under guard. The Capt. told the corporal (John West) to take Mike's gun from him. John could not do it, was afraid to do it & well he might be. The Capt. took it himself knocking Mike down with the butt of a gun. Clark rode to the front & saw the Maj. as to what should be done with Caton & then rode again to the rear & asked of West, Where is the man that I took the gun from? At that moment Mike having got his gun again fired & shot the whole top of Clark's head off. Mike is now being court marshaled. I reckon he will be shot. He is a good soldier when sober, but he killed a good capt., one of our best. The Nashville

Union of today reports the rebels at Murfreesboro 100,000 strong. That is but 30 miles from here. Our forces are moving out that way. A heavy battle is pending. We are going out to-morrow—I don't care how soon the battle comes. I guess we can clean them out. We shall not stay here this winter. I don't know when you will get to come. I guess you will have to start when you get ready & keep coming till you catch us. I reckon we will stay close along the railroad. I. D. is well & so am I. Have only had one letter from you since the Perryville battle. Write often.

Truly,
Webb

Camp in the field 25 miles south of Nashville, Dec. 28, 1862
Dear Mother:

We left Nashville Friday morning. It rained all day. We had to carry our blankets, pup tents & all our clothes, & three days rations & 100 rounds, a pretty good load when the roads are good, & a big one when the rain is pouring down & the mud half knee deep. We had a heavy skirmish in the evening. We took one piece of artillery & 10 prisoners. Just in the evening a ball struck John Hawkins square on the belt buckle. It made him grunt, but was so far spent that it [did] no farther damage, but dropped at his feet. He picked it up & is around every day now bragging that he is bullet proof. Another division passed us in the night & were skirmishing all day yesterday. They took 6 pieces of artillery. As usual it rained all day. We have laid over today—I don't know why—perhaps because it is Sunday. If Gen. Bragg tries us on at Murfreesboro, I expect we will go into them tomorrow. If he falls back I reckon we will follow to Chattanooga where we expect to have a roaring fight. Wherever the fight comes I hope we will not make a Fredericksburg of it. Henry Beavers & John Moore were left at Nashville. The boys are all well & in fine spirits. I. D. will not write today.

Truly yours,
Webb

Camp 2 miles south of Murfreesboro, Tenn., Jan. 10, 1863

Dear Mother:

Yours of the 26th ult. just came to hand last evening & I was glad to hear that all are well. It does us much good to hear from home. There was a hard fight here & a heavy loss but Rosecrans gained the victory & the rebs. are gone. McCook was driven back 2 miles by the massed force of the enemy on our right before we were reinforced. The secesh got our knapsacks & blankets. I have been having the chills. Am well now. I am better satisfied now that John's remains are at home. It is not worthwhile for you to attempt to come & see us now. We are likely to follow the enemy right up & I hope we will keep at it till the job is done—don't like to waste so much time. I don't mind fighting for my country if we will only do it but I hate to lay round while the work remains to be done. I. D. is well. With kindest regards.

Truly,
Webb

Camp near Murfreesboro, Tenn., Jan. 19, 1863

Dear Mother:

We are on picket today four miles south of M[urfreesboro]—a flag of truce came in this morning. I don't know what for. He carried a sealed dispatch to Gen. Rosecrans. Rebs seem to be prowling over the country in every direction. The enemy reinforced is reported at Shelbyville 22 miles away. If we do not go to them perhaps they will come to us. It has rained nearly every day for 10 days. It closed up with a light snow just enough to cover the ground. This climate suits me. I am coming here to live after the war is over. It is as warm as a May day today. The 123 Rgt. is here. Was over to see the boys the other day. I. D. is well. John Moore is at Gallatin with part of the regt.

Your affectionate son,
Webb

Camp near Murfreesboro, Tenn., Jan. 25, 1863

Dear Mother:

We are still here in camp. Nothing of importance in our vicinity. Our forage parties have some skirmishing nearly every day. We hear that Bragg has been reinforced with 40,000, & we are receiving reinforcements & there may be a battle. If we don't go to the rebs they will come to us. It has rained more than half the time since we left Nashville. Saw Dave today, he is well.

Your affectionate son,
Webb

Franklin, Tenn., Feb. 8, 1863

Dear Mother:

We left Murfreesboro on the 31st of Jan. & after a three days march through mud, rain & snow we arrived at this place. I suppose we started in pursuit of Forrest, thinking perhaps that he might give us a fight, at this place; but when we got here he had been gone two days. Gen. Davis' division with one brig[ade] of cavalry was all that came. After we got here we learned that he went to Harpeth Shoals on the Cumberland river & got decently cleaned out & himself mortally wounded & taken prisoner. That may not be true. Davis turned the divis[ion] command over to Col. Carlin & took the cavalry & left. I suppose to cut off the retreat of Forrest's men. We are in readiness to go to his support if he needs us. If you hear of a fight near Franklin now you may know we are in it. The Emancipation Proclamation has stirred things up considerable. Some of the boys are very bitter about it. They say that they did not come to war to free niggers, but I guess this will bring the South to a compromise. Anyway, I hope the war will soon be over.

This is the prettiest country I ever saw though at present it is devastated, & like a ruin. The few people who are left are very friendly, & of refined manners. They are most all secesh. They say they never will submit to the usurpation of their rights. But I guess they will. I have not had a letter from home since

Christmas. It seems long. The boys are all well. Hope this will find you well.

> With much love your affectionate son,
> Please write often,
> Webb

Murfreesboro, Tenn., Feb. 20, 1863

Dear Mother:

After we returned from our Franklin scout I received two letters from you—It is very wet & muddy & disagreeable though it is warm. There is talk that we will move on Chattanooga soon—I wish we could move soon & talk less—Somehow I hope the war will close before another summer passes—I don't know how the settlement is to come but somehow I look for it to come.

> With kindest regards. Truly,
> B. W. Baker

Camp near Murfreesboro, Tenn., March 6, 1863

Dear Mother:

I wrote you on the 8th of Feb. & Mary on the 13th & you again on the 20th & yet no answer—I. D. says he will not write again till he gets a letter—We have done nothing since we came back from Franklin. There is some skirmishing among the foraging parties. One of our parties killed 10 rebs the other day & got 80 prisoners, several wagons & 300 cavalry saddles & accoutrements. The weather is cool & clear & the talk is of an immediate advance. No set battle is expected till we get to Chattanooga, but every inch of ground between here & there will be contested so our advance will be slow but I think sure— How do the fellows up north like the conscription bill? The soldiers like it I tell you. Hope those braggy fellows at home will all get pulled in. There is talk now of granting furloughs a few at a time. If that is done I may get home some time this summer.

We have been mustered for 6 months pay. The talk is that we will get 4 months soon. It will not be before we need it.

The 123 regt. is about 2 miles from us. Dave Adams has sore eyes—John Moore is well.

There has been a good deal of deserting since the Proclamation, but I guess it will stop now—I understand that the law is to be executed to the limit on deserters, & that means death—for my part I would as soon die any other way as to be set up against a stump & shot at.

With much love,
Webb

Murfreesboro, Tenn., March 16, 1863

Dear Mother:

Yours of the 5th inst was here [when] we got in. We have been on a ten days' scout. Nothing of importance transpired while we were gone. We got a drenching for 36 hrs. but it is clear & warm now. This is really a summer day. The trees are putting forth their leaves & the earth will soon be covered again with verdure. Already the grass is about good enough for cattle to live grazing. I would rather be here than at home till [the] war is over. I don't understand how loyal men can remain at home. I am sorry there is so much division in the North. The Proclamation serves a good purpose, as an excuse for some rebel sympathizers in the north. It can't do the slave much good till he gets inside of our lines. I suppose it will be hard on him till after that. The boys many of them don't like the idea of making soldiers of negroes. But after all they will do to shoot at as well as anybody if we could only think so.

Truly yours,
Webb

Murfreesboro, Tenn., March 25, 1863

Dear Mother:

Tom Temple who was taken prisoner at Stones River is just in from home, & we are asking questions till he is nearly tired out. It does us so much good to see one from home who has seen the folks. We are just in from picket duty. The enemy is in force in front of us. We have ⅓ of the army on picket all the time now I guess & the rest are under orders to be ready to march with three days rations at a moments warning. It looks as if we were going to have a fight. Let it come—I am anxious for the war to be over. I guess the fellows back there don't like conscription very much do they? If they resist they will have to be whipped, too.

There is nothing much to write.

Truly yours,
Webb

Murfreesboro, Tenn., Apr. 7, 1863

Dear Mother:

Capt. Taggert got in yesterday & I received my presents. I am very thankful. The train ran off of the track at Munfordsville, KY, & though none were killed several were badly shaken up. Capt. has a bad wound on his head. I have not talked with the capt. much yet. He said that you took dinner with him. Did you like him? And his wife! Nice isn't she? Did you know that she was a Catholic?

I carried the cake that you sent to me to George Hutton, poor fellow he is very sick. I was all night with him last night. The 123 are out on a scout. Those who are left behind are hardly able to help each other so George is having a hard time. He expects to get his discharge in about two weeks. His papers went out today.

We are jubilant over the fact authentic that Charleston, S.C., the mother of secession is fallen.

Ever your affectionate son,
Webb

Picket Post 4 miles south of Murfreesboro, Tenn., May 19, 1863

Dear Mother:

The excitement over the late battle of the Rhapahannock is subsiding in a measure. We are disappointed to some extent, though not so much perhaps as we would have been if the Potomac army had never been beaten before, but anyway we expected something of Fighting Joe, & we got something, i.e. a good drubbing. We should have liked it better if the result had been different but we are not here to complain. I guess Burnside & Hooker are not the men to handle great armies. They are good fighters directed, but not to direct.

Don't know what we are going to do. I have said we are going to move so often I don't want to say it any more, though I think we will sometime.

I wish you would collect my long Point money if you please & the John Jones money if you can.

Oh, it is such a treat to get out on this kind of picket duty. It is like getting out of town after a hard day when there is a large gathering. We expect to stay here 5 days. Wish it was a month. Write soon.

Your affectionate son,
Webb

Manchester, Tenn., June 30, 1863

Dear Mother:

Your kind letter of the 12 came to hand yesterday. It was so welcome. We are finally out of Murfreesboro as you see. We left there on the 24 & have been making slow progress. We are in 13 miles of Tullahoma, the advance of the army is reported 8 miles beyond that. We have to repair the railroad as we go in order to get supplies. We have been out this is the 7th day. It has rained every one of the six preceding days & looks as if it would today. It is very muddy. We are going 5 or 6 miles a day. We are fighting for every step we gain. The fighting is only skirmishing, but it makes slow marching.

Wilder's Brig. is in the advance. John Moore is here. He was left on picket when his Reg. went out. He is well. One of our boys has word that there is a company of rebs. organized in Hutton Township & a regt in Coles County. I wonder if it is so. I hope every one of them will be drafted into our army & sent to the very front. I hope this may find you well.

Truly your affectionate son,
Webb

Winchester, Tenn., July 12, 1863

Dear Mother:

Your Fourth of July letter was very welcome. I read it with pleasure & interest. I am truly sorry to hear of so much discord & contention at home. The war is for the restoration of the union. Will the people of the North be so blind as to invite civil war into their own homes? The northern people do not know what war is. Suppose a busy army of 20,000 should camp on Mr. Moore's farm. In the morning there would not be a chick or pig or cow on the farm. The potatoes & onions & all eatables in the house would be gone. The fences would all be burned. If they stayed a week in the neighborhood the whole community would be a common, utterly devastated—no pen, let alone mine, can describe the horrors of civil war.

I never wrote Albert Moore an abolition letter. I am not an abolitionist, though I would rather be one than to be a secessionist. I never advised anyone to desert. I would not advise any man to dishonor himself & disgrace his friends.

Please Ma, don't be despondent. Your trouble is hard, I know, but not so hard as some. I met a widow here who had 5 sons. All went into the southern army. Three of them have been killed, & the other two are at Vicksburg.

Write soon to your affectionate son,
Webb

Winchester, Tenn., Aug. 1, 1863

Dear Mother:

I did not write you last week, but I seldom fail, & I wrote Mary last week, so you will hear & I reckon that will do. Our company is still on pious duty here & having the best kind of time—I have gotten acquainted with several families. The people are sociable & intelligent & very obliging to the soldiers, in spite of the insults that they are exposed to from drunken, worthless fellows, who, if they ever had any breeding, sense, or humanity, have lost all traces of it since they left home. This town is very healthy & beautifully situated. It has been favored with large schools. There has been as high as 600 young ladies here at school at one time. I have gotten acquainted with a Mr. & Mrs. Merritt here who are very kind to me. The Regt. expects to stay here.

Truly your son,
Webb

Winchester, Tenn., Aug. 8, 1863

Dear Mother:

When I wrote you last, I thought we were going to stay here, but now we have been taken from town duty back to the Regt. & are doing picket duty every other day. It is excessively hot, & raining a little almost every day. We are under marching orders with 10 days rations draw, & will go tomorrow or next day probably. The indications are that we go to the vicinity of Chattanooga. I hate dreadfully to leave here. The Dixie gals are awful nice, & it is very pleasant here. I had a letter from Levi Baker. It came from Cashville Col. in about 20 days, was not that a quick trip. We had a grand Division meeting on Thursday. Several chaplains spoke & then Gen. Davis was called. He made a few appropriate remarks & then said he was no speaker, but that if he was on charley & we were on our way to Chattanooga & Bragg was between us & that town, he would know how to talk. We cheered him heartily. Gen. McCook then was repeatedly called & finally stood up to say that he could not talk, but promised us the advance, the post of honor as we go to Chattanooga. I believe I would rather guard the train, or some nice town like Winchester, ha ha. I did intend to send home a little money but somebody went through the regt. after pay day & took all he could find. He got mine, $50. I think I know who did it, but am not certain. He got out of the regt. 3 or 400 dollars— it is too bad. We hear that there is a great excitement at home over the draft, & that the Copperheads are drilling to resist it. Hear that six hundred drilled in Mattoon. Is it true—I love to hear from home every week. Please write as often as you can.

Webb

Camp near Stephenson, Alabama, Aug. 25, 1863

Dear Mother:

We left Winchester on the 17 & came out to the mountains 7 miles. On the 18 we climbed to the top of the mountain 2 miles & on the 19 helped the wagons up & marched on the mountain 10 miles. It was a hard day's work. We did not get to camp till 12 at night. Be sure we were all tired, & glad when our days work was done. On the 20th we helped the wagons down—we fastened ropes to them & let them down the steep places by hand while the teamsters got down with the mules. Sundown found us in camp in the valley close to a splendid spring. After feasting on sow belly & hardtack with plenty of green corn & green apples & a good bath, I never slept better in my life. On the 21 we went into camp at 10 o'clock in a regular gutter up Alabama swamp where the mosquitoes are nearly as big as horse flies, & where nobody ever lived but mosquitoes. Here we are in this swamp today & will stay here till we march I think. We are 23 miles from Stephenson & 25 miles from Chattanooga on the Memphis & Charleston Railroad. I. D. & all are well.

Truly your son,
Webb

Camp in Front, Alabama, Sept. 1, 1863

Dear Mother:

Sure enough we stayed in that swamp till we marched. We left camp with a pontoon train & came to the river 4 miles & camped for the night, our brigade in advance. Gen. McCook kept his word. There were 4 regts. in the brigade. Early Saturday morning we were divided into companies of 25 each & loaded into the pontoons with 100 rounds & our guns loaded, & at the command of the general all the boats pulled for the south shore of the Tennessee where we expected a battle for the rebs were in sight & a few shots were fired. It looked like risky business going out into the river in those boats facing the enemy. There was a sure thing that nobody could run. The river is 800 yards wide. It was a beautiful sight to see the boats in line of battle nearly a mile long pulling together regularly. It looked too many for the few rebels on the south shore for they took at once to the bushes. We landed all together. Gen. McCook went over with us making his promise good that he would give us the advance & go with us. We guarded the southern shore while the Pioneer Brigade put down the Pontoon Bridge. The first to come over on the bridge were Rosecrans, Davis, Negley, Sheridan, Garfield & their staffs. Part of the second brigade came over & relieved us & we marched out to the foot of Sand Mountain & went into camp. We rested Sunday & on Monday we came up & went into camp here where we are. The rest of the Division came up last night. Today Gen. Johnson's Division is crossing. We are about 6 miles from the river. McCook complimented us highly for our efficiency in throwing across the Pontoon Bridge. Another week will show us new things perhaps. The boys are all well.

Truly yours,
Webb

Camp between Sand Mountain & Lookout, Sept. 15, 1863
Dear Mother:

We are here in Alabama & 30 miles south of Chattanooga. Bragg has skedaddled & left us in undisputed possession of the mountains of Alabama. Rosecrans is in Chattanooga with his headquarters. As soon as the Railroad is repaired to Chattanooga we intend to make Bragg hunt his hole. We are all well & in fine spirits. We are full of good rumors. I am sorry to hear that an early frost has spoiled the corn. Hope it is not as bad as you think. Some of the boys have had letters about Copperheads. Tell me the names of those Copperheads. I think they ought to be rode on a rail.

Truly,
Webb

Murfreesboro, Tenn., Sept. 27, 1863
Dear Mother:

This is my first opportunity to write you since the battle. I hope it will reach you before the details so that you will not be uneasy about me. I received a wound in the left shoulder through the deltoid muscle. The ball lodged in the shoulder near the joint. The surgeon is going to cut it out next week perhaps. The wound is already sloughing & doing well. I hope to be well in a month. I was wounded in Saturday's engagement. In that engagement, Hogan, Westley, Wm Goodrich, Hawkins, Hatmaker, Meyers, McLain, H. Beevers, Wallace, & R. Cartwright & some others whose names I do not know were wounded. Out of 33 who went into the battle only 13 stacked arms. None of our boys were killed on Saturday. I was the last to leave the company on Saturday. I saw I. D. as I was leaving the field. He had not received a scratch, but they had shot his hat away. He was bareheaded & laughing. On Sunday the boys were in again & only stacked six guns at night. T. Devick & I. D. are still with the company & unhurt. Bill Beevers was wounded & taken. Several of the boys are lost from the company, perhaps killed. You will get a description of the battle from those whose business it is to describe in the papers & in the reports of the officers. I am in Hospital No 1 Ward A. Henry Beevers is here. He is wounded in the leg. Send me a Charleston Ledger please.

Truly yours,
B. W. Baker

General Hospital No 1 Ward A
Murfreesboro, Tenn., Sept. 27, 1863

Dear Mother:

I avail myself of the first opportunity of writing you since the battle. Am in hopes this will reach you before you get the details of the battle so you will not be uneasy about me. I received a slight wound in the left arm, the ball penetrating about three inches below the point of the shoulder & ranging upward it lodged somewhere about the point of the shoulder. The surgeon is going to cut it out this morning. The wound is already running and doing first rate. Think I will join the company in a month. I was wounded in Saturday engagement together with Hogan, Westley, Williams, Goodrich, Hawkins, Hatmaker, Meyers, McLain, Henry Beevers, Wallace, & Red Cartwright. There is some others reported but I do not recollect their names or know certain that they are wounded. One thing certain, out of 33 men our company only stacked 13 guns. I believe there was none killed in our company. I was pretty near the last man wounded on Saturday. I saw I. D. just as I was leaving the field. He had not received a scratch but they had shot his hat away—he was bareheaded & laughing. On Sunday the Division had another hard engagement & was driven from the field. I saw some of the boys from the company—told me they only stacked six guns Saturday night. Tom Devick & I. D. were still with the company & unhurt. Bill Beevers was supposed to be wounded & have fallen into the hands of the enemy—don't know certain. Several of the boys were lost from the company that they knew were not hurt. There has been no musketry engagements since I left Chattanooga. It is of no use for me to attempt a description of the battle for I saw but a small portion of it & it will be described by some that will have nothing else to do. None of our officers were wounded. I will close. Write me soon,

DIRECT, B. W. BAKER
GEN. HOSPITAL NO 1 WARD A
MURFREESBORO, TENN.

Henry Beevers is here. He is wounded in the leg. Will you please send me a Charleston Ledger.

Webb

Murfreesboro, Tenn., Oct. 6, 1863

Dear Mother:

I resume my seat this morning to again address you. I wrote you immediately after my arrival here but lest it should not reach you & you would become uneasy about me, I will write again. I never enjoyed better health than at present & my arm is getting well fast. If I have no bad luck I will join the reg in two weeks. There is no news from the front [but] Forrest's rebel cavalry 10,000 strong succeeded in crossing the river & made a raid in Tenn as far up as here, cutting the telegraph & tearing up the railroad. They threatened this place all day yesterday. Everything was moved into the fortifications & skirmishing all day not half mile from town. We expected an old fashioned twist this morning. All the boys that stopped here when I did drew guns & ammunition & took our places behind the fort—some with one good leg & some with one good arm. The chaplain of our hospital was our capt. You would have laughed to have seen us there. They called us the Quinine Brigade. But just at night 15,000 of our cavalry from Chattanooga, Wilder's Brigade included, made their appearance & rebs skedaddled in the direction of Shelbyville & our fellows have gone in pursuit this morning. The train will be running to the front in a day or two. I saw the 123rd this morning. Johnny & Dave is fat as pigs. The boys are all well. Just tell all the folks you see they wished me to send word for them, said they did not know when they would get [home]. I can learn nothing from the 25th. Better guess I would like to see the boys. I hardly know how to stay here. If I would hear [what was going on, I] would be better satisfied. As the mail is going out in a few moments I will close for if I don't get this started today you will not get it Friday.

Give my love to all. Write me soon & believe me as ever your affectionate son,

Webb

DIRECT
C/O HOSPITAL NO 1 WARD A, MURFREESBORO, TENN.

Murfreesboro, Tenn., Oct. 11, 1863

Dear Mother:

Another week has passed & still finds me at the hospital & no word from home. It seems to me I should have had a letter from home ere this for I think you got my first a week ago last Friday. I have not heard from the regiment yet but that is not strange for the railroad has been torn up between here & there so that the mail could not go through. But the track is [now] repaired so the train has gone through. This is the third day. On the evening of the seventh our cavalry & Wilder's Brigade of mounted infantry had a sharp engagement of an hour & a half resulting in the capture of 20 pieces of artillery & 300 prisoners. Not, however, without a loss on our side. Col. Monroe with several of his boys were killed. Among them, Johnny Moore, but I know the sad intelligence will have reached you before you get this. Poor little Johnny. On the morning before the battle, as the reg passed through here, I talked with him & he seemed to be so glad to see me & was so pleasant & in such high spirits. I cannot realize the fact that I will never see him again. If I could only have been there to have marked the place where he lays. It is only 36 miles from here & Lieut. Easton told me the place would be easy found. If I stay here this week I shall look hard for Mr. Moore, but I am so lonesome I shall leave for the reg. if I can get away. I know the boys must be lonesome. So many of us away & my arm is almost well. The soreness is all gone & it will soon be healed up. From the best information I can get from the front, there will not be any more fighting at Chattanooga soon, if there is at all. I saw Major McIlvain of the 35th Ill belonging to the third brigade. He said that all was quiet & they had settled down to fortifying & the general opinion of military men [is] that there would be no fighting soon. I believe it will be like the siege of Corinth. About the time we are ready to strike, the rebs will leave. As we are going to have preaching & the chaplain is already to begin, I will close hoping this will find you all well as it leaves me. Tell Mary to write if she pleases for I have not had a letter from her for a long time. Write soon & believe me,

Truly your son,
Webb

Murfreesboro, Tenn., Nov. 2, 1863

Dear Mother:

Your kind letter of the 25th came to hand a few moments ago & was perused with interest & pleasure. It is the second letter from you since I came here. I got one paper, the other has not come. Certainly you do not Direct right or I would get them—you should be careful about that. I had a letter from I. D. & Tom Devick but I believe I wrote you that in my last. I do not recollect certain any thing that John [Moore] said only that he had a letter just before the battle at Chickamauga & wished me to tell you that he was well & in truth I never saw him look better. I saw Dave Adam & Capt. Wiley yesterday enroute to Nashville for fresh horses for their Brigade. This last raid has killed nearly all their horses. In speaking of John, they said he was killed by a ball passing through his head from the flank while among the foremost in a charge shouting for victory. They seem to feel nearly as bad as if he was their own brother. He was the company's pet & always ready to do his part. If Mr. Moore & Uncle Adams wishes to visit the army it will be useless for them to come at present for a citizen can go no further south than Stevenson. As soon as they can go through I will write. I don't know how long I will stop here. They have put me on duty today & perhaps will keep me all winter as I can't get away till the surgeon sees fit to send me. I am not caring much. I have a good bed & warm room & plenty of grub & that is more than I would get at the front. Besides, I have lots of good books & plenty of time to read them. Then why should I not be contented to stop just as long as they have a mind to keep me? At present I am reading the history of ancient Greece & hardly know how to take time to drill! Gen. Sherman's corps of Grant's Army four days ago was at Florence, Alabama, & by this time I expect he is at Stevenson. Gen. Hooker with the 11th & part of the 12th corps has crossed the river at Stevenson & driven the rebels off of Lookout Mountain so that communication is open via the river from Bridgeport to Chattanooga so the boys will get more rations. They have been on one third rations for some time. I know they will be glad to get full rations. I think Sherman & Hooker will cross the mountain the way we went & by so doing completely flank Bragg so he will be compelled to fall back on Atlanta without giving battle. I do not believe there will be another battle at Chattanooga. Every thing seems to work in our favor.

Henry Beevers' leg seems not to mend as fast as it ought to. I never enjoyed better health in my life. I weigh 210 lbs. Hope this will find you well as it leaves me. My love to all. Write me soon & believe me as ever. Truly your affectionate son,

Webb

P.S. Direct Gen. Hospital No. 1 Ward B, Murfreesboro, Tenn.

Murfreesboro, Tenn., Gen. Hospital No 1, Nov. 8, 1863
Dear Mother:

It is now four o'clock. I did think I would not write today; but as I have nothing else to do, I might as well spend a few moments in writing, as to be doing nothing! We have just had [a church] meeting at the hospital. I do not know the ministers name, but do know that he preached as good a sermon as I have heard since I have been in the service. But that is not all—there were three ladies came with him & did the singing. O! they were such good singers. Perhaps I thought so because it is the first singing I have heard at church since I left home. It waked a train of reflections on bygone days that is easier imagined than described. When you read this you will say that I am homesick, but I aver that such is not the case. Of course, I should like to be at home a few days, but don't expect I would stay long if I was there. I did want to come with Henry, but could not get to so I am contented as it is. I guess I will stay here till Henry comes back. I will if it is possible. I have not heard from the regiment except the letter from I. D. & Tom. There is no news from the front since the 1 of this month. Every thing seems to be quiet except at Charleston.

It is cool today, almost cool enough to snow. I expect you are having cold weather now. We have rain nearly every day. I wish you to tell me how Henry's leg is & if they have heard from Bill & where he is—be sure & don't forget it. I have no news to write so I will close for this time.

Give my love to all the family & best respects to all enquiring friends. Write me soon & believe me truly,

Your affectionate son,
Webb

Hospital No 1, Murfreesboro, Tenn., Nov. 20, 1863

Dear Mother:

Your kind letter of the 8th inst is just at hand and has been perused with interest and pleasure. I was glad to hear that Henry had got home all right. The reason I did not send a letter to him [is] I had written you the day before he started. Tell him the letter he sent me came through all right. I expect I will stay here till he comes back in hopes to hear from home. It is raining today & somewhat disagreeable though not cold. I am having a very pleasant time about now. Have not had a letter from the regiment but one since the battle, though the papers report all quiet at the front & the boys in fine spirits. Gen. Sherman's corps has arrived at Chattanooga. Bragg is said to be largely re-inforced & a battle is again anticipated in that region such as the world never saw, but my opinion it will be a Corinth affair, at least I hope so. If you are afraid the fair one will cost too much, just lay her in the cupboard & she will do well enough.

Dave is still here. He is up in my room now disputing with

me as to which belongs to the best fighting corps, old fashioned, you know how we used to do.

Tell Harriet she should not tell tales out of school if she would have the good opinion of the scholars. A still tongue makes a wise ear & a tattler is disliked by everybody. Give my respects to all.

Write me soon & believe me as ever truly your affectionate son,

Webb

I did not get my descriptive roll, consequently I got no pay & have no stamps so you will have to pay the postage.

Murfreesboro, Tenn., Nov. 29, 1863

Dear Mother:

I resume my seat this morning to address you a few lines. It was pretty cold last night, snowed, but is warm today, & the snow has nearly disappeared!

We have good news from Chickamauga: a dispatch today to the effect that we have fifteen thousand prisoners; & have driven the rebs seven miles below Chickamauga, & are still pursuing them! Chickamauga is eight miles from Chattanooga. Bully for Grant. Reports say that Meade has crossed the Rapidan, perhaps so. & that Gillmore has, ere this, made an assault on Charleston. That's old. Our prospect is bright at present. Dave Adams [Company] A left for his regiment on Tuesday & I have left No. 1 to nurse at No. 4. A few days if I should slip in between now & Christmas, don't be surprised though you need not look for me unless you see me coming. But as strange things has happened.

You may Direct your next letter to No. 4 Ward 2, Murfreesboro unless you hear from me before. I have not heard from the regiment since I wrote you. My health is good. I will close for church has begun. Write soon & believe me as ever truly your affectionate son,

Webb

Benjamin Webb Baker

B. W. B.

Hospital No. 4, Murfreesboro, Tenn., Jan. 1, 1864

Dear Mother:

This New Year evening finds me safe in Murfreesboro and attempting to write you. I was five days on the road. Had a very good time and pleasant journey. I found the boys about as I left them and though I might possibly enjoy myself better at home, yet I am having and like to have a very good time here while I remain. Can't tell how long that will be. Henry Beevers is here. I saw him today after I got here. He is in good health and getting along finely. I got his cake all mashed up before I got here. As for Wm Beevers, I hunted for him all day in Louisville but he is not there. Henry told me that he (Bill) is in Ill, somewhere so, of course, I did not give him his cake but I gave it to Henry. I don't know whether I will see I. D. soon or not but if I don't, if you will send me his address (I have forgotten it). I will send the socks by mail. From all that I can learn from the regt it is east of Knoxville. A great many are reenlisting. As I came through, I saw several entire regt that had reinlisted and were enroute for home to recruit. They were enthusiastic. One thing certain, they like soldiering better than I! I should like to know how you are getting [on] from your late fall & how you all enjoyed the new year. I can not get a pass for Mr. Moore here, but if he will get a pass or recommend[ation] from the Governor or some prominent man in Ill., he will have no trouble. At least I saw three men going out front told me they had no trouble in getting through and I went to Gen. Van Cleve today and he told me the same. I am in good health.

My love to all the family. I did not see the girls in town. Tell Hez and Anna [Webb's stepbrother and stepsister] that I forgot their books, that they shall have them yet. Remember me to all enquiring friends. Write me very soon & believe me as ever,

Truly your son,
Webb

DIRECT HOSPITAL NO. 11 WARD 2, MURFREESBORO, TENN.

Convalescent Camp, Stevenson, Alabama, Jan. 15th (Eve), 1864

Dear Mother:

Though differently situated from what I was when last I wrote you perhaps I would not spend the time better than in writing you this evening. Left Murfreesboro on Tuesday enroute for the regt and came here where I with others have been waiting since for transportation. Probably we will get away tomorrow, can't tell. The regt is at Kaggerville, east of Knoxville. We can not get there now, but the camp equipage is at Chattanooga and the boys that are sent front are stopping there. Some that left for the front about the time I started home are there yet. The weather is very nice here. It is trying to snow today, but think it will turn to rain if it don't clear off for it is not cold enough to freeze. The railroad is repaired, so the trains run through to Chattanooga today. All that are able for duty and some that are not are being sent to their commands by order Gen. Thomas. Everything seems quiet out here. Still a great many regts. are going home having gone into the veteran service. Did hear the old 25th had reenlisted but can't tell whether it is the truth or no.

I wrote Mary a few days before I left Murfreesboro. If she has not written before you get this she may direct to the regt for I do not expect to have a permanent stopping place till I get there. You will have to excuse this being written with a pencil for I have no ink. Have you got over your fall? and be sure to tell how Grandma and Uncle Will is. I will not write any more today. Hope this will find all well. Give my love to all. Write soon and believe me as ever affectionately your son

Webb

DIRECT TO THE REGT AND TO CHATTANOOGA

Chattanooga, Tenn., Jan 20, 1864

Dear Mother:

Arrived here today. A detachment is going to the regt next week and I shall go. I. D. is gone.

Convalescent Camp, 1st Regt, 3rd Divis,
4th Army corps
Chattanooga, Tenn., Jan. 30, 1864

Dear Mother:

Again I embrace the privilege of writing you. When I mailed my last letter I thought I would be with the regiment ere this but the prospect is no better now than when I first arrived here. Do not know when I will get to go. The first Division of the 4th [?] army corps passed through here today enroute for Knoxville. The prospect for a battle is said to be good up there. The eleventh and twelfth corps are ordered up. Longstreet is said to have twenty thousand reinforcements with Lill [?] to command. If so the struggle will be sanguinary. Fellows from there report our forces driven in to the breastworks but don't know whether true or not. We have the finest weather here I ever saw since I have been here. As warm as summer and no storms. There is nine of our company here and we are having our own fun. Nothing to do and plenty to eat and a good shelter and we are not particular whether they send us to the regiment till after the fight. Health is good. I have not had any letter from home since I left. Of course, I would like to hear but don't expect to till I get to the regiment. I would have my letters directed here but it is uncertain how long I will stay here. I wrote to Plude last week, no news. Write me soon. Direct to the regt. Believe me as ever truly your son,

Webb

Newmarket, Tenn. March 3rd, 1864.

Dear Mother:

I embrace this opportunity of addressing you a few lines in response to yours of the 17th ult which came to hand the day I. D. started for Ill. I should have answered it sooner but we have been on the march or expecting to march every day since we are just off of a scout or rather returning from a reconnaissance in force. We have been as far as Morristown forty miles from Knoxville on the east Tennessee and Va railroad. We found no enemy though they are reported at Bulls Gap only twenty miles farther. Why we did not go farther I do not know. One thing I do know, yesterday we took the back track and came back 20 miles. Today we are resting though under orders to march. Where to, I do not know. Rumor says that the bulk of Longstreet's army has gone to Dalton to reinforce Johnston and that we are going back to Chattanooga. How true I can't say. The probability is though that there will be no general engagement in this department soon. We can not advance very far on acct. of transportation and the rebs dare not advance on us in our fortifications. The rainy season will set in soon and then all movement will be suspended for the wet term. Today is very nice and warm. The two preceding days have been rainy and disagreeable. No news of importance to write so I will close hoping this will find all well as it leaves me.

Write soon and believe me as ever your affectionate son,
Webb

P.S. Excuse this being written with pencil. Ink has played.

Morristown, Tenn., March 15, 1864

Dear Mother:

I embrace this opportunity of writing you lest I should not have another soon. We are under marching orders to be ready at a moments warning. We are only about 11 miles from the front and skirmishing is going on constantly. An engagement may be brought on at any hour though I do not think it likely there will be one soon! If there is, our Divis[ion] is in the reserve and will not be called in to action unless we are like to lose the day. A rumor in camp today that we are ordered back to Chattanooga but I will not vouch for the truth. By the way, have you seen anything of Plude in your part though, of course, you have! I have not heard from home since he started on the 11th of last month or from him either. The weather this month has been very nice so far though today is pretty cold. Real March grub is scarce enough you may believe though the prospect is good for it to be more plenty shortly as the railroad is in operation this far for the last two days. We are now 40 miles from Knoxville, though such a thing might be that we would be less before we are more, though if an engagement does not come off inside of a week, a great many of our veterans will be back. No apprehension seems to be felt for our safety. No news of importance to write so I will close hoping this will find you well as it leaves me. My love to all.

Write me soon and believe me as ever your affectionate son,
Webb.

P.S. You can [give] Hez and Anne their books for me if you please. If you see Plude, tell him to write as I suppose he will not be back soon.

Strawberry Plains, Tenn., March 25, 1864
Dear Mother:

I embrace this opportunity of responding to yours of the 10th inst which came to hand on the 20th inst and was perused with pleasure for it had been a long time since I heard from home. I am truly glad to hear that you are again enjoying good health. I believe I wrote you last while at Morristown 20 miles from here on the railroad. We were ordered back here near a week ago and are now doing post duty i.e. for our Brig[ade]. The rest of the Divis[ion] has gone farther up the river. I suppose we will stay here till ordered somewhere else. The capt got a letter from Maj Taggert the other day stating that the detachments sent there for recruits were kept to carry recruits to Louisville and Memphis. He said that he was going to Memphis with some recruits so we do not look for them back till our time is out. I guess you was all surprised to see Plude. I bet I would have laughed if I had been looking in at the window when he came in ha—ha—ha—hoopee. Now you think that all imagination, well, it is, and all made at that. We had the heaviest [snow] on the 22nd I have seen since I have been in the army. It snowed so it layed a foot deep all night, but it went off the next day. It snowed again last night and is raining today. We are cooped up in our pup tents having lots of fun. Tom and I are writing, not to our ducks, for I haven't any, neither has he. Wish we had one a piece. I am sure we would spend an hour to the best advantage in writing them. Well, I have filled this sheet with bad sense and will quit for fear I make it worse. Say to Mary I think her letter a long time on the road. My love to all.

Write me soon and believe me as ever truly your son,
Webb

Strawberry Plains, Tenn., April 1, 1864

Dear Mother:

Yours of the 19th ult came to hand today and be assured it was read with pleasure and delight. If you do not get a letter every week it is no fault of mine. There is no news to write—everything seems quiet. The river is up and rising rapidly. We have had considerable rain and snow within the last week, but today is clear and warm and a prospect for settled weather now is good. There is a good deal of talk as to the time we will get out. Some think the first of June, but I think August. One thing I don't care, so they don't keep us another winter and I guess that will hardly be. The prospect I believe is good for our Brigade to stay here till June though can't tell certain. Got a letter from Hattie and Ellen yesterday and Martha Titus all combined, two days later than yours. It says that Louis and Frank Jones are both married. Well, I don't care who gets married, hope they will all have good luck, but Hutton Township is getting behind. I don't like to hear that. I am ashamed to send this letter but for fear I would not do any better I will send it. I will be able to do better next week. I am pretty near mad this morning, have not had any breakfast and am not likely to get any till evening. About every fifth day we have to fast whether we will or not.

With this I will close hoping this will find you well as it leaves me. My love to all. Write me soon and believe me as ever,

Your affectionate son,

Webb

Cleveland, Tenn., April 16, 1864

Dear Mother:

I resume my seat this morning to again address you after a march of ten days we again find ourselves with the Army of the Cumberland ready to participate in the contest that from the concentrated movements of the army is to come off soon. Ours, that is the 4th corps, commanded now by Gen. Howard of Chancellorsville notoriety is being concentrated at or in the vicinity of Cleveland 30 miles north of Dalton on the Knoxville and Dalton Rail Road and 30 miles east of Chattanooga.

Whether there will be a battle or not I can't tell. Some say that we are relieving Hookers 1st army corps off of the railroad so they can go back to the army of the Potomac where the great campaign is expected to open. For my part I have quit prophesizing and come to the conclusion that I know nothing about it and care less so I get plenty of grub. With regard to the Charleston riot, I hardly know what to say or whether to say anything, but will venture to say if the reports that I have got are true, that every man engaged in the assault upon the soldiers is a traitor and ought to be hung as a criminal in the double capacity of murderer and traitor. But I can't think that I have true reports. Yet when I think of it I am vexed and have a notion to throw down my pen and never scratch another line to Coles County. I have not had a line from there later than the 10th of March, while others have at least a month later. Now if you should ever take a notion to write me or see anybody that does take a notion, please tell or have the person writing to tell me if there was others besides Cooper from our neighborhood engaged in the affray, and I should like to have the truth as to what gave rise to the trouble and who was in the fault. As to our regt I can say nothing where [we] will go, what we will do or how long we will stay. I don't know anything about it. Orders has just come to march. I guess we will go to Chattanooga or in that direction. I will have to close. Give my love to all.

Write me soon and believe me as ever your affectionate son,

Webb

Camp of 25th Ill., Cleveland, Tenn., April 30, 1864

Dear Mother:

After a short delay owing to the amount of duty on hand, I resume my seat this evening to respond to your kind and ever welcome letter of the 10th of this month which was perused with interest and pleasure! I hardly know what to write that will interest you. I will begin by saying I am very well satisfied with the development of certain characters referred to in yours. If all parties are as well satisfied with the marriage contract of Mr. and Mrs. Lawyer, late Miss Gill, as I am, there will be no trouble from dissenting voice! We have been very busy this week preparing for active service. We had general reviews by Gen. Howard, our Corps Commander, yesterday. A very good sign of an advance and others equally as good that an advance in intended. We have been mustered for pay today. Don't know when we will get the pay, though if we stay here another week think we will get a little tobacco money. Col. Nodine returned today. He says we will be discharged the first of June, that is only a month. But a month is a long time at this stage of the game, at least it is long enough for many a poor fellow to go to his long home. But our corps is [in] reserve and the engagement will be desperate if we are engaged. Capt. Salee got a letter from Maj Taggert yesterday. He had just got back from Vicksburg having been down with recruits. He (the maj) said that Gen. White promised to send them (that is the detachment) to the regt as soon as there was a squad of recruits to bring to Chattanooga, so we will look for them before long! Politics is very little discussed here. The army, like the citizens, are divided though they do not carry things to such extremes. I fear the results [if] Lincoln should be elected again. There is no news. I will close hoping this will find you well as it leaves me. Give my love to all.

Write me soon and believe me as ever your affectionate son,

Webb

Cleveland, Tenn., May 9, 1864

Dear Mother:

I embrace this opportunity of responding to your kind and ever welcome letter of April 6th which came to hand several days ago. I should have written sooner but thought I would wait till we got settled. On Monday last, the army receiving orders, pulled up stakes for Dalton when the army left. Our regt with the sixth Ohio were ordered here for garrison duty where we are likely to remain some time perhaps till the 4th of August as Gen. Grant's late order will detain us till that time. But if we stay here the time will soon pass. We will stay here at least till the present progressing battle is over. Maj Taggert with his squad arrived yesterday. They are right from the front. Heavy skirmishing was going on and our forces within six miles of Dalton, a general engagement will hardly be kept off longer than Monday, not more than till the middle of the week, no way. I. D. is in good health. He says he has not heard from home since he left there. He has had a fine time. This is a pretty town, half the size of Charleston and there is lots of pretty girls here though I have not got acquainted with any yet. But we have been here only since Tuesday and have been busy putting up quarters, but saw for it we are certain to have a good time this summer. Can go to town whenever we are not on duty. Believe I have given all the news. Will close hoping this finds all well as it leaves me. My love to all.

Write me soon and believe me as ever your affectionate son,

Webb

Camp in the field, June 8, 1864

Dear Mother:

I embrace this opportunity of again writing you. We left Cleveland on the 31st of May being relieved by the second Ohio heavy artillery. We took the cars and came to Kingston, from there we escorted a train through where we arrived last evening and joined our Brigade, our corps having been in advance all the time for the last month were relieved for a few days and what is left of them are enjoying themselves very well now, though about one third have been killed or wounded. We have orders to march in the morning with nine days rations and sixty rounds of cartridges, so suppose we will take the front again. The rebel pickets are within two miles of camp. I hear them skirmishing with ours while I am writing, but the main force is said to be nine miles from here where they have the last but one strong position this side of Atlanta, and they have none as strong as some they have left. We do not expect any very hard fighting this side of Atlanta as we can easily flank their position and when we get to Atlanta, if they do not leave, we will starve them out. According to the way they are relieving troops, we will be relieved the 20th of next month. That would not be long under any other circumstances except those by which we are surrounded at the present time. Though if a fellow has good luck it will not be long. The weather is very warm and if it gets much warmer, we will be compelled to lay up till fall. I. D. is well and the boys generally. We have forty in our camp, many more than we ever went into an engagement with. Believe I have given you all the news so I will close hoping this will find you well as it leaves me. Give my love to all enquiring friends.

Write me soon and believe me as ever your affectionate son,

Webb

Camp B near Louisville, Ky.
[Undated, but written in September 1862]

Dear Mother:

It is with pleasure that I take my pen in hand to write you a few lines to tell you that I am well. I would have written sooner but I was on guard on Sunday. On Monday I was breaking mules. Tuesday we all was throwing up breastworks. The secesh is [with]in 90 miles of us but we are ready for them. We have all our things. We quit our work about sundown, got supper, then it was night. It is getting late, I will have to quit. The boys is all well.

Direct of camp near Louisville 123 Ill volunteers, Co K in care of Capt. Wiley

John Baker

ACKNOWLEDGMENTS

This book has had many friends in the making. In compiling archival material essential to it, I am deeply obliged to the conscientious industry of Barbara Krehbiel, Librarian and Genealogist of the Carnegie Public Library in Charleston, Illinois; to Anke Voss-Hubbard, Archivist and Special Collections Librarian of the Ames Library of Illinois Wesleyan University; to Roger V. Hillman, University Archivist of Eastern Illinois University; to Jocelyn Tipton, Librarian of the Booth Library of Eastern Illinois University; to Catherine W. Knight, Archivist of the Illinois Great Rivers Conference of the United Methodist Church; to Bob Cavanagh and Mary Michals of the Illinois State Historical Library; and to the staffs of the New York Public Library and Butler Library of Columbia University. I would also like to thank my brother, Peter, for noticing a useful source; my friend Anthony Chiappelloni (a walking encyclopedia of Civil War material) for a number of fruitful suggestions; my agent, Russell Galen, for his enthusiasm throughout; my editor, Bob Bender, for his embrace of the text; and his assistant, Johanna Li, for her help with details. Yet this book could not have been written—indeed, would not even have been conceived—but for the priceless family papers that came to me from my late grandfather, James Chamberlain Baker, and by way of two kind and generous cousins, Alice Lackey and David Heck. To David and Alice—as well as to my wife, Hilary, who gave me every kind of support along the way—I most gratefully dedicate this book.

NOTES

CHAPTER ONE

3   "I see a cloud": *Congressional Globe*, 33rd Congress, 1st Session, 340, quoted in Brock, *The Character of American History*, p. 127.

6   "Ruth had gleaned": Brush, *Growing Up with Southern Illinois*, p. 31.

7   "the Buckle on the Corn Belt": Hamand, "Coles County in the Civil War," p. 83.

8   "Come leave the fields": quoted in Trestrail, *Illinois*, p. 29.

8   "read, rite, and cipher": An implicit comparison to Lincoln, funeral eulogy by Joe Bell, *Minutes of the Central Illinois Conference of the Methodist Church*, 1909.

CHAPTER TWO

11   "an object of general worship": G. Smith, *The United States, Political History*, p. 178.

12   "be disposed of": ibid., p. 129.

12   "was equal in size": Macy, *The Anti-Slavery Crusade*, p. 17.

13   "like a firebell": Jefferson, *Writings* (letter to John Holmes, April 22, 1820), p. 1434.

13   "While the Union lasts": quoted in G. Smith, op. cit., p. 181.

13   "Turn this question": quoted in Fiske, *Essays Historical and Literary*, v. 1, p. 394.

14   "a kind of intense": Brock, op. cit., p. 119.

15   "If Kansas wants": quoted in Stephenson, *Abraham Lincoln and the Union*, p. 49.

16   "A minor shift": Brock, op. cit., p. 127.

16   "Notwithstanding that slavery": quoted in Brush, op. cit., p. 241.

17   "in every respect": quoted in Johannsen, *Stephen A. Douglas*, p. 645.

17   "scraped clean": Thomas, *The Words of Abraham Lincoln*, p. 22.

17   "retaining them all": ibid., p. 99.

17   "with large features": ibid., p. 23.

18   "I shall have my hands full": quoted in Cole, *The Era of the Civil War*, p. 168.

18   "A house divided": quoted in Thomas, op. cit., pp. 27–28.

19   "kind, amiable": quoted in Johannsen, op. cit., pp. 643, 642.

19   "trailing into town": Cole, op. cit., p. 169.

20   "Westward the Star of Empire": "Lincoln–Douglas Debate Centennial Booklet," p. 7.

21   "cider to cut": Coleman, *The Lincoln–Douglas Debate*, p. 43.

21   "The government was made": Zarefsky, *The Complete Lincoln–Douglas Debates*, p. 233.

21   "with the air": "Centennial Booklet," p. 11.

21   "like a plantation owner": "Centennial Booklet," p. 11.

22   "as high-pitched": *New York Tribune*, September 18, 1858; Horace White, *The Lincoln and Douglas Debates*, p. 20.

22   "Lincoln Worrying Douglas": *Charleston Daily Courier*, September 18, 1908, Semi-Centennial Celebration of the Lincoln–Douglas debate, p. 3.

22   "Let us have nothing offensive": Coleman, op. cit., p. 48.

22   "Negro Equality": ibid.

23   "I should like to know": quoted in Johannsen, op. cit., p. 574.

23   "in any way the social": quoted in Zarefsky, op. cit., p. 235.

23   "jet black": ibid., p. 265.

24   "like so many fish": quoted in Turner, *The Underground Railroad in Illinois*, p. 147.

24   "white basis": Zarefsky, op. cit., p. 266.

25   "When are we to have peace": ibid., p. 268.

26   "one of the chief": Stephenson, op. cit., p. 54.

26   "some blind Samson": ibid.

26   "saint, to make the gallows": quoted in Brock, op. cit., p. 132.

26   "No, I never expect": quoted in Stephenson, op. cit., p. 61.

27   "The negro, by nature": quoted in G. Smith, op. cit., p. 243.

28   "We seek no conquest": quoted in Brock, *The Civil War*, p. 7.

28   "foreign power": Brock, *The Character of American History*, p. 136.

28   "denied his own right": Stephenson, op. cit., p. 87.

28   "showed conclusively": William H .Seward, quoted in ibid., p. 85.

29   "bloodshed or violence" and "In your hands": Lincoln's *First Inaugural Address*.

29   "linked to the fate": Brock, *The Character of American History*, p. 150.

30   "who, for various reasons": Brock, *The Character of American History*, p. 142.

31   "it also had to do the invading": Catton, *The Civil War*, p. 32.
32   "You might as well use": quoted in Urwin, *The U.S. Infantry*, p. 89.
32   "the hero of two wars": Steele, *American Campaigns*, v. 1, p. 131.

CHAPTER THREE

37   "the great rights and hopes": quoted in Catton, *This Hallowed Ground*, p. 30.
38   "Men, we are going to": quoted in ibid., p. 49.
39   "solitude and desolation": Schmucker, *A History of the Civil War in the United States*, p. 204.
45   "a military intellectual": Shea and Hess, *Pea Ridge*, p. 3.
46   "With a comparatively small": ibid.
49   "for hard fighting": ibid., p. 1.
50   "his prompt and ardent": *Dictionary of American Biography*, v. 19, p. 153.
50   "a massive limestone": Shea and Hess, op. cit., p. 10.
50   "have to travel light": ibid., p. 11.
52   "ripped apart from the uppers": ibid., p. 13.
54   "Who knows but that": quoted in ibid., pp. 21, 22.
54   "the hell-for-leather": ibid., p. 22.
57   "strolled over": ibid., p. 69.
57   "like a black cloud": Abbott, *The History of the Civil War*, v. 1, p. 232.
58   "he sent half his force": Foote, *The Civil War: vol. 1, Fort Sumter to Per-ryville*, p. 283.
59   "Carr was sent": ibid., p. 284.
60   "were whooping": ibid., p. 285.
60   "occasional flashes": Shea and Hess, op. cit., p. 217.
61   "slashing retreat": Foote, op. cit., p. 289.
62   "the most sustained": Shea and Hess, op. cit., p. 235.
62   "Billows of smoke": ibid., p. 252.
63   "as lively as if": ibid., p. 229.
63   "Oh, dot was lofely": quoted in Foote, op. cit., p. 291.
64   "blown to fragments": Abbott, op. cit., p. 243.
64   "To add to the horrors": Headley, *The Great Rebellion*, v. 1, p. 310.
64   "sunk into the earth": quoted in Shea and Hess, op. cit., p. 253.
64   "Victory! Victory!": quoted in ibid.
65   "It is redicklous": ibid.
65   "I don't believe he could": ibid.
65   "had been brought": Catton, *The Civil War*, p. 154.

66 "were busy cutting": Shea and Hess, op. cit., p. 210.

66 "The scene is silent": quoted in Foote, op. cit., p. 293.

67 "but as they approached": *Mattoon Independent Gazette*, September 28, 1862, quoted in Hamand, op. cit., p. 21.

68 "cylindro-conoidal ball": Urwin, *The U.S. Infantry*, p. 101.

CHAPTER FOUR

74 "though not inconclusive": quoted in Shea and Hess, op. cit., p. 317.

77 "brief but brilliant": Steele, op. cit., p. 190.

78 "effectively sealed up": ibid., p. 192.

CHAPTER FIVE

81 "Kentucky gone": quoted in McDonough, *War in Kentucky*, p. 61.

81 "We cannot escape history": Annual Message to Congress, December 1861.

83 "In this enlightened age": quoted in Brock, *The Character of American History*, p. 139.

83 "I can anticipate": quoted in ibid.

83 "I had to meet the question": quoted in ibid.

84 "incapable of making": Miles, *Piercing the Heartland*, p. 85.

84 "thoroughly upright": quoted in ibid.

85 "always gave the impression": Engle, *Don Carlos Buell*, p. 81.

85 "a fixed way": ibid., p. 82.

86 "To take and hold": quoted in Office of the Chief of Military History, p. 254.

86 "no greater disaster": McWhiney, *Braxton Bragg*, p. 268.

87 "slows": Engle, op. cit., p. 273.

87 "Where is Buell?": quoted in ibid.

88 "to keep abreast": Miles, op. cit., p. 73.

92 "from the tyranny": quoted in McDonough, op. cit., p. 155.

93 "If you want to avoid": quoted in Abbott, op. cit., p. 190.

93 "with all the honors": McDonough, op. cit., p. 181.

93 "His dress was that": quoted in Engle, op.cit., p. 293.

94 "The brave men": quoted in Hamand, op. cit., p. 16.

95 "Damn your souls": quoted in McDonough, op. cit., p. 141.

95 "a damned puppy": quoted in ibid., p. 142.

96 "The years creep slowly by": quoted in Hafendorfer, *Perryville*, p. 195.

97   "Our prospects are not": quoted in Miles, op. cit., p. 74.

98   "bushwhackers had sniped": Buell, *Warrior Generals*, p. 184.

98   "Should it be a real attack": quoted in McWhiney, op. cit., p. 301.

98   "too much scattered": ibid.

99   "tired-looking threads": Miles, op. cit., p. 82.

99   "for a few muddy drops": McDonough, op. cit., p. 203.

99   "I never saw men suffer": quoted in ibid., p. 210.

99   "I have directed": quoted in ibid., p. 204.

100   "kept up a running": ibid., p. 207.

100   "sweep every living thing": *War of the Rebellion*, Document 128, p. 500.

101   "a brown, chunky": quoted in McDonough, op. cit., p. 219.

102   "the great disparity": quoted in Foote, op. cit., p. 734.

102   "evidently taking": McDonough, op. cit., p. 243.

102   "their bayonets glistened": quoted in ibid.

103   "in skirmishes": Abbott, op. cit., p. 236.

103   "their thinned": Hafendorfer, op. cit., p. 258.

104   "the rest of the blue": Noe, *Perryville*, p. 210.

104   "the exhausted": ibid., p. 211.

104   "to a skirt": ibid.

104   "It was a life to life": quoted in McDonough, op. cit., p. 276.

105   "the doctrine of probabilities": Hafendorfer, op. cit., p. 123.

105   "all drifted": ibid., p. 125.

106   "Their synchronized stomachs": McDonough, op. cit., p. 235.

106   "I was astonished": quoted in Miles, op. cit., p. 82.

106   "from stillness": quoted in ibid.

106   "There is some mistake": quoted in ibid., p. 80.

106   "he meant by shooting": ibid.

107   "The sun was declining": quoted in McDonough, op. cit., p. 287.

107   "as the first streak": *Battles and Leaders*, 1862, v. 3, pp. 61–62.

107   "the bloodiest battle": *War of the Rebellion*, Document 128, p. 567.

107   "For the time engaged": ibid., p. 519.

108   "The severest action": ibid., p. 511.

108   "was enough to make": quoted in McDonough, op. cit., p. 291.

108   "the moaning and sighing": quoted in ibid.

108   "Some lay with with tongues": ibid., p. 293.

108   "It seemed the climax": quoted in ibid., p. 291.

109   "For God's sake": quoted in ibid., p. 305.

111   "At once the dogs of detraction": quoted in McWhiney, op. cit., p. 235.

CHAPTER SIX

113 "forestalled European mediation": McPherson, *Battle Cry of Freedom*, p. 858.

114 "We may have our own": quoted in Stephenson, op. cit., p. 178.

115 "I would save the Union": Thomas, op. cit., pp. 169–170.

116 "the tide of blood": quoted in ibid.

116 "If we shall suppose": quoted in G. Smith, op. cit., p. 265.

CHAPTER SEVEN

119 "the hero of Iuka and Corinth": Hicken, *Illinois in the Civil War*, p. 100.

120 "Everywhere in the Army": ibid., p. 106.

120 "Can't get shoes": quoted in Abbott, op. cit., v. 2, p. 359.

122 "crumbled under": Buell, op. cit., p. 187.

122 "The President is very": quoted in Steele, op. cit., p. 325.

122 "I have lost no time": ibid.

123 "Spread out your skirmishers": Headley, op. cit., v. 2, p. 130.

124 "who contested every": Haskew, "Winter Fury Unleashed," p. 5.

125 "The turnpike as far": quoted in ibid., p. 6.

125 "half-burned clearings": Headley, op. cit., v. 2, p. 134.

126 "committed himself": ibid., v. 2, p. 135.

127 "In five minutes": Catton, *This Hallowed Ground*, p. 193.

128 "with a swift, rushing": Headley, op. cit., v. 2, p. 132.

128 "God has granted": quoted in Haskew, op. cit., p. 7.

128 "This army can't retreat": quoted in Buell, op. cit. p. 202.

129 "We have retired": Abbott, op. cit., v. 2, p. 365.

129 "God bless you": quoted in ibid.

129 "You gave us a hard-earned": quoted in Williams, *Lincoln and His Generals*, pp. 208–209.

CHAPTER EIGHT

132 "a tunnel had been choked": Fiske, *The Mississippi Valley in the Civil War*, p. 253.

135 "The enemy must either": quoted in Steele, op. cit., p. 332.

135 "The rebel army is now": ibid.

136 "sooner or later": ibid., p. 333.

137 "on hoof": Cist, *Army of the Cumberland*, p. 157.

138 "If we can hold": Korn, *The Fight for Chattanooga*, p. 18.
138 "Lee's army overthrown": quoted in ibid., p. 30.
139 "You do not appear": quoted in ibid.
142 "suspected persons": Stephenson, op. cit., p. 161–162.
143 "The Constitution as it is": quoted in Hamand, op. cit., p. 80.
143 "Down with the rich": quoted in Stephenson, op. cit., p. 159.
146 "The broad Tennessee": quoted in Hicken, op. cit., p. 195.
149 "a sharp fire": quoted in Korn, op. cit., p. 52.
149 "as was his habit": Cozzens, *This Terrible Sound*, p. 297.
150 "As the wind whistled": quoted in ibid.
150 "were slammed out of place": quoted in Fiske, op. cit., p. 269.
151 "Are you the same man": quoted in Davis, *Stand in the Day of Battle*, pp. 289–290.
152 "The minie ball striking bone": quoted in Freemon, *Gangrene and Glory*, p. 48.
153 "an ounce of Rebel lead": obituary, *Watseka Republican*, June 23, 1909.

CHAPTER NINE

155 "had been beaten": Steele, op. cit., p. 442.
155 "our whole camp": Fullerton, in *Battles and Leaders of the Civil War*, v. 3, p. 719.
156 "that a heavy wagon": ibid.
156 "their very bones": Coppée, *General Thomas*, p. 164.
156 "in addition": ibid.
159 "The Secretary handed me": quoted in Steele, op. cit., p. 298.
159 "Hold Chattanooga": quoted in Stoddard, *Ulysses S. Grant*, p. 200.
160 "stunned and confused": quoted in Williams, op. cit., p. 285.
160 "Instead of looking down": Stoddard, op. cit., p. 203.
160 "If the Rebels give us": quoted in ibid.
164 "whether or not": quoted in Eicher, *The Longest Night*, p. 613.

CHAPTER TEN

167 "without seacoast or harbors": Stoddard, op. cit., p. 200.
167 "like a team of balky": quoted in Bailey, *Battles for Atlanta*, p. 20.
167 "Grant is the first": quoted in Stoddard, op. cit., p. 211.
168 "to break it up": quoted in Steele, op. cit., p. 470.
169 "locomotives and freight cars": Korn, op. cit., p. 156.

170   "it was Lee's army": Steele, op. cit., p. 518.

171   "it was ideal country": Bailey, op. cit., p. 8.

174   "to cut in behind": Fuller, *The Generalship of Ulysses S. Grant*, p. 310.

174   "one big Indian fight": quoted in Bailey, op. cit., p. 75.

177   "heavy siege guns": ibid., p. 76.

177   "the domes and minarets": Connolly, *Three Years in the Army of the Cumberland*, p. 234.

177   "Send up": ibid.

178   "the repair train": quoted in G. Smith, op. cit., p. 277.

178   sent forward and deployed: Hamand, op. cit., p. 27.

178   "They'll only beat": quoted in Connolly, op. cit., p. 248.

CHAPTER ELEVEN

179   "The tendency of war": Baker Papers, author's private collection.

180   "the cheerful manhood": *Report of the Adjutant General of the State of Illinois*, v. 2, p. 353.

181   "With malice": quoted in Thomas, op. cit., p. 239.

181   "They will need them": quoted in G. Smith, op. cit., p. 280.

181   "The war is over": quoted in Brock, *The Character of American History*, p. 151.

181   "hanging or killing": quoted in Stephenson, op. cit., pp. 257–258.

182   "a ranting actor": G. Smith, op. cit., p. 281.

182   "when the telescope": Baker Papers, author's private collection.

182   "By the interposition": ibid.

183   "You can more easily": ibid.

183   "from the Aegean Sea": ibid.

184   "the achievements of history": Marshall, *Grandest of Enterprises*, p. 91.

185   "press reading upon the people": Baker Papers, author's private collection.

185   "disabled from obtaining": ibid.

185   "It seems providential": ibid.

185   "Especially today": ibid.

186   "Dr. Baker impressed": Bell, *Minister of the Central Illinois Conference*, p. 3.

187   "All flesh is grass": ibid.

BIBLIOGRAPHY

Abbott, John S. C. *The History of the Civil War in America*. 2 vols. New York: Henry Dill, 1863–1865.

Adams, George Worthington. *Doctors in Blue*. Baton Rouge: Louisiana State University Press, 1952.

Adams, Lois Genevieve. *Hutton Township. Coles County, Illinois. With a Genealogical Supplement*. Charleston, IL: Coles County Historical Society, 1995.

Angle, Paul M., ed. *The Complete Lincoln–Douglas Debates of 1858*. Chicago: University of Chicago Press, 1958.

Annual Report of the American Historical Association, 1913. Vol. 1. Washington, DC, 1915.

Army Medical Department, 1818–1865. www.armymedicine.army.mil.

Bailey, Ronald H. *Battles for Atlanta: Sherman Moves East*. New York: Time-Life Books, 1985.

Baker Papers. Author's private collection.

Battle of Chickamauga 19–20 September 1863. www.aotc.net.

Battle of Murfreesboro (Stones River) 31 December 1962 and 2 January 1963. www.aotc.net.

Battle of Perryville, Kentucky, 8 October, 1862. www.aotc.net.

Battles and Leaders of the Civil War. Vols. 1–3. New York: Century, 1884–1888.

Baxter, William. *Pea Ridge and Prairie Grove*. Fayetteville: University of Arkansas Press, 2000.

Bell, Joe. "Funeral Eulogy of Benjamin W. Baker," *Minutes of the Central Illinois Conference of the Methodist Church*, 1909.

Beveridge, Albert J. *Abraham Lincoln, 1809–1858*. 2 vols. Boston: Houghton Mifflin, 1928.

Bond, John W. *The Battle of Pea Ridge, 1862*. Rogers, AR: Pea Ridge National Park, n.d.

Bowman, John S., ed. *Encyclopedia of the Civil War*. North Dighton, MA: JG Press, 2001.

Braxton Bragg and the Army of Tennessee. www.aotc.net.

Brock, W. R. *The Character of American History*. New York: St. Martin's Press, 1960.

———, ed. *The Civil War.* New York: Harper & Row, 1969.

Brush, Daniel Harmon. *Growing Up with Southern Illinois.* Chicago: Lakeside Press, 1944.

Buell, Thomas B. *The Warrior Generals: Combat Leadership in the Civil War.* New York: Three Rivers Press, 1997.

Caring for the Men: The History of Civil War Medicine. www.civilwarhome.net.

Carr, Clark E. *The Illini: A Story of the Prairies.* Chicago: A. C. McClurg, 1904.

Catton, Bruce. *The Civil War.* Boston: Houghton Mifflin, 1987.

———. *This Hallowed Ground.* New York: Doubleday, 1956.

Chickamauga Reports. www.aotc.net.

Cist, Henry M. *The Army of the Cumberland.* New York: Charles Scribner's Sons, 1882.

Cole, Arthur Charles. *The Era of the Civil War, 1848–1870.* Springfield: Illinois Centennial Commission, 1919.

Coleman, Charles H. *The Lincoln–Douglas Debate at Charleston, Illinois. September 18, 1858. Eastern Illinois University Bulletin,* no. 249, December 1963.

Connolly, James A. *Three Years in the Army of the Cumberland.* Bloomington: Indiana University Press, 1959.

Coppée, Henry. *General Thomas.* New York: D. Appleton and Co., 1905.

Coy, David Kent. *Recollections of Abraham Lincoln in Coles County, Illinois.* Charleston, IL: PrintCo., 2000.

Cozzens, Peter. *No Better Place to Die: The Battle of Stones River.* Urbana: University of Illinois Press, 1991.

———. *This Terrible Sound: The Battle of Chickamauga.* Urbana: University of Illinois Press, 1996.

Davis, William C. *Stand in the Day of Battle.* New York: Doubleday, 1983.

Degregorio, William A. *The Complete Book of U.S. Presidents.* New York: Barricade Books, 1991.

Dictionary of American Biography. 3. vols. New York: Scribner's reprint, 1971.

Dwight, Timothy, ed. *American Orators.* New York: Colonial Press, 1900.

Eicher, David J. *The Longest Night: A Military History of the Civil War.* New York: Simon & Schuster, 2001.

Engle, Stephen D. *Don Carlos Buell.* Chapel Hill: University of North Carolina Press, 1999.

"Eyewitness Accounts of the Battle of Perryville." Perryville's Battlefield Preservation Association, *www.perryville.net.*

Fiske, John. *Essays Historical and Literary.* Vol. 1. New York: Macmillan, 1903.

————. *The Mississippi Valley in the Civil War.* Boston: Houghton Mifflin, 1902.

Flanagan, James W. "Battle for the Bluegrass." America's Civil War, *www.thehistory.net.*

Foote, Shelby. *The Civil War: A Narrative.* 3 vols. New York: Vintage Books, 1986.

Freemon, Frank R. *Gangrene and Glory: Medical Care During the Civil War.* Chicago: University of Illinois Press, 2001.

Fuller, J. F. C. *The Generalship of Ulysses S. Grant.* New York: Dodd, Mead, 1929.

Giffin, Evelyn Cox. *In Other Days: History of Hutton Township, Coles County, Illinois.* Charleston, IL: Prairie Publications Press, 1977.

Hafendorfer, Kenneth A. *Perryville.* Owensboro, KY: McDowell Publications, 1981.

Hamand, Lavern M. "Coles County in the Civil War, 1861–1865." *Eastern Illinois University Bulletin,* no. 234, April 1961, 1–112.

Haskew, Michael E. "Valley of the Shadow." America's Civil War, *www.thehistorynet.*

————. "Winter Fury Unleashed." American's Civil War, *www.thehistorynet.*

Hattaway, Herman, and Archer Jones. *How the North Won: A Military History of the Civil War.* Urbana: University of Illinois Press, 1991.

Headley, J. T. *The Great Rebellion.* 2 vols. Washington, DC: National Tribune, 1898.

Hicken, Victor. *Illinois in the Civil War.* Urbana: University of Illinois Press, 1966.

History of Coles County, Illinois. Chicago: Wm. Le Baron, Jr. & Co., 1979.

Hospitals, Surgeon, and Nurses. www.civilwarhome.net.

Illinois in 1837; A Sketch. Philadelphia: S. Augustus Mitchell, 1837.

Johannsen, Robert W. *Stephen A. Douglas.* New York: Oxford University Press, 1973.

Korn, Jerry. *The Fight for Chattanooga: Chickamauga to Missionary Ridge.* New York: Time-Life Books, 1985.

Koznarsky, Michael. "Anesthetic in Field and General Hospitals of the Confederate States of America during the Civil War 1861–1865." *www.civilwarinteractive.net.*

"Lincoln-Douglas Debate Centennial Booklet," Charleston, Illinois, September 18, 1958.

Long, E. B. *The Civil War Day by Day.* New York: Doubleday, 1971.

Macy, Jesse. *The Anti-Slavery Crusade.* New Haven: Yale University Press, 1921.

Marshall, Helen E. *Grandest of Enterprises, Illinois State Normal University, 1857–1957.* Normal, IL: 1956.

McDonough, James Lee. *War in Kentucky: From Shiloh to Perryville.* Knoxville: University of Tennessee Press, 1994.

McPherson, James M. *Battle Cry of Freedom: The Civil War Era.* New York: Oxford University Press, 1988.

————, ed. *Battle Chronicles of the Civil War, 1862.* New York: Macmillan, 1989.

McWhiney, Grady. *Braxton Bragg and Confederate Defeat.* Vol. 1. Tuscaloosa: University of Alabama Press, 1969.

Medicine in the Civil War. www.aretesurf.net.

Miles, Jim. *Piercing the Heartland: A History and Tour Guide of the Tennessee and Kentucky Campaigns.* Nashville, TN: Rutledge Hill Press, 1991.

Monaghan, Jay. *Civil War on the Western Border, 1854–1865.* New York: Bonanza Books, 1955.

Moore, Frank, ed. *The Rebellion Record: A Diary of American Events, 1860–1862.* New York: G.P. Putnam, 1862.

Nevins, Allan. *The War for the Union.* Vol 2. New York: Scribner's, 1960.

Noe, Kenneth W. *Perryville: This Grand Havoc of Battle.* Lexington: University of Kentucky Press, 2001.

Office of the Chief of Military History, United States Army. *American Military History. www.army.mil.*

Piston, William Garrett, and Richard W. Hatcher. *Wilson's Creek: The Second Battle of the Civil War and the Men Who Fought It.* Chapel Hill: University of North Carolina Press, 2000.

Pollard, Edward Albert. *The Lost Cause.* New York: Century, 1867.

Report of the Adjutant General of the State of Illinois. Vol. 2, *1861–1866.* Springfield, IL: Phillips Bros., 1900.

Sanders, Stuart W. "Every Mother's Son." *Civil War Times,* October 1999, 50–60.

Schmucker, Samuel M. *A History of the Civil War in the United States.* Philadelphia: Bradley & Co., 1863.

Shea, William L., and Earl J. Hess. *Pea Ridge: Civil War Campaign in the West.* Chapel Hill: University of North Carolina Press, 1992.

Smith, Goldwin. *The United States, Political History, 1492–1871.* New York: Macmillan, 1901.

Smith, Jean Edward. *Grant.* New York: Simon & Schuster, 2001.

Steele, Matthew Forney. *American Campaigns.* Vol. 1. Washington, DC: United States Infantry Association, 1943.

Stephenson, Nathaniel W. *Abraham Lincoln and the Union.* New Haven: Yale University Press, 1921.

Stoddard, William O. *Ulysses S. Grant.* New York: Frederick A. Stokes Co., 1886.

Thomas, Isaac, ed. *The Words of Abraham Lincoln*. Chicago: Western Publishing House, 1898.

Trestrail, Joanne. *Illinois*. New York: Abrams, 1999.

Turner, Glennette Tilley. *The Underground Railroad in Illinois*. Glen Ellyn, IL: Newman Educational Publishing, 2001.

Urwin, Gregory J. W. *The U.S. Infantry*. New York: Sterling, 1991.

War of the Rebellion: A Compilation of the Official Records of the Union and Confederate Armies. 129 vols. Washington, DC: U.S. Government Printing Office, 1880–1901.

Warner, Ezra J. *Generals in Blue*. Baton Rouge: Louisiana State University Press, 1964.

———. *Generals in Gray*. Baton Rouge: Louisiana State University Press, 1959.

Weigley, Russell F. *A Great Civil War: A Military and Polical History, 1861–1865*. Bloomington: Indiana University Press, 2000.

Wellborn, Fred W. *The Growth of American Nationality, 1492–1865*. New York: Macmillan, 1943.

Wheeler, Richard. *Voices of the Civil War*. New York: Thomas Y. Crowell, 1976.

White, Horace. *The Lincoln and Douglas Debates: An Address before the Chicago Historical Society, February 17, 1914*. Chicago: University of Chicago Press, 1914.

Wiley, Bell Irvin. *The Common Soldier in the Civil War*. New York: Grosset & Dunlap, 1952.

Williams, T. Harry. *Lincoln and His Generals*. New York: Knopf, 1952.

Wilson, Charles Edward. *Historical Encyclopedia of Coles County, Illinois*. Chicago: Munsell Publishing Company, 1906.

INDEX

Page numbers in *italics* refer to illustrations.

Abolitionism, 12, 23–24, 26, 43,
    115, 139–40, 171, 230
  Harper's Ferry raid, 26–27
Adam, Dave, 161–62, 216
Adams, Elijah, 5, 9, 159, 199
Adams, John, 5, 12
Agriculture, 5, 6, 8, 9, 11, 39
  cotton, 12
Alabama, 27, 81, 87, 144–47, 165,
    181, 231–33, 242
Alexandria, 32
Allatoona, 174
Amputation, 152–53
Anderson's Crossroads, 156
Antidraft riots, 143, 144, 172, 173,
    247
Antietam, Battle of, 113–14, 116,
    119, 136, 171
Antiwar movement, 141–44, 147,
    173, 180, 231, 233, 247
Appalachians, 138, 167
Appomattox Court House, Lee's
    surrender at, 181
Arkansas, 30, 50, 53, 204–7, 213
  Civil War in, 53–66, 70–72
  Pea Ridge, 4, *34*, 56–66, 70, 72, 77,
    108, 205–8
Arkansas River, 70
Arlington Heights, 32
Army of Mississippi, 167
Army of Northern Virginia, 167,
    181
Army of Ohio, 97, 171

Army of Tennessee, 160, 167, 171
Army of the Potomac, 159, 173
Arnold, Benedict, 5
Artillery, 62–63, 124–25, 177
Asboth, General Alexander S., 49,
    53, 58, 59, 60
Atlanta, 161, 171, 173, 249
  Battle for, 178, 180, 181
  fall of, 181
  Sherman's march on, 4, 168,
    174–78, 180, 181

Back pay, 133
Baker, Benjamin W. ("Webb"), *ix*,
    2–9, 20
  in Arkansas, 53–68, 70–75, 81,
    204–7, 213
  birth of, 5
  camp life, 39–42, 46–47, 69–74,
    88–89, 120–24, 126, 132,
    144–45, 161, 166, 169, 194,
    202, 204, 205, 216–17, 222, 238
  at Chickamauga, 148–53, 160,
    233–37, 240
  childhood of, 5–9
  Civil War letters of, 193–250
  death of, 186
  death of brother John, 109–11,
    140, 179, 220–22
  discharged from army, 179
  education of, 51–52, 182–84
  furlough, 165
  in Georgia, 174–78, 250

Baker, Benjamin W. (*cont.*)
  on guard duty, 39–40, 132, 194, 217
  homesickness, 47–48, 71–72, 202,
    239
  joins Illinois Volunteer Infantry,
    35–36
  in Kentucky, 81–111, 220–21
  at Lincoln-Douglas debate, 20–25
  in Missouri, 39–53, 193–204,
    208–12
  at Pea Ridge, 56–66, 70, 72, 77,
    205–8
  postwar life, 182–86
  religion of, 184–85
  at Stones River, 124–29, 131, 227
  as a teacher, 183–84
  in Tennessee, 119–29, 131–41,
    144, 151–66, 168–71, 218–19,
    224–50
  views on slavery, 133–34, 139–40,
    186, 201, 225, 227, 230
  views on war, 179, 183, 185–86
  wounds of, 63–64, 66, 67–68, 70,
    151–53, 161, 165, 179, 207,
    233–34
Baker, John, 5, 71, 72–73, 75, 89–90,
    102, 137, 217
  Civil War letter of, 193, 250
  death of, at Perryville, 109–11,
    140, 179, 220–22, 224
  joins army, 94–95
Baker, John B., 4–5, 6, 9
Baker, Martha Francis Henry, 184,
    186
Baker, Sarah. *See* Moore, Sarah
Bald Knob, 176–77
Banking, 16
Bardstown, Kentucky, 97, 98, 99
Baton Rouge, 91
Bayonets, 63, 102–4, 127, 206
Beauregard, General P.G.T., 33,
    75–77, 84
Bell, John, 27
Bell, Joseph, 186

Blacks, free, 116
  emancipation and, 47–48, 113,
    114–17, 133, 140, 181, 186,
    201, 225, 227
  in Union Army, 116, 134
Blue Ridge Mountains, 170
Booth, John Wilkes, 182
Boston Mountains, 64
Bowling Green, Kentucky, 67,
    92–93, 120, 121
Bragg, Braxton, 82, 83–88, 90–111,
    113, 119–20, 123–29, 131, 136,
    137–41, 142–53, 155–65, 223,
    225, 233, 239
  at Chattanooga, 161–65
  at Chickamauga, 148–53
  at Perryville, 99–111, 113
  at Stones River, 123–29
Brandenburg, Brink, 74, 212
Breckinridge, John C., 26–27
Bridgeport, Alabama, 155
Brown, John, 26–27, 43
Buchanan, James, 15, 28
Buckner, Simon Bolivar, 67
Buell, General Don Carlos, 67,
    85–88, 90–111, 114, 119, 121,
    123, 219
  at Perryville, 99–111
Bull Run, First Battle of, 33, 37, 38,
    77, 85, 119, 171
Bull Run, Second Battle of, 79, 83,
    94, 136
Burnside, Ambrose, 119, 125, 134,
    136, 164, 228

Cairo, Illinois, 37, 66
Calhoun, John C., 13
California, 14
Camp Butler, 180
Camp Hoffman, 70, 208–11
Camp life, 39–42, 46–47, 69–74,
    88–89, 120–24, 126, 132,
    144–45, 161, 166, 169, 194,
    202, 204, 205, 216–17, 222, 238

Camp Terry, 94
Camp Wilfley, 69–70
Cannons, 62–63
Cape Girardeau, 75, 214
Carr, Colonel Eugene A., 49, 53, 58, 59, 60, 62
Casualties, 30, 40–41, 64–65, 70, 107–8, 128, 129, 136, 140, 158, 164, 170, 179, 198, 208
Catholicism, 126
Catton, Bruce, 127
Cemetery Ridge, 136
Chancellorsville, 135–36, 171, 172
Charleston, South Carolina, 29, 135, 228
Charleston Riot (1864), 144, 172, 173, 247
Chattahoochee River, 175–78
Chattanooga, 30, 85–88, 91, 125, 137, 138, 141, 144, 146–51, 155, 158–61, 168, 169, 233, 235, 237
  Battle for, 161–67
Chattanooga Valley, 162–66
Cherokee Indians, 53, 58
Chicago, 8, 19
Chicago Times, 142
Chickamauga, Battle of, 4, *130*, 148–53, 160, 163, 171, 233–37, 240
Choctaw Indians, 53
Cicero, 142
Cincinnati, 81, 95
Cincinnati Gazette, 108
Civil War:
  Atlanta, 174–78, 180, 181
  battle sites, maps of, *2, 34, 80, 118, 130*
  casualties, 30, 40–41, 64–65, 70, 107–8, 128, 129, 136, 140, 158, 164, 170, 179, 198, 208
  Chattanooga, 161–67
  Chickamauga, 4, *130*, 148–53, 160, 233–37, 240

  end of, 181–82
  events leading to, 11–29
  Pea Ridge, 56–66, 70, 72, 77, 108, 205–8
  Perryville, 4, *80*, 99–111, 113, 220–21
  start of, 29–33
  Stones River, 4, *118*, 124–29, 227–28
  Union invasion of South, 167–79
  Wilson's Creek, 38–40, 45, 49, 198–99
  See also Confederate Army; North; South; *specific battles, cities, states, and officers;* Union Army
Clay, Henry, 20
Cleveland, Tennessee, 172, 173, 247–49
Coal, 81
Cold Harbor, 170
Coles, Edward, 22–23
Coles County, Illinois, 4, 5–9, 18–23, 35, 94, 111, 144
Columbus, 81, 82
Comanche Indians, 38
Company E, 25th Regiment, Illinois Volunteer Army, 35, 51, 53, 69, 71, 127, 141, 193
Compromise of 1850, 26
Confederate Army, 30–33, 116
  Chattanooga, 161–67
  Chicakamauga, 4, *130*, 148–53, 160, 233–37, 240
  Pea Ridge, *34*, 56–66, 70, 72, 77, 108, 205–8
  Perryville, 4, *80*, 99–111, 113, 220–21
  shortage of men, 142
  Stones River, 4, *118*, 124–29, 131, 227–28
  Wilson's Creek, 38–40, 45, 198–99
  See also specific battles and officers
Congress, 12, 13, 26, 28–29, 115, 164, 180

Congress (*cont.*)
  pre-war slavery debate, 11–29
Constitution, 12, 13–14, 24, 143
  Thirteenth Amendment, 181
Convalescent Camp, 161, 165, 166, 242
Copperheads, 141–44, 147, 180, 231, 233
Corinth, Mississippi, 69, 76, 78, 84, 86, 101
Corn, 8–9
Cotton, 12
Creek Indians, 53
Crimean War, 77
Crittenden, Thomas L., 87, 97, 100, 101, 105, 109, 123–26, 144, 148
Crockett, Davy, 37
Crook, Colonel George, 157
Cumberland Gap, 82, 87, 88, 91, 109, 137, 139, 146, 155–56, 163, 171, 246
Cumberland River, 67, 82, 132
Cumberland Valley, 136, 146
Curtis, Brigadier General Samuel R., 49–66, 72, 74, 212

Dalton, 171, 172
Davis, Jefferson, 27–29, 76, 85, 97, 111, 142, 167, 178
Davis, Colonel Jefferson C., 49, 53, 58, 59, 60, 62, 95–96, 132, 141, 225, 231, 232
Declaration of Independence, 23, 25
Delaware, 115
Democratic Party, 16, 26–27, 113, 180–81
  Copperheads, 141–44, 180, 231, 233
  1860 presidential election, 26–27
  1864 presidential election, 180–81
Deserters, 120, 133, 226–27
Disease, 41, 47, 48, 65, 74, 200, 201, 202
"Dixie" (song), 126

Doctors, 65–66, 68, 108, 149, 151–53, 161
Doctor's Creek, 100, 101
Donelson, Daniel S., 102
Douglas, Stephen A., 14–15, 16, 27
  -Lincoln debates, 17, 18–26
Douglass, Frederick, 24
Draft, 142, 143
  riots, 143, 144, 172, 173, 247
Dug Springs, 38
Dysentery, 65

Early, Jubal, 171
East Tennessee & Georgia Railroad, 86
Economy, 11
  Confederate, 12, 116, 173
Edwards, Richard, 184
Elkhorn Tavern, 57–60, 62, 64, 66
Emancipation, 47–48, 113, 114–17, 133, 140, 181, 186, 201, 225, 227
Emancipation Proclamation, 113, 116–17, 133, 225, 227
Emerson, Ralph Waldo, 26
England, 11, 30, 47, 77, 114
Erie Canal, 7

Famine, 156, 215
Farragut, Admiral David, 181
Fayetteville, Alabama, 55
1st Brigade, 1st Division of the Army of Southwest Missouri, 69
1st Brigade, 3rd Division, 4th Army Corps, 17, 179
1st Brigade, 4th Division of the Army of the Mississippi, 76
Florence, Alabama, 160
Florida, 27
Foote, Commodore Andrew, 66–67
Foote, Shelby, 59
Ford's Theater, Lincoln assassinated at, 182

Forrest, Nathan Bedford, 87, 132, 149–51, 225, 235
Forsyth, Missouri, 72–74, 211–12
Fort Donelson, 66–67, 82
Fort Henry, 67, 82, 214
Fort Sumter, 29–30, 49
France, 30, 31, 71–72, 114
Frankfurt, Kentucky, 98, 99, 101
Fredericksburg, 119, 125, 134
Freeport Doctrine, 20, 26
Free-Soilers, 15
Frémont, John C., 16, 38, 40, 41, 44, 46, 49, 115
Frost, Enoch, 64
Fugitive Slave Law (1793), 12, 14, 29
Furlough, 165

Galena, 72–73
Gallatin, Tennessee, 88
Garesche, Colonel Julius P., 126
Garfield, James A., 146
Georgia, 16, 26, 87, 138, 250
    Chickamauga, 4, *130*, 148–53, 160, 233–37, 240
    Civil War in, 147–53, 167–78, 180, 181
Germany, 50
Gettysburg, Battle of, 136–37, 138, 171
Gibson, Colonel W. H., 179
Gilbert, Charles C., 97, 100, 101, 105, 106
Gillmore, Major General Quincy A., 164
Gladstone, Sir William, 114
Gold Rush, 38
Grant, Ulysses S., 66–67, 70, 82, 86, 92, 107, 119, 123, 138, 159, 160, 162, 167–68, 170–71, 180, 181, 238, 248
    at Chattanooga, 160–65
    Lee's surrender to, 181
    Memoirs, 84

Greece, 183
Greeley, Horace, 115, 143
Guard duty, 39–40, 132, 194, 217
Guerrilla operations, 72, 82
Gulf Coast, 83
Gunboats, 66–67

Halleck, Major General Henry W., 45–46, 49, 76, 78, 86, 96, 122, 212
Hardee, William J., 85, 98, 99–101, 126
Hardtack, 42, 43, 160
Harper's Ferry raid, 26–27
Hawes, Richard C., 98
Hawkins, John, 124
"The Hebrew Maiden's Lament" (song), 149–50
Heg, Colonel Hans Christian, 145
Henry Clay (steamboat), 75, 214
Hickok, Wild Bill, 55–56
Home Guards, 81
"Home Sweet Home" (song), 126
Hood, John Bell, 148, 178, 181
Hooker, Joseph, 134–36, 159, 160–64, 170, 172, 228, 238, 247
Horses and mules, 155–57
Hospitals, 66, 108, 151–53
House of Representatives, 12, 13, 29
Howard, Major General Oliver H., 171–73, 176, 246, 248
Howard University, 171
Hunter, General David, 45–46, 115

Illinois, 4–9, 14, 17–23, 36, 94, 144, 173
    pre-war slavery debate, 16–25
Illinois State Normal University, 184
Illinois Volunteer Infantry, 35–36, 51
    25th Regiment, 35, 51, 53, 69, 71, 127, 141, 145, 165, 179–80, 193
    123rd Regiment, 94, 102–8, 137

Illinois Wesleyan, 184, 185
Immigration, 11, 145
Indiana, 94
Indianapolis, 159
Indianapolis Daily Journal, 87
Indian Cavalry Brigade, 53–54, 58, 60, 65
Indians, 38, 51, 53–54
  in Civil War battles, 53–54, 58, 60, 65
Industry, 36, 81, 173
  wartime, 36–37, 173
Iowa, 49
Iron, 81
Island No. 10, 67, 73, 74, 212

Jacinto, Mississippi, 76, 88–89, 215–18
Jackson, Andrew, 54
Jackson, General James S., 102, 105
Jackson, Stonewall, 33, 77, 79, 171
James River, 72, 73, 171, 211
Jefferson, Thomas, 12, 13
Jefferson City, Missouri, 40, 195–96
Jenkins, John, 111
"John Brown's Body" (song), 96
Johnston, Albert Sidney, 84
Johnston, Joseph E., 78, 167, 171–78
Jones, Hezekiah, 9

Kansas, 14, 15, 23, 25, 70
Kansas-Nebraska Act, 3, 14–15, 18, 24, 26, 115
Kennesaw Mountain, 174, 175, 176
Kentucky, 16, 17, 22, 36, 66, 220–21
  Civil War in, 80–111, 113, 115, 123
  drought, 98–99
  Perryville, 4, *80*, 99–111, 113, 220–21
  secession, 81–82
Knights of the Golden Circle, 143–44

Knoxville, 85, 87, 109, 164, 165–66, 168, 243, 244

Lane, General James Henry, 43–44, 197
Lebanon, Missouri, 52, 53
Lee, Robert E., 26, 78–79, 82–86, 94, 113–14, 123, 135–38, 148, 166, 167–68, 170–71, 181
  on slavery, 83
  surrender to Grant, 181
Lee and Gordon's Mill, 148, 149
Leesburg, 113
Lexington, Missouri, 40–41, 195, 196
Lightning Brigade, 137, 147, 157–59, 235–36
Lincoln, Abraham, 4, 17–25, 27, 36, 47, 49, 77, 78, 81, 86, 87, 101, 114–15, 119, 122, 123, 129, 132, 134, 142, 160, 164, 167–68
  assassination of, 182
  childhood of, 17
  -Douglas debates, 17, 18–26
  1860 presidential election, 26–27
  1864 reelection, 173, 180–81, 248
  emancipation of slaves, 47–48, 113, 114–17, 133, 181, 201, 225, 227
  First Inaugural Address, 29, 191
  Grant and, 167–68
  McClellan and, 78
  power of, 142
  Second Inaugural Address, 181
  views on slavery, 23–25, 29, 114–17, 181
Little Rock, 72
Little Sugar Creek, Arkansas, 55–56
Longstreet, James, 148, 149, 150, 166, 171, 243, 244
Lookout Mountain, 138, 146–48, 155, 161, 162, 164, 171

"Lorena" (song), 96
Lost Mountain, 174, 176
Louisiana, 27, 30, 85
Louisiana Purchase, 11
Louisville, Kentucky, 81, 82, 93–96, 122, 159, 250
Louisville & Nashville Railroad, 88, 132
Lyon, Brigadier General Nathaniel, 37, 38–39, 45, 199

Macon & Western Railroad, 178
Mail, 70–71, 120
Maine, 12
Manassas Junction, 33
Maney, George, 102–3
Marietta, 174
Maryland, 81, 82, 94, 113, 115, 136
Mattoon Independent Gazette, 94
McClellan, General George, 77–78, 83–84, 86, 113–14, 119, 135, 180–81, 212
McCook, Alexander, 87, 97, 100, 101, 106, 107, 123–26, 131, 141, 144, 145–49, 231, 232
McCulloch, Benjamin, 37–38, 43, 53, 55, 60, 61, 197
McDowell, Brevet-Major Irvin, 32–33
McMinneville, 156
McPherson, James, 113, 171, 174, 178
Meade, George Gordon, 136, 164
Measles, 47, 48, 200
Medical treatment, 65–66, 68, 108, 149, 151–53, 161
Memorial Day, 185
Memphis, 70, 71, 76, 245
Memphis & Charleston Railroad, 86
Methodist Church, 184, 185
Mexican War, 31, 37, 49, 54, 78, 82–83, 84, 85, 135
Mexico, 11

Military Division of the Mississippi, 159
Military tactics, 21, 31, 62, 67, 77–79, 82, 85, 100–105, 135
Mill Springs, Kentucky, 123
Mine Run, 170
Minié, Captain Claude E., 67
Minié ball, 67–68, 152–53
Missionary Ridge, 148, 149, 151, 155, 162–64, 171, 172
Mississippi, 27, 69, 72, 81, 167, 214–18
Mississippi River, 30, 36, 67, 78, 82, 136, 159
Missouri, 12, 30, 35, 70, 81, 193–204, 208–12
  Civil War in, 35–53, 61, 66, 115
Missouri Compromise, 12–13, 15, 29
Missouri River, 39, 49
Mitchell, General Robert B., 105
Mobile, 83, 177, 181
Monroe, Colonel James, 94, 103, 158
Moore, Isaiah D., 9, 35, 40, 152, 234
Moore, John W., 9, 94, 158–59, 236, 237
Moore, Robert, 9, 139, 158, 159, 237, 241
Moore, Sarah, 4–5, 9, 40, 71, 90, 109–11, 120, 131, 133, 139–40, 168, 180
  Baker's Civil War letters to, 193–250
Morgan, John Hunt, 97
Morphine, 153
Mosquitoes, 145
Mumps, 48
Munfordville, 93
Murfreesboro, Tennessee, 125, 129, 131, 132, 137, 151–52, 156–57, 224–29, 233–41
Music, 125, 149–50
Musketry, 63

Nashville, 67, 86, 88, 92, 121, 122, 128, 159, 169, 181, 219, 221–23
Nashville & Chattanooga Railroad, 86, 125
Nashville Railway, 157
Nebraska, 14
Nelson, William "Bull," 95
New Hope Church, 174
New Madrid, 74, 82
New Mexico, 14
New Orleans, 78
New York, 143
New York Tribune, 115
Nodine, Major Richard H., 71, 173, 209, 248
North, 11, 30–31, 116
  antiwar movement, 141–44, 147, 173, 180, 231, 233, 247
  postwar, 182
  pre-war slavery debate, 11–29
  start of Civil War, 29–33
  See also specific cities, states, and battles; Union Army
North Carolina, 30, 119
Norwegians, 145

Ohio, 94, 95
Ohio River, 81, 94, 95, 159
Open Knob, 102–5
Opium, 68
Orchard Knob, 162–63
Osage River, 49
Osterhaus, Colonel Peter, 49, 53, 58, 59, 60
Ozark Mountains, 50, 51

Palmerston, Lord, 114
Parsons, Charles, 102, 104, 107
Peace Democrats, 141–44, 147, 180, 231, 233
Pea Ridge, Battle of, 4, *34*, 56–66, 70, 72, 77, 82, 108, 205–8
Pelican, Peter, 60

Peninsular Campaign, 77–78, 135, 171
Pennsylvania, 136–37
Pensacola, 83
Percussion-lock rifles, 67–68, 103
Perryville, Battle of, 4, *80*, 99–101, 113, 220–21
Petersburg, 171, 180
Pickett's Mills, 174
Pierce, Franklin, 15
Pigeon Mountain, 147
Pike, Albert, 53–54, 58, 60
Pine Mountain, 174, 175
Pittsburg Landing, 67, 74, 75–76, 212
Plains Indians, 54
Pneumonia, 65
Polk, Leonidas K., 85, 97, 99–100, 106–7
Pope, General John, 67, 76, 78–79, 83, 91, 215, 218
Population, 11
Port Hudson, 78
Potomac River, 78, 113
Price, Sterling, 37, 38, 41–46, 51–66, 72, 87, 92, 119, 195, 197, 198, 199, 200, 203, 204, 206
Puritans, 183

Railroads, 7, 11, 81, 86, 88, 122, 125, 132, 137, 155, 157, 165, 168, 169, 173, 178
Rain, 73–74, 124, 131–32, 137, 223
Rations and supplies, 42–43, 73, 76, 120, 121, 124, 132, 137, 155–57, 169, 173
Reconnaissance, 148–49
Religion, 126, 161, 183, 184–85
Republican Party, 16, 27, 142
  1860 presidential election, 26–27
  1864 presidential election, 180–81
Resaca, 174
Revolutionary War, 5, 30, 39, 82

Richmond, 30, 78, 86, 119, 136, 168, 215
Rocky Face, 174
Rolla, Missouri, 46–47, 49, 200–203
Rosecrans, General William S., 111, 119–29, 131–32, 136–53, 159–65, 219, 232, 233
  at Chickamauga, 148–53, 160
  at Stones River, 124–29
Rossville Gap, 163, 164
Round Forest, 127–28, 151

St. Louis, 35, 36, 37, 39, 45, 46, 49, 50, 54, 193–94
Salee, Captain William J., 48
Sanitation, lack of, 65–66
Schofield, Major General John M., 171
Scott, General Winfield, 32, 43, 82, 197
Scott (Dred) case, 15, 19, 24
Scurvy, 41, 132
Secession, 27–30, 81–82, 83
Sedalia, Missouri, 41–42, 44, 197, 198
Seminole War, 84, 85, 135
Senate, 12, 17, 29
Sequatchie Valley, 156
Seven Pines, Battle of, 78, 171
Shelbyville, Tennessee, 137, 157
Shenandoah Valley, 136, 171, 181
Sheridan, Philip H., 51, 101, 102, 105, 171, 181, 232
Sherman, General William Tecumseh, 32, 46, 74, 123, 160, 162, 171–78, 219, 238, 239
  march on Atlanta, 4, 168, 174–78, 180, 181
Shields, General James, 73
Shiloh, Battle of, 67, 74, 75, 76, 84, 86, 95
Sigel, General Franz, 37, 38, 46, 49, 50, 51, 56–63, 70, 77, 91, 196, 200, 205, 215, 219

Slavery, 11–12, 81, 83, 86, 139–40, 143, 181
  emancipation, 47–48, 113, 114–17, 133, 140, 181, 186, 201, 225, 227
  pre-war debate, 11–29
Smallpox, 47, 48, 201, 202
Smith, Kirby, 85, 87–88, 91, 97–100, 109, 219
Snake Creek Gap, 174
South, 11, 30–31, 167
  antiwar sentiment, 142
  Confederate government, 27–29, 141–42
  economy, 12, 116, 173
  ports blockaded, 114
  postwar, 182
  pre-war slavery debate, 11–29
  secession, 27–30, 81
  start of Civil War, 29–33
  Union invasion of, 167–69
  See also Confederate Army; specific cities, states, and battles
South Carolina, 13, 27, 29, 116, 135
  secession, 27
Spence, Joseph B., 52
Spencer repeating rifles, 137
Spotsylvania, 170
Springfield, Missouri, 49, 51, 53, 54, 72, 198–99
Stanton, Edwin M., 134, 138, 159
Steamboats, 75, 169, 214
Stephens, Alexander, 26, 27, 85
Stevenson, Alabama, 165
Stones River, Battle of, 4, 118, 124–29, 131, 227–28
Suffrage, 186
Supply wagons, 155–57, 160, 175
Supreme Court, 15
  Dred Scott decision, 15, 19, 24
Surgery, 65–66, 108, 152–53

Taggert, Captain Westford, 35, 228, 248

Taylor, Zachary, 49
Tennessee, 16, 22, 30, 66, 67, 70, 71,
    81, 86–91, 218–19, 224–50
  Chattanooga, 161–67
  Civil War in, 119–29, 131–41, 144,
    151–66, 168–71, 181
  Stones River, 4, *118*, 124–29, 131,
    227–28
Tennessee River, 67, 82, 88, 138,
    144–46, 162, 169, 214
Terrill, General William Rufus,
    102–5, 107
Texas, 26, 27, 30, 54, 83
Texas cavalry, 57
Texas Rangers, 37
3rd Brigade, 1st Division, 20th
    Army Corps, 139, 149
Thirteenth Amendment, 181
Thomas, General George H., 96,
    109, 123–26, 144, 147–51, 159,
    162–64, 165, 171, 174, 176–78,
    181, 242
Trail of Tears, 51
Tullahoma, Tennessee, 137, 138,
    139
Tunnel Hill, 162, 163, 174
Tupelo, 76, 85, 87
Typhoid, 65

Uniforms, 41, 173, 196
Union, 11–12, 115
  Copperheads, 141–44, 147, 180,
    231, 233
  pre-war slavery debate, 11–29
  secession, 27–30, 81–83
  See also specific cities and states
Union Army, 31–33
  blacks in, 116, 134
  Chattanooga, 161–67
  Chickamauga, 4, *130*, 148–53,
    160, 233–37, 240
  disorganization of, 159–60
  draft, 142, 143
  invasion of South, 167–69

pay, 133, 141
Pea Ridge, *34*, 56–66, 70, 72, 77,
    108, 205–8
Perryville, 4, *80*, 99–111, 113,
    220–21
Stones River, 4, *118*, 124–29, 131,
    227–28
Wilson's Creek, 38–40, 45, 198–99
See also specific battles and officers
Union Navy, 31–32
Utah, 14

Van Cleve, General Horatio
    Phillips, 165
Van Dorn, Earl, 54–66, 85, 87, 119
Vicksburg, 85, 119, 137, 138, 140,
    160
Virginia, 30, 54, 123, 136, 148, 167
Volunteer armies, 32, 78, 94, 104.
    See also specific armies

Wallace, Lew, 95
Waltrip, Mike, 64
War Department, 116, 136, 137
War of 1812, 11
Washington, D.C., 32, 171, 180
Washington, George, 5, 123, 142
Water, 65–66, 151
Weapons, 32, 39, 52, 58, 60, 62–63,
    65, 67–68, 102, 103, 124, 137,
    152, 177. *See also specific weapons*
Webster, Daniel, 13
Webster, Colonel George, 105
Wesley, John, 185
West, 11
  Civil War battles, *2*, 36–37, 39–68,
    70–75, 80–111, 205–7
  expansion, 14
  pre-war slavery debate, 14–29
  See also specific cities and states
Western & Atlantic Railroad, 86
West Point, 31, 77, 78, 83, 84, 85,
    101, 102, 123
West Virginia, 77

Wheeler, Joseph, 124–25, 156–57
Whigs, 26
Whiskey, 56, 121, 205, 222
Wilder, Colonel John T., 93, 137
  Lightning Brigade of, 137, 147,
    157–59, 235–36
Wilderness, 135, 170
Wilmot Proviso, 14
Wilson's Creek, Battle of, 38–40, 45,
  49, 198–99
Winchester, Tennessee, 139, 140,
  144, 229–31
Winter camp, 46–47, 52–53, 61, 69,
  204, 207–8

Wisconsin, 145
Women's suffrage movement,
  186
Wood, General Thomas J., 171,
  177
Wounds:
  amputation, 152–53
  types of, 63, 65–66, 67–68, 108,
    109, 151–52, 178, 207

"Yankee Doodle" (song), 126

Zagonyi, Major Charles, 44
Zagonyi Cavalry Charge, 44